C0-ATN-653

# The Compact Disc

# The Computer Music and Digital Audio Series

John Strawn, *Series Editor*

*Volume 1*
**Digital Audio Signal Processing**
Edited by John Strawn
With contributions by J. W. Gordon, F. R. Moore, J. A. Moorer,
T. L. Petersen, J. O. Smith, and J. Strawn

*Volume 2*
**Composers and the Computer**
Edited by Curtis Roads
Contributions by or about H. Brün, J. Chowning, J. Dashow, C. Dodge,
P. Hamlin, G. Lewis, T. Machover, J.-C. Risset, C. Roads, and I. Xenakis

*Volume 3*
**Digital Audio Engineering**
Edited by John Strawn
With contributions by J. McGill, F. R. Moore, J. A. Moorer, P. Samson,
and R. Talambiras

*Volume 4*
**Computer Applications in Music: A Bibliography**
Deta S. Davis

*Volume 5*
**The Compact Disc: A Handbook of Theory and Use**
Ken C. Pohlmann

*Forthcoming Volumes*

**The Little Book of Computer Music Instruments**
Dexter Morrill

**A Computer Music History**
Curtis Roads

**MIDI: An Introduction**
Joseph Rothstein

**Computer Analysis of Musical Style**
David Cope

Volume 5    The Computer Music and Digital Audio Series

*Ken C. Pohlmann*

# The Compact Disc

## A HANDBOOK OF THEORY AND USE

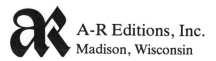 A-R Editions, Inc.
Madison, Wisconsin

Everybody, including myself, was astonished to find that it was impossible to distinguish between my own voice, and Mr. Edison's re-creation of it.

—Anna Case, Metropolitan Opera soprano, 1915.

**Library of Congress Cataloging-in-Publication Data**

Pohlmann, Ken C.
   The compact disc: a handbook of theory and use.

   (The Computer music and digital audio series ; v. 5)
   Includes index.
   1. Compact discs.   2. Compact disc players.
I. Title.   II. Series.
TK7882.C56P64   1988            621.389′32            88–70723
ISBN 0–89579–228–1 (paper)
ISBN 0–89579–234–6 (cloth)


A-R Editions, Inc.
801 Deming Way
Madison, Wisconsin 53717-1903
(608) 836-9000

© 1989 by A-R Editions, Inc.
All rights reserved
Printed in the United States of America

10 9 8 7 6 5 4 3 2 1

TK 7882.C56 music
P 63

# Contents

**4 CD Player Design**

**5 Practical Concerns**

**6 Diverse Disc Formats**

**7 Disc Manufacturing**

# A Note about
# This Series

The Computer Music and Digital Audio Series was established in 1985 to serve as a central source for books dealing with computer music, digital audio, and related subjects. During the past few decades, computer music and digital audio have developed as closely related fields that draw from a wide variety of disciplines: audio engineering, computer science, digital signal processing and hardware, psychology (especially perception), physics, and of course all aspects of music.

The series includes, but is not limited to, works in the following forms:

- textbooks at the undergraduate and graduate levels
- guides for audio engineers and studio musicians
- how-to books (such as collections of patches for synthesis)
- anthologies
- reference works and monographs
- books for home computer users and synthesizer players

As for content, the series addresses audiences from a wide variety of disciplines. Also, the series addresses both beginning and experienced practitioners in the field. Therefore, it is not surprising that some material in the series or even within a given volume will seem too advanced or too elementary for a given reader. But by including material for all levels and all types of readers, the series serves as a source of introductory material as well as a unified reference collection. Thus far, the books in the series have been written with an academic slant. This book is the first in the series to address the informed but general reader. Even though many technical matters are discussed here, Ken Pohlmann maintains an accessible style and tone.

A book on compact discs (CDs) was included in the plans for the series from its very inception. This work is distinguished from other books on CDs by its breadth, depth, and emphasis on topics that have not yet been treated extensively in book form, such as engineering. Pohlmann is a well-respected author and teacher. Over the years, he has gathered a wealth of information, much of which has not been available to other authors. This volume develops a theme started in the series with *Digital Audio Engineering,* where consumer applications were discussed, though in less detail than in this volume. Future volumes in the series will continue to treat consumer and studio applications.

John Strawn
San Rafael, California

# Preface

A bit of innocent eavesdropping prompted me to write this book. I was browsing through CDs in a record store when I overheard someone explaining the compact disc to his buddy. Knowingly, he told him, "It's the same as an LP, only it's silver."

Although I didn't say so at the time, that remark bothered me considerably. In an unknowing way, his explanation was adequate. The compact disc is indeed a counterpart and successor to the long-playing record, but it's also much more. The sophistication of the technology underlying the CD system should command considerably more understanding and respect than is reflected in a simple comparison to a mechanical groove.

Along those lines, I decided that a book might help illuminate the technological beauty of the CD. My goal was to explain things without generating more confusion. There is enough of that surrounding high technology already. The result, of course, is now in your hands. When you have finished reading, I hope your impression will be that the book was very simple, even though you will have learned a great deal about compact disc technology. A good teacher is just like a good nurse with a hypodermic needle—you never feel the pain.

There is at least one philosophical question that I will not try to answer directly: Is digital audio inherently better than analog? This question is similar to asking whether or not there is life after death. Each of us may ascertain the answer, but not until later.

Meanwhile, I hope this book helps to expand your insight into the CD. And the next time you're in a record store, please try not to embarrass yourself.

Ken C. Pohlmann

# Introduction

"00000000 00000011 00000000 00000011 00000000 00000011
00000000 00000011 00000000 00000011 00000000 00000010
01101000 11010000 11001110 11001110 00000000 00000001
00000000 00000001 00000000 00000001 11111111 11111101
11111111 11111101 11111111 11111100 00101100 01000111
01110011 10000110 00000000 00000011 00000000 00000011
00000000 00000011 00000000 00000100 00000000, etc."

First, a word of explanation. From its Dutch and Japanese origins in June 1980, the compact disc system has prospered beyond the wildest dreams of its inventors. The original audio CD was one of the most successful new electronic products ever introduced; everyone was surprised by its rapid acceptance by music lovers. Over the next few years the biggest news concerned shortages, particularly of discs themselves. Then the disc caught the attention of data lovers as well. CD-ROM quickly started its own acceleration into the market of mass storage. CD-V added high fidelity video to the family. As if that wasn't enough, CD-I's future looks similarly promising as an interactive audio-video medium. Of course, while reading data is fun, writing data is even more fun. Thus a standard for write-once CDs was introduced, and erasable CD technology has been developed. Furthermore, CDs with graphics and MIDI information, and mini-CDs were also introduced into the marketplace. In short, the compact disc family is a hit and already encompasses more topics than one book could comprehensively cover.

Exactly how important is it to bone up on a new technology such as the compact disc? How significantly will it influence our everyday lives, and for how long? There are a number of factors that determine the lifespan of a technology. Manufacturing cost, product performance, market penetration, user boredom, and innovative competition all move technological evolution forward and heighten expectations. As far as the CD family goes, it is safe to say that the future looks bright indeed. Its market share is just beginning to expand, and new and consequential applications are undoubtedly waiting to be discovered by insightful entrepreneurs. Of course, no technology, except the very primitive kind, lasts forever, and someday (perhaps relatively soon) the CD will be only a curiosity. Fittingly, the discs themselves should long outlast their usefulness.

Meanwhile, this handbook covers all the fundamentals of the audio CD and should prove useful to anyone delving into this technology, especially for the first time. Hopefully, it will answer all your questions about audio CDs, and pave the way to a greater understanding of the derivative CD formats.

This little opus, composed of seven chapters, starts from the basics and proceeds onwards and upwards. Theoretical topics are treated expeditiously, and mathematics have been avoided almost entirely. The emphasis is on practical, understandable, useful information.

Chapter One is an introduction to the fundamentals of digital audio theory. Digital signals are contrasted to the analog variety, and the pros and cons are discussed. Just for fun, a brief history of the events leading to the CD is chronicled. In addition, the compact disc is weighed against its predecessors. The first chapter, like all the chapters, concludes with a list of references for further reading.

Chapter Two begins our technical discussion. Sampling and quantization, the key analytical methods of digitally interpreting analog signals, such as audio waveforms, are presented. Aliasing, a negative attribute of sampling, and dither, a panacea for problems arising from quantization, are examined. Pulse code modulation, a particularly clever method of encoding digital audio data, is presented. Finally, a practical audio digitization system is used to consolidate all the theory.

Chapter Three examines the technical theory underlying the compact disc system. The bit stream leading to the plastic disc is examined. The disc itself is an impressive piece of handiwork, particularly at the microscopic level, so the intricacies of data pits are presented. The use of error correction is unprecedented in audio storage; the methods used to safeguard the CD's data are discussed. The bit stream from the disc is processed just as heavily, and oppositely, to the input bit stream. The signal processing circuitry comprising every CD player is examined.

Chapter Four zeros in on CD player design, starting with the laser pickup as it reads data from the disc at a rate of 4.3218 million bits per second. To assist the pickup in its difficult task, electro-mechanical circuits are used for focusing the beam and keeping it on track. These systems are discussed as well. Data decoding involves considerable signal processing. The digital-to-analog converter's job is to transform data back into an audio waveform. Either analog or digital filters must be used to help process the waveform before it is presented to the ears. These output stages are summarized with a look at a specific chip set. The chapter concludes with a look at the non-audio subcode data which is stored on every CD and used to control playback, and a serial transmission format used to convey data from one digital audio device to another.

Chapter Five brings the discussion back to the macroscopic level of the consumer. User notes are presented on a variety of topics. Different player designs are examined and critiqued. Specifications provide a means to distinguish good players from the merely mediocre; measurement techniques are examined. Tips are given to assist in purchasing a CD player. Player care is also important, including the do's and don't's of preventative maintenance. Your disc collection will probably represent a bigger investment than the player; it is wise to take care of your discs, and to be able to evaluate any defects that may be present.

Chapter Six carries the discussion to the diverse versions of the compact disc system. The audio CD was only the first of several CD family members. CD-ROM uses the CD's vast storage potential for non-audio applications, such as data bases and software programs. CD-I merges video with audio on CDs. Imagine a new kind of publishing: combined illustrated, printed, and talking books. To make room for video information on CD-I, adaptive delta pulse code modulation can be used to encode audio data. DVI provides yet another format for interactivity. CD-V merges the CD's digital audio format with that of high quality analog video optical storage. The CD-WO format offers users the chance to permanently record their own data. Several fully recordable/erasable CD methods, including magneto-optics and phase-change technology, allow users to record and erase data. CD + G utilizes subcode storage capacity to provide graphics output from audio CDs. Finally, CD-3 is a mini-sized CD for applications where shorter playing times are sufficient.

Chapter Seven is an examination of the technology of compact disc manufacturing. The discussion concentrates on the foremost production method, injection molding of polycarbonate plastic. Preparation of master tape, the mastering of the glass disc, the production of pressing molds, injection molding, metallization, spin coating, printing, packaging, and quality control are all discussed. Alternative manufacturing methods promise to simplify the task of making discs; these new methods are explained.

A glossary containing definitions of key technical terms and abbreviations rounds out the presentation.

In summary, this book attempts to cram as much pleasant and useful information into the smallest possible space, rather like the compact disc itself.

Oh, the bits that began this introduction are from a compact disc recording of Tchaikovsky's 1812 Overture, the very beginning, as the male chorus opens the piece in this particular rendition. Of course, with all the multiplexing, modulation, interleaving, and error protection, it's a little difficult to catch the melody. And since the bits represent less than 200 microseconds of the recording, the guys really haven't finished inhaling their first breath. So, these bits aren't that great. It's a lot more exciting when the cannon go off.

# Chapter One

# Introduction to the Compact Disc

## INTRODUCTION

Let's try a conceptual experiment. From your conceptual seat in your conceptual concert hall, you lean forward in anticipation as the conceptual orchestra begins its conceptual performance of Beethoven's Tenth Symphony. (No, I'm not conceptualizing; he really did start a Tenth.) Your job is to write down all the information you hear. Ready? Begin!

Whew! After only a few bars, you give up. Even writing down the score in musical notation is overwhelming, much less recording all the timbres, aesthetic considerations, hall acoustics, and so forth.

We have to conclude that music is a surprisingly complex phenomenon; it is filled with information. To store it, we require a system which can deal with incredible amounts of information. It is not surprising that historically the latest and highest technology has always been utilized to make recordings, because only the best technology satisfies our current expectations of what a good recording should sound like. As higher technology was devised and pressed into service, our expectations were redefined. All of which brings us to the topic at hand: digital audio and the compact disc.

## ANALOG VERSUS DIGITAL

To understand the nature of analog and digital systems, along with their differences, let's try another conceptual experiment. Suppose that you are stationed in the Arctic Circle. (Since I'm writing this book in Miami in July, this concept has particular appeal to me.) The Audubon Society has charged you with the important mission of noting the effect, if any, of barometric pressure on the mating habits of penguins.

A barometer measures changes in atmospheric pressure. Attached to the barometer is a recording device, a cylinder with graph paper attached to it, and a pen with ink (and anti-freeze). As the atmospheric pressure changes, the pen traces a line on the slowly rotating cylinder. At the end of every day, the cylinder has completed one rotation, and you change paper. You are thus left with a graph of barometric pressure over time.

What you have is an analog recording. It is analog because it is a continuous representation, an analogy, or a model of the actual phenomenon. It's very nice, but its accuracy is limited by numerous factors, including the precision of the cylinder's rotation and the flow of ink. Its usefulness is also limited by the fact that its representation is graphical. For example, to communicate your findings to the Audubon Society headquarters, you would have to send the actual graph paper or a copy which might not be as accurate as the original.

You figure there might be an alternative, and there is. Instead of relying on the graph paper, you decide to document individual readings themselves. You design a device that reads the pressure from the barometer every minute and prints out the number. At the end of a day, there are 1,440 numbers, representing the changing pressure.

What you have is a digital recording. It is digital because the signal is subjected to measurement at discrete points in time, and the information is stored as discrete numbers. It's very nice because the numbers are inherently more robust than the analog graph, and if your digital device is well designed, the numbers are probably more precise. In addition, it is far easier to communicate your findings; simply reading the numbers over the radio would do the job. Moreover, when the scientists at headquarters write down the numbers, they will have an exact copy of your results.

Suppose, however, that the scientists back at headquarters squawk that the numbers are not as good as a graph and complain that there is no record of pressure between each measurement. You could point out that you aren't as stupid as you look. Atmospheric pressure can change only so fast. For example, suppose the barometric pressure was 30.034 inches at 11:01:00 P.M., and 30.036 inches at 11:02:00 P.M. Although you didn't take a reading at 11:01:30 P.M., you can calculate that the pressure was 30.035, and not, say, 29.022. The atmosphere would not work like that. Thus by knowing how fast things change, you can sample often enough to obtain complete information about what's happening.

On the other hand, an event outside the interest of our barometric experiment, such as the overpressure created by a nearby penguin exploding at precisely 11:01:30 P.M., would not be documented. But that doesn't affect our study. By defining how fast things of interest change, we can ignore those events which happen faster.

At any rate, satisfied that the barometric pressure will be accurately documented, you can get down to the primary scientific task of watching the penguins.

Our conceptual experiment illustrates fairly well the relevant differences between analog and digital representations. In fact, barometric pressure is a close analogy to audio signals, since both are simply pressure changes in air. Of course, changes in barometric pressure would produce a very low frequency (about 0.00001 Hz), but if you speeded it up about 100 million times, it might sound musical, or at least like punk rock.

Back to reality. Let's nail down our comparison between analog and digital systems. The principal distinction lies in the way they represent information. Digital information can exist only in pieces, as discrete values, as numbers. This is vastly different from analog information, where one continuous, infinitely indivisible value is recorded.

Analog and digital systems thus differ considerably. There is no doubt about that. Nevertheless, the basic question has still eluded us: Why digital? At first glance, the use of digital technology for audio purposes seems very cumbersome. After all, we must convert sound into a series of numbers, each of which must accurately describe the sound at that instant in time. We must first store these billions of numbers and then convert them back into sound to hear what's going on. That's a lot of work. Moreover, since analog audio technology seemed perfectly adequate for a hundred years, is it really necessary to replace analog with digital?

One answer is this: Sure, digital audio is a lot of hassle, but it's worth it. One justification for digital audio lies in the very nature of its signal. Sound is an analog phenomenon, and so is noise. An analog audio device cannot distinguish between them; hence, the noise of an analog signal is the sum total of all the noise introduced in its path. For example, every time an analog tape is copied, its noise increases. The numbers comprising a digital signal will carry an error, introduced when they are first selected, but they are impervious to noise; for example, rerecording does not add noise. A digital number cannot become noisy; it is right or wrong.

Analog reproduction is more frail than digital. An analog system introduces distortion as it attempts to convey the exact analog nature of its information. In contrast, a digital system, at least philosophically, has an easy job. It must be able to distinguish only between 1s and 0s to reproduce the signal. The only theoretical limitations are those dictated by the quantity and accuracy of the numbers. In other words, with digital we can more precisely manipulate and process information, and thus achieve a more accurate result.

Along similar lines, digital audio is advantageous because its signal is robust. It is a cruel world out there, and under adverse conditions, a digital signal suffers less degradation than an analog signal. Moreover, a digital signal suffers no degradation at all until conditions have deteriorated beyond a known level. The design performance of a digital system is designed into its circuits. Performance is thus always a known, defined quantity.

Another justification for digital audio is its consistency of performance. Analog devices can work quite well when they are new, but frequent adjustment and maintenance are necessary to ensure consistent performance. Because digital systems often permit a higher degree of circuit integration, they exhibit greater long-term accuracy, with less performance variation or failure. In fact, when a digital system fails, the problem is often an analog part inside.

Digital circuits are also very efficient because logical functions and operational features can be easily designed and implemented. Moreover, such functions and features can be quickly altered or updated; often the hardware circuit remains unchanged, and a change in programming achieves the new result.

Finally, digital audio's sonic performance is excellent. First-generation digital audio products rivalled the result of a century of analog evolution, and digital's evolution guarantees the gap will widen.

Of course, digital audio isn't perfect—far from it. Its complexity breeds considerable challenges that are not found in analog systems. To use and appreciate such equipment properly, a fair amount of technical understanding is required, as demonstrated in the following pages.

**LP VERSUS CD**

Many methods of audio storage have evolved since Edison made the first audio recording in 1877 on a cylinder covered with tin foil. Early acoustical recordings were made on wax cylinder and shellac disc, and many electrical recordings used 78 rpm and long-playing records. Subsequently, numerous magnetic tape formats were developed. However, all of these audio systems shared identical foundations; they recorded and reproduced an analog signal by using a mechanical pickup in contact with the medium. Overall, this technology is now a mature one and has virtually exhausted the possibilities available within the limitations of analog master tape, phono cartridges, analog circuitry, motors, and mechanical systems.

The difference between analog and digital audio technologies can be illustrated by a close look at a long playing record, and a compact disc, illustrated in figure 1.1.

The LP stores its information as an analog groove. Variations in its side-to-side amplitude and depth represent the original audio signal. If someone hit a big drum, the groove would take a big swing. The frequency of the drum sound determines the frequency of the groove's swing, and the amplitude of the drum sound determines the amplitude of the swing. In short, the groove is a physical analogy to the original sound wave. Left and right audio channels are stored on either side of the groove walls. To reproduce the information, a stylus runs through the groove and the phonograph cartridge converts the stylus's mechanical movements into an electrical signal which is later amplified. Analog tapes follow the same

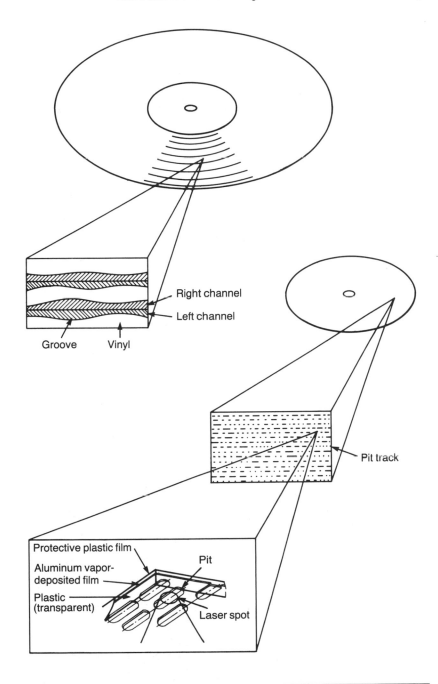

Right channel

Left channel

Groove    Vinyl

Pit track

Protective plastic film

Aluminum vapor-deposited film

Plastic (transparent)

Pit

Laser spot

Figure 1.1    *LP grooves storing analog information contrasted to CD pits, storing digital information.*

principles, but instead of groove undulations, the analog signal is stored in orientations of magnetic particles.

The CD stores its information digitally. The length of its data pits represents a series of 1s and 0s—numbers (binary bits, actually) which represent the original audio signal. If someone hit a big drum, the numbers would be different than if there was no drum. Generally, the frequency of the signal is reflected in the rate of change in the numbers, and the amplitude is represented by the magnitude of the numbers. Both audio channels are stored along the same pit track. To read the data, we use a laser beam light source. The numbers are read from the disc as flashes of light and are used to reconstruct the original audio signal. Because nothing (except light) touches the pits, they never wear out.

In practice, the compact disc offers numerous advantages over previously existing audio storage media such as the LP record: the LP must be handled with care to preserve its mechanical groove; groove damage is audible; tracking with a stylus damages the groove; and performance specifications are limited. For example, the signal-to-noise ratio is about 60 dB, channel separation is about 30 dB, and frequency response is not flat.

Phonograph turntables have inherent problems associated with analog devices. The mechanical transport introduces audible artifacts such as wow and flutter because the medium's speed is directly linked to audio reproduction. Electrical circuitry is prone to aging and to temperature drift and instabilities. Considerable phase shift is introduced by analog circuits, and considerable signal equalization is required. The stylus suffers wear and requires periodic replacement to maintain fidelity and prevent accelerated damage to the medium. Turntables are usually operated through mechanical controls that are limited in utility and prone to wear and tear.

The compact disc is designed for better performance in these areas. A CD is more robust because the data surface is embedded inside the disc itself. Because data is read by a focused laser beam, there is no degradation from repeated playings, and the effect of dust and surface damage is minimized. Digital signal processing permits use of error correction and other techniques to improve the reliability of the stored data.

The importance of digital error correction is apparent when we consider the question of scale, which is illustrated in figure 1.2. An LP microgroove is extemely narrow, about the width of a human hair. However, over thirty laps of a CD pit track would fit into one LP groove. The data rate from that track would be 4.3218 million bits every second.

The volume of numbers stored on a compact disc necessitates error correction. An analog signal presents basic conceptual problems for any attempt to diagnose and correct errors in the signal. If a groove is distorted, or the record scratched, the turntable's stylus cannot distinguish the defect from the real thing. A digital system easily accommodates and desperately requires error protection. The density of information on a CD is about 100

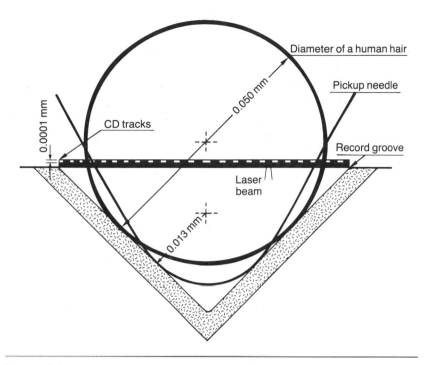

Figure 1.2 *A scale drawing illustrates the small dimensions of compact disc tracks compared to those of an LP micro-groove.*

times greater than that on an LP. With three billion or so pits crammed onto its surface, a CD is vulnerable to defects and scratches. Fortunately, the data may be recorded with error protection codes which permit detection, correction, or concealment of errors. A CD player can thus correct disc errors, whereas a turntable cannot.

A compact disc player offers numerous other improvements over turntables. The transport's performance does not affect the quality of audio reproduction. Data conversion is independent of variations in disc rotational speed, hence wow and flutter are negligible. Digital circuitry is more immune to aging and temperature problems. A CD player with a digital oversampling filter introduces negligible phase shift. The laser pickup is self-regulating and has great longevity. In addition, the pickup can never damage the medium. Specifications are improved; for example, signal-to-noise ratio and channel separation are both over 90 dB, and frequency response deviations are minimized. The CD also offers longer playing time, smaller size, programmability of tracks, and a subcode for display, control, and optional user information. Integration of circuitry permits portability of players and low manufacturing costs.

Digital applications extend far beyond the task of storing audio data; digital logic, including the use of microprocessors, controls the operation of all CD players. Turntables could also benefit from digital control, but the marriage of stored digital data and digital control offers many advantages. For example, the data on a compact disc not only stores the music, but also directly controls the rotating speed of the disc and the tracking and focusing of the laser pickup reading the stored data. That would be tough for an analog storage device. Finally, digital control circuits permit flexibility of operation, including programmability and a simpler mechanical interface.

In summary, the introduction of the compact disc revitalized audio technology by changing three fundamental design criteria. First, digital data is used to store and process the audio signal. Second, error correction is employed to make the stored data more robust. Third, the compact disc system uses an optical, non-contact pickup.

Part of the compact disc's strength lies in its noble lineage. Its technology embodies over 100 years of scientific and engineering advances. With that in mind, a quick look at the origins of the compact disc may help to establish a better perspective on this technology.

## ORIGINS OF THE COMPACT DISC

"The exaggeration of sibilants by the new method is abominable, and there is often a harshness which recalls the worst excesses of the past. The recording of massed strings is atrocious. . . ." Clearly, not everyone always agrees that advances in audio technology are a good thing. Change is not always welcome, particularly when it occurs with something as intimately and subjectively felt as the perception of musical sound. That was certainly true when Compton Mackenzie, editor of *The Gramophone,* described the new electrical recording process in 1925.

Understandably, change is hard to accept. The introduction of any new technology prompts both praise and condemnation, both of which are sometimes misguided because the context of the technology is misunderstood. The compact disc system is both an evolutionary and revolutionary step in the history of audio technology—nothing more and nothing less. To appreciate the compact disc fully, it may help to consider a very brief chronology of events in its development. Several references at the end of this chapter contain extensive information on the history of audio.

Significant events in the nineteenth century set the stage for digital audio as we know it today. In 1841 Augustin-Louis Cauchy proposed an early sampling theorem. In 1842, Charles Babbage proposed his analytical engine for performing and storing calculations. Construction of this first computer was never completed. In 1854 George Boole published *An Investiga-*

*tion Into the Laws of Thought* which contained the axioms of switching algebra, the basis of digital circuits. In 1855 Leon Scott de Martinville invented the phonautograph, a machine for recording vibrations using a carbonized paper cylinder and a hog's bristle. In 1876 Alexander Graham Bell publicly demonstrated the telephone. A breakthrough, and the true birth of audio reproduction, occurred in 1877 when Thomas Alva Edison invented the analog phonograph. Ironically, this occurred while he was experimenting with a device for storing digital data—a telegraphic code repeater. Edison's wax cylinder was quickly challenged in 1887 as Emile Berliner invented the audio disc.

The opening years of the twentieth century saw a number of important inventions in the new field of electricity. In 1904 John Ambrose Fleming invented the diode vacuum tube, the first active circuit component. In 1907 Lee DeForest invented the triode amplifier vacuum tube, thereby initiating the modern era of electrical recording and reproduction. The 78 rpm record was introduced in 1915. In 1922 J. R. Carson published a mathematical analysis exploring the nature of time sampling in communications. A major breakthrough occurred in 1928 when Harry Nyquist published *Certain Topics in Telegraph Transmission Theory* which contains proof of the sampling theorem—the basis of digital audio. In the same year R. V. L. Hartley stated the information capacity of an ideal channel, and $33^{1}/_{3}$ rpm records were demonstrated. In 1937 A. Reeves invented pulse code modulation, and H. Aiken of Harvard proposed the design of an electromechanical computing machine to IBM.

The Second World War stimulated development of computing devices and electrical components. In 1943 the Electronic Numerical Integrator and Computer (ENIAC) was developed at the University of Pennsylvania by the U.S. Army. This dinosaur weighed thirty tons. In 1947 the first magnetic tape recorders were sold in the United States. In 1948 John Bardeen, William Shockley, and Walter Brattain invented the transistor in Bell Laboratories. In the same year Claude E. Shannon published *A Mathematical Theory of Communication,* containing work on information theory, including a measure of information and the capacity of a data channel. In 1949 Peter Goldmark developed the microgroove LP record, and 45 rpm records were introduced.

In 1950 Richard W. Hamming published work on error detection and error correction codes, another critical piece in the subsequent development of digital audio. In 1952 D. A. Huffman described a minimum redundancy coding scheme. In 1958 C. H. Townes and A. L. Schawlow invented the laser, and stereo LPs were marketed. Also in 1958, Jack S. Kilby invented the integrated circuit while in the employ of Texas Instruments. In 1959 A. Hocquenghem published error correction codes. In 1960 R. C. Bose and D. K. Ray-Chaudhuri published binary group error correction codes. Early computer music experiments took place at Bell Laboratories and other facilities. I. S. Reed and G. Solomon published a multiple error correction code, later to be incorporated into the compact disc. T. H. Mainan demonstrated the first working model of a laser.

By the 60s, the essential components required to build a digital audio recorder/reproducer were in place. In 1967 the NHK Technical Research Institute publicly demonstrated a PCM digital audio recorder with 30 kHz sampling and 12-bit companding using a one-inch helical scan video recorder for the storage medium. In 1969 Sony Corporation demonstrated a PCM digital audio recorder with 47.25 kHz sampling and 13-bit quantization, using two-inch video tape for storage. In 1969 Philips initiated the development of optical storage, the final major technology required for the development of the compact disc. In 1971 large scale integrated (LSI) circuits, such as the microprocessor, were introduced by Intel and other manufacturing companies. The first digital audio device, the digital delay line, was introduced into recording studios. Optical disc technology was publicly demonstrated by Philips in 1972. In 1973 Denon and the BBC began using digital recorders for master recording.

In 1974 Philips experimented with optical audio disc storage and standardized the 120 millimeter disc diameter. In 1976 Sony experimented with large diameter optical audio discs. In 1977 Mitsubishi, Sony, and Hitachi demonstrated digital audio disc prototypes at the Tokyo Audio Fair. Also in 1977, JVC developed a digital audio processor. In 1978 Philips announced the ongoing development of the compact disc as an audio playback medium. Philips also introduced video disc players using optical readout. Also in 1978, Sony marketed the PCM-1600 and PCM-1 digital audio processors, as well as stationary head digital tape recorders for professional use. The Digital Audio Disc Convention was held in Tokyo; thirty-five manufacturers attended.

In 1979 Philips demonstrated a prototype compact disc player in Eindhoven. In 1979 Philips and Sony agreed to collaborate on the design of the compact disc system. Toshi Doi reported on the suitability of error correction codes on digital audio signals. In 1980 the Philips/Sony compact disc standard was proposed, including an EFM signal format, polycarbonate disc material, and Reed-Solomon error correction codes. The Digital Audio Disc Committee and Matsushita adopted the compact disc standard in 1981. The semiconductor laser was introduced in 1982 and Philips demonstrated an oversampling digital audio filter. Later in 1982 the compact disc system was finally introduced in Japan and Europe, and the first commercially manufactured compact disc was made at the CBS/Sony factory in Japan. Philips began work on a car CD player. Low cost LSI 16-bit A/D converters became available as well.

In 1983 the compact disc system was introduced into the United States. The Compact Disc Group was formed to aid in marketing efforts. CD audio discs with video prototypes were demonstrated. CD-ROM prototypes were also demonstrated. In 1983, 30,000 players and 800,000 discs were sold in the United States. In 1984 second generation CD players were introduced, along with automobile CD players. The first CD pressing plant in this country was opened in Terre Haute. Portable CD players were then introduced, followed in 1985 by third generation CD players and CD-ROM computer drives. The CD-I concept was introduced in 1986, the same year that over three million players and over 53 million discs were sold in the United States. In 1987 the CD-I standard was finalized, and both CD-V and CD-3 discs were introduced. In 1988 the CD-WO write-once standard was introduced, the development of erasable/recordable CDs was announced, and CD-I products were marketed. Analysts predicted that the domestic market would grow from 100 million to 150 million discs in 1988.

And there you have it—a very brief look at how we got to where we are now. It's certainly not a complete chronology, but it includes many of the technological prerequisites to the compact disc and to digital audio in general. It serves to demonstrate that any advance in technology is an effect with many causes. The compact disc exists today because of a unique sequence of many technological events. Omit any of these breakthroughs, and the CD as we know it today would have been a technological impossibility.

Of course, the compact disc does not signal the end of development in audio technology. In much the same way that other breakthroughs, such as Edison's wax cylinder, engendered startling consequences, the CD will undoubtedly have the same effect, if not an even more radical one.

## FOR FURTHER READING

Blesser, B., B. Locanthi, and T. G. Stockham, Jr., eds. *Digital Audio.* New York: Audio Engineering Society, 1983.

Deloraine, E. M., and A. H. Reeves. "The 25th Anniversary of Pulse Code Modulation." *IEEE Spectrum* 2(5):56–63, May, 1965.

McGill, James F. "An Introduction to Digital Recording and Reproduction." In John Strawn, ed. *Digital Audio Engineering: An Anthology.* Los Altos, Calif.: Kaufmann, 1985.

Nijsen, C. G. "And the Music Went Round and Round on Rolls, Disks, or Reels." Part 1, *Journal of the Audio Engineering Society* 32(3):162–78, March, 1984. Part 2, *Journal of the Audio Engineering Society* 32(4):262–73, April, 1984.

Read, O., and W. L. Welch. *From Tin Foil to Stereo: Evolution of the Phonograph.* Indianapolis: Sams, 1976.

Shannon, C. E. "A Mathematical Theory of Communication." *Bell System Technical Journal* 27:379–423, 623–56.

## Chapter Two

# Fundamentals of Digital Audio

## INTRODUCTION

The essence of digital audio lies in its numerical basis. A digital audio system converts an analog waveform into numbers, stores, transmits, or processes those numbers, and then converts them back to an analog waveform. These steps may be divided into the digital audio recording of a music performance, the storage of that performance on a compact disc, and the reproduction of the performance with the CD player.

The digital audio chain, from the recording studio or concert hall to your living room, is predicated on several basic phenomena. First, the analog waveform must be discrete-time sampled at a precise, unvarying rate. This divides the waveform into discrete intervals. With sampling, the signal must be filtered to prevent aliasing, a form of distortion. Next, each sample must be converted to a number; this is the process of quantization. To minimize an inevitable error associated with quantization, a dither signal must be introduced. In most digital audio recorder/reproducers these steps take place in a linear pulse code modulation system. This chapter examines all of these fundamental elements.

## SAMPLING

Analog is continuous. Digital is discrete. To transform the original analog audio waveform into a digital audio signal, we examine the waveform at specific points in time. We must choose points on the original analog signal. This decision process is called discrete-time sampling, or simply sampling.

Since we're speaking of time, let's try a clock analogy to illustrate how a digital music system uses sampling. Time seems to flow continuously, and the hands of an analog clock sweep across the circle of hours, covering each part of time. A digital readout clock also tells time, but with a discretely valued display and at discrete points in time. In other words, it displays a sampled time. It's the same with audio. Audio varies continuously in time and may be recorded and reproduced either in continuous analog form or time-sampled digital form. Just as both clocks tell time, both types of recordings play the same music. In summary, sampling means dividing a signal into evenly spaced, discrete points in time.

However, there is a price to pay, in the form of several tricky decisions. The first question we are faced with involves how many measurements we want. In other words, how often do we record a data point? How fast do we sample? And if a digital system samples discretely, what happens to information between samples? To answer these questions, let's go back in time.

### Harry's Theorem

It is February, 1928. Shiny new Model A's bounce noisily along barely paved roads. *The Jazz Singer,* the first talking motion picture, is opening in theatres across the country. The stock market is spiraling to new heights; everyone's future prosperity is assured. The winter convention of the American Institute of Electrical Engineers is being held in New York City. An engineer from American Telephone and Telegraph Company delivers a paper entitled "Certain Topics in Telegraph Transmission Theory." The engineer apologizes, saying that it is necessary ". . . to include a certain amount of material which is already well known to telegraphic engineers." But at least one of his topics isn't so familiar. He shows that a waveform may be sampled discretely in time; furthermore, the waveform may be completely reconstructed if it is sampled correctly.

The engineer, named Harry, has just completed his paper. We catch him as he steps from the podium to ask him a few questions.

"Harry, the mathematics are great, but can you state this theorem in plain English?"

"That's easy. To understand it, let's consider how a movie camera works. A strip of film runs past the shutter so that a series of still images is photographed. When the movie is projected, these still pictures create a moving image. The frame rate is important: to capture a fast moving object, we would need a fast frame rate. Digital audio is the same. Instead of taking still photographs to create a movie, you take still audio samples to create sound. My theorem tells you how fast you should take samples."

"Is that all there is to it?"

"Pretty much. An audio waveform is a variation in air pressure; it exists continuously in time, over a continuously variable amplitude range. If you

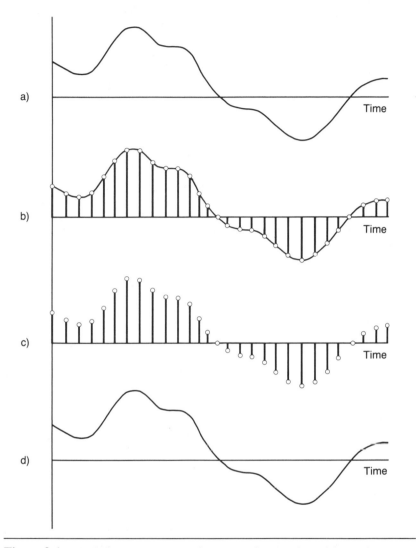

Figure 2.1   *With discrete-time sampling, an audio waveform (a) may be sampled (b), and the sample points (c) may be used to reconstruct the waveform (d).*

put a pencil to paper and start drawing in one direction, and never go in the opposite direction, or let the pencil line intersect with itself, you're drawing a representation of an analog audio waveform (figure 2.1a). Now if you go back and periodically tap your pencil along the line (figure 2.1b), you've sampled the waveform (figure 2.1c). The interesting part is that if you follow my theorem, your sample points can be used to reconstruct the original analog waveform, without loss of information" (figure 2.1d).

"That's incredible, Harry. Are you sure about this?"

"The math is impeccable. Discrete time sampling is legitimate. Given correct conditions, the theorem says that no information is lost due to sampling in a digitization system. The samples contain the same amount of information as the unsampled signal. The trick is to follow the correct conditions.

"It's just like in our film. Once we determine the speed of the fastest object we wish to photograph, we can set the frame rate accordingly. For sound, the samples correspond to the film frames, the sampling rate corresponds to the frame rate, and the high-frequency signal corresponds to the fast moving object. Just as we need some relationship between the frame rate and the speed of moving objects, we need to define the relationship between sampling frequency and audio frequencies. That's where my theorem comes in. It states that if we take samples at a frequency at least twice that of the highest audio frequency, complete reconstruction can be accomplished."

"What about the waveform between samples?"

"Not to worry. By definition, the samples have all the information we need to provide complete reconstruction. Of course, the frequency criteria must be strictly observed. If you were making a movie and someone shot an arrow across the set, it might pass by without being recorded on a frame. The same thing is true with sound; a frequency that is too high would not be properly encoded and would even create a kind of distortion called aliasing. To prevent that, we limit the frequency content of the input signal with a low-pass filter. Its job is to ensure that all frequencies greater than one half the sampling frequency are attenuated below the amplitude resolution of the system (figure 2.2). To limit the sampling rate required to achieve a given audio bandwidth, we design low-pass filters with a very sharp characteristic—the so-called brickwall filters."

"They have a cutoff at the half-sampling frequency?"

"Actually, we design them to begin cutting a little before that point to give the filter's response an opportunity to achieve full attenuation before the half-sampling frequency. Conversely, we place the half-sampling point a little above the highest audio frequency we want in our flat passband. For example, to achieve flat response to 20 kHz, we might sample at 44 kHz; the filter would have 2 kHz, from 20 to 22 kHz, to achieve full attenuation. Whatever the numbers, the idea is clear—the filter bandlimits the input signal, thus ensuring that the theorem's criteria will be upheld. Thanks to sampling, we can reconstruct the waveform later."

"What if we want a higher frequency response?"

"No problem—just raise your sampling frequency. But a 20 kHz bandwidth should be okay, since that's the limit of most people's hearing."

"So choice of sampling frequency determines the highest frequency reproducible by the digitization system?"

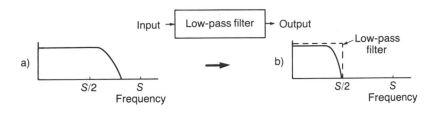

**Figure 2.2** *The sampling theorem dictates that the frequency content of the audio signal be less than or equal to the half-sampling frequency. The input signal may contain frequencies greater than the half-sampling frequency as shown by its spectrum (a). A low-pass filter removes high frequencies (b) to produce a spectrum of frequencies below the half-sampling frequency.*

"Right. And that's the essence of the theorem. $S$ samples per second are needed to represent a waveform with a bandwidth of $S/2$."

"Hey, I just thought of something. If you're sampling at 40 kHz, the 20 kHz waveform will have only two samples. How can that work?"

"As you stated, when the sampled frequencies become higher, the periods are shorter, and there will be fewer samples per period. At the theoretical limiting case of critical sampling, at an audio frequency of half the sampling frequency, there will be two samples per period. Consider a 20 kHz input sine wave (figure 2.3a). The digitizer would generate two samples, and this would be used at the output to produce a 20 kHz square wave (figure 2.3b).

"Of course, a square wave is quite unlike a sine wave, which brings us to the final piece of system hardware. At the output of every digitization system is another low-pass filter, essentially identical in design to the input low-pass filter. Its job is also to remove all frequencies above the half-sampling frequency. We have to do that again because sampling has generated new frequencies above the audio band, that is, all the high-order har-

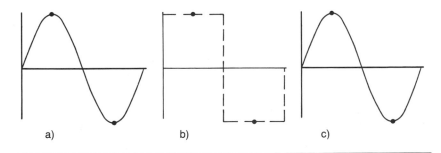

**Figure 2.3** *With critical sampling, a sine wave input (a) would be reconstructed as a square wave (b), low-pass filtered and output as a sine wave (c).*

monics in the square wave. The output filter removes all the unwanted harmonics above the half-sampling frequency, leaving only the original 20 kHz sine wave" (figure 2.3c).

"But what if the input wasn't a sine wave?"

"It had to be. Our input filter would have removed the harmonics from any 20 kHz waveform, leaving only the fundamental sine wave."

"We're losing all the harmonics!"

"Sure. But that's okay. All complicated waveforms, which are everything other than a sine wave, are basically comprised of a fundamental sine wave and a series of harmonic sine waves at multiples of the fundamental. For example, a 1 kHz waveform would have a fundamental of 1 kHz, and harmonic sine waves at 2 kHz, 3 kHz, 4 kHz, 5 kHz, etc. However, that information is useful only in your hearing range. You probably can't hear harmonics above 20 kHz, so there's no reason for a digital system to 'hear' them either. A complex 20 kHz waveform has harmonics at 40 kHz, 60 kHz, 80 kHz, 100 kHz, etc., and most people cannot hear anything past the fundamental. There is no need for a digitization system to attempt to record such high frequencies."

"I guess your sampling idea holds water."

"It sure looks like it. Of course, it's all still theoretical, but sooner or later someone might find an application for the theory—there could be some real possibilities."

### The Nyquist Theorem

The engineer's name is Harry Nyquist, and his paper contains the sampling theorem that has transformed audio and is used in all digital audio systems. There is no evidence that the other engineers at the convention stood to their feet and cheered after Harry delivered his paper. Indeed, if he had tried to describe to them the music digitization systems we take for granted today, they probably would have laughed. Nevertheless, he established the foundations of digital audio.

There are still some people around who either do not believe Nyquist's sampling theorem or simply distrust it. For one reason or another, they do not see how little pieces of a continuous bandlimited waveform can be used to reconstruct a waveform. In all fairness to them, the theorem is somewhat like a brainbuster in the comics section of the Sunday paper, because it seems counterintuitive.

Briefly, let's reconsider Harry's analogy. Just as the discrete frames of a movie create moving pictures, so the samples of a digital audio recording

$\longrightarrow$

Figure 2.4    *An audio digitization system showing sampling and de-sampling.*

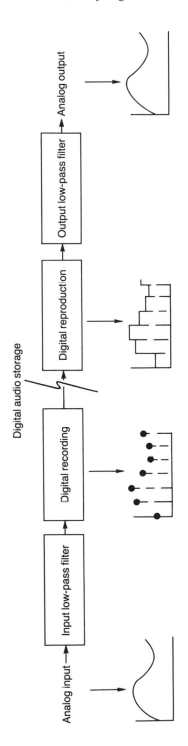

create time-varying music; there is little conceptual difference between the visual and aural systems. In a digital audio system, such as the one shown in figure 2.4, we must limit the highest frequency in the incoming signal to a frequency of one-half the sampling frequency (the half-sampling frequency is also known as the Nyquist frequency). Specifically, the signal is low-pass filtered at 20 kHz or so. When this filtering is accomplished, we can successfully sample the signal such that there is no loss of information due to sampling between the sampled signal at the output and the filtered signal at the input. When the input is filtered, we can restore all the intervening values, without error due to sampling, and thus re-create the original waveform filtered at the upper limit of audibility. An output filter smooths the waveform to return it to its original state.

We merely observe the theorem's dictate that we must sample at a frequency at least twice that of the highest input frequency. In the case of the compact disc, the sampling frequency is 44.1 kHz (a sample every 22.6757 millionths of a second). This permits an audio frequency response from 0 to over 20 kHz. Thus, each channel of a CD outputs a sample 44,100 times per second. With stereo, that's 88,200 times per second. And over the course of an hour, that's about 320 million values. Fortunately, such high data rates are well within the scope of mass-produced technology. At any rate, the point is clear: a filtered signal may be sampled, stored in discrete values, de-sampled, and reproduced without loss due to sampling.

Why 44.1 kHz? There is no special reason; it's just a question of circumstance. Early digital tape recorders used video cassette recorders for storage (some digital PCM recorders still do). A sampling frequency of 44.1 kHz was derived from the video scan frequencies of the television system.

However, there are other important considerations pertaining to sampling. We still must discuss exactly why we must have a low-pass filter at the input and the output of a digital music system and what happens if we don't.

## ALIASING

One particular challenge to the audio digitization system designer is that of aliasing, a kind of sampling confusion that can take place in the recording side of the chain. A criminal at large can assume an alias to confuse his identity. Similarly, a sampled signal can masquerade as another; this is aliasing. An alias frequency appears as another, new frequency. It is thus the designer's obligation to prevent aliasing from ever occurring. As we will see, an input low-pass filter (sometimes called the anti-aliasing filter) will accomplish this, but only if its cutoff frequency is carefully chosen.

Aliasing is a digital system's improper response to any frequency greater than half the sampling frequency. Nyquist has shown that the highest signal frequency in a sampling system can be no more than half the sampling frequency. As the signal frequency becomes higher and higher, the number of sample points per cycle becomes fewer. When the signal frequency reaches half the sampling frequency, there are only two samples per cycle, which is the absolute minimum needed to record a waveform. A higher frequency would cause the digitization system to alias.

### Stagecoach Wheels

What is aliasing? One example occurs in western movies. When the marshall climbs up onto the stagecoach and drives away, the spokes on the stagecoach's wheels begin rotating forward, faster and faster. Then a funny thing happens. The spokes first appear to slow down, and then appear to rotate backwards, even though the stagecoach is obviously picking up forward speed. As the stagecoach goes even faster, the spokes start moving forward again. The problem lies in the rate of the film's frames. If the camera is taking 24 pictures per second, the sampling theorem dictates that a maximum change of 12 spokes per second can be properly reproduced. Thus a twelve-spoke wheel could reach a maximum speed of one revolution per second for proper reproduction. If the speed increased to 13 spokes per second, the camera would show 11 spokes per second. At 14 spokes per second, a rate of 10 would be reproduced. The reproduced spoke rate is wrong; a form of aliasing is occurring.

Audio waveforms behave similarly. When a waveform is under-sampled—that is, when its frequency is greater than the half-sampling rate—aliasing can create new frequencies. Figure 2.5 shows an input waveform, sample points, and a new reconstructed waveform. Both waveforms are valid for those samples, but the new waveform is an alias frequency.

A more complete understanding of aliasing may be obtained when sampling is considered as a modulation process. One result of that modulation is the creation of a spectrum, or frequency response, having sidebands, or image frequency responses, centered on multiples of the sampling frequency. These sidebands are a consequence of sampling and result even when the Nyquist theorem is observed.

Figure 2.6 shows an input audio signal (a), the sampling signal (b), and the resulting sampled audio signal (c). To the left is the familiar time-domain representation of the waveforms. To the right is the waveform's spectrum, or frequency-domain representation. The input audio signal has been properly bandlimited to the half-sampling frequency of $S/2$. The sampled audio signal contains the original spectrum, as well as images of that spectrum, centered at multiples of the sampling frequency. The output filter would remove the high-frequency image spectrum, leaving only the original. The sampling theorem has been observed, and all is well.

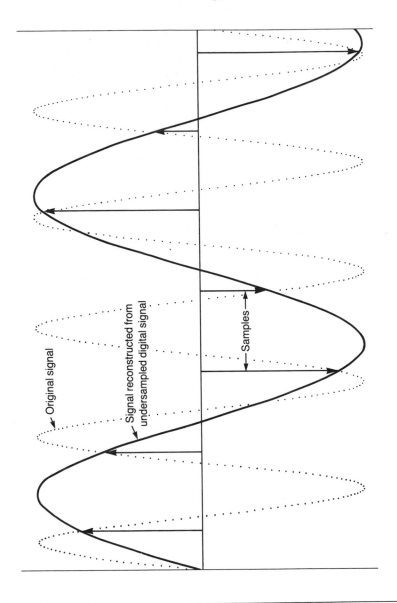

Figure 2.5   *As a result of undersampling, aliasing can create a new frequency.*

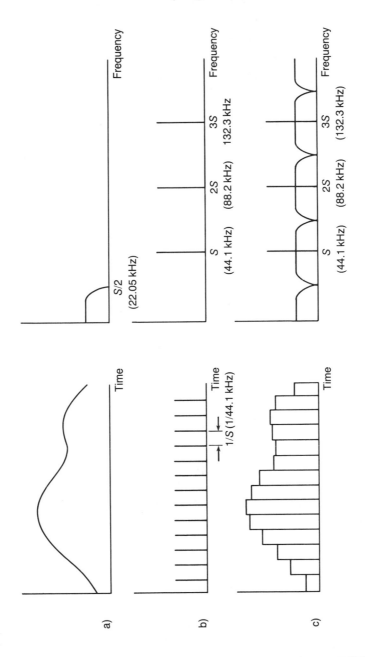

Figure 2.6 *When a bandlimited audio signal (a) is sampled by a sampling signal (b), a series of high frequency image spectra (c) are created at multiples of the sampling frequency.*

### *Foldover Frequencies*

Aliasing takes place when the sampling theorem is not observed. Fortunately for our understanding, we can draw a simple picture of aliasing. Figure 2.7 shows what happens when the input frequency exceeds the half-sampling frequency; aliasing can be seen as overlap between the signal bands. It is evident that the output filter can remove the higher-frequency image spectra and their aliasing; however, the aliased frequency below $S/2$ cannot be removed from the audio signal. In this case, the upper frequencies of the audio band become contaminated with the lower frequencies of the side band. The result? Distortion.

As a digital audio system samples these disallowed input frequencies, the spurious new frequencies are "recorded" as well. As the deviate input frequencies ascend, new descending frequencies are created. Specifically, if $S$ is the sampling frequency and $F$ is a frequency higher than half the sampling rate, then a new frequency $A$ is also created at $A = \pm NS \pm F$ where $N$ is any integer. In practice, the $S-F$ is the most troublesome component. For example, if $S = 44$ kHz, a 23 kHz input signal will alias to produce another frequency at 21 kHz. If we attempt to sample a 24 kHz signal, 20 kHz appears. In other words, a new frequency appears back in the audio band, folded over from the sampling frequency, as the placement of the sidebands predicts. In fact, aliasing is sometimes called foldover.

To elaborate further upon this sad scenario, in which a false frequency accompanies the actual frequency following the sampler, we must remember that a low-pass filter is used at the output of a digitization system to smooth the staircase function and thus recover the original signal. This output filter (sometimes called the anti-imaging filter) will be designed to cut at half the sampling frequency; thus the errant input frequencies which were above that value will be filtered out, and we would be left with only the aliased frequencies in the audio band.

Aliasing can produce some rather strange results in the audio band. If you were sampling at 44 kHz, an input frequency from 0 to 22 kHz would sound fine, but as the frequency ranged from 22 to 44 kHz, we would hear it returning as a frequency descending from 22 kHz to 0 kHz. If we raised the input frequency from 44 to 66 kHz, it would appear again from 0 to 22 kHz. The process would continue infinitely, folding back one sideband after another.

Our sine wave example limited foldover to one fundamental frequency. With complex tones, aliasing frequencies could be generated separately for each harmonic. For example, a complex tone of 5 kHz would normally have harmonics at 10 kHz, 15 kHz, 25 kHz, 30 kHz, etc. With sampling at 44 kHz, however, the 25 kHz fifth harmonic would fold over to 19 kHz, and the sixth harmonic at 30 kHz would pop in at 14 kHz, just shy of the 15

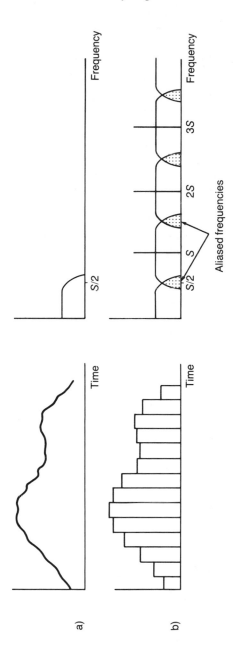

Figure 2.7 *When an audio signal is not properly bandlimited (a), the image spectra (b) overlap. This is aliasing.*

kHz third harmonic. This is illustrated in the spectrum in figure 2.8. A distortion akin to intermodulation distortion would result.

As difficult a problem as aliasing might be in theory, in practice it can be alleviated. In a well designed digital recording system, aliasing does not occur. The solution is simple. We merely bandlimit the input frequencies with a low-pass filter. Its job is to ensure that all frequencies above the half-sampling frequency are attenuated to below the amplitude resolution of the system. The system will not attempt to record these extreme low-level signals. To achieve a maximum audio bandwidth for a given sampling rate, filters with a very sharp characteristic, often called brickwall filters, are employed. Only certain fundamentals or harmonics are allowed to enter the sampler; thus aliasing cannot occur. In other words, when sampling, one must obey the sampling theorem.

However, time sampling is only one consideration; a digital system must also be able to determine the actual numerical values it will use at sample time to represent the original waveform's amplitude. That process, amplitude quantization, has its own quirks.


## QUANTIZATION

Whenever there's good news, there is invariably a little bad news, too. At least that's the case with amplitude quantization, the counterpart to time sampling. Whereas sampling is counterintuitively wonderful, quantization is intuitively not wonderful. Hence the need for the short, apologetic introduction that follows.

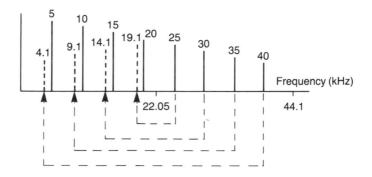

Figure 2.8    *The harmonics of a sampled waveform generate alias frequencies.*

In essence, the objective in recording and reproducing music can be simply formulated: we want to form a representation of the music. Obviously, the closer our representation is to the original, the better. Unfortunately, reality is stubborn in its ability to defy re-creation, and we are left with a challenging endeavor as we attempt to create an approximation of the original event. The essential problem lies in the complexity of even the simplest acoustic waveform and in the problem of measuring the waveform's infinitely varying amplitude.

As we've seen, sampling is a method of periodically taking a measurement. An audio measurement is meaningful only if both the time and value of the measurement are stored. Sampling represents the time of the measurement; quantization represents the value of the measurement or, in the case of audio, the amplitude of the waveform. Both sampling and quantization are parameters which determine the limitations of an audio digitization system.

While sampling is perfect within its prescribed context, quantization is imperfect. The problem lies in measuring the waveform's amplitude. In the same way that length, an analog quantity, can be measured (e.g., in inches), an audio waveform can be measured (e.g., in volts). In the same way that a measurement of length is always prone to error, quantizing is prone to error.

### Digital Error

Let's take a quick ride in my Porsche 911 to demonstrate that, yes, even digital has error, and let us differentiate this error from the one inherent in an analog system. Suppose that I've connected three speedometers, one analog and two digital types, like the ones in figure 2.9. Suppose also that I read the first two speedometers just as a police officer pulls up behind me, red lights flashing. Given a good meter face and a sharp eye, I read the analog needle as approximately 75 MPH. My digital speedometer reads 77.3 MPH. The trooper writes me a ticket.

Now, any type of speedometer is always in error. The analog speedometer errs because of the ballistics of the mechanism. That is, it takes the needle a certain amount of time to settle to the correct value. With the digital speedometer, precision is limited by the number of digits displayed. The more digits, the greater our precision, but the last digit will always round off relative to the actual value. For example, 77.3 MPH may have been displayed for an actual 77.34 MPH speed. Under the best conditions the last digit would be completely accurate; for example, 77 MPH would be shown as 77.0 MPH. Under the worst conditions, the rounding off will be one half increment away; for example, 77.55 MPH will be rounded off

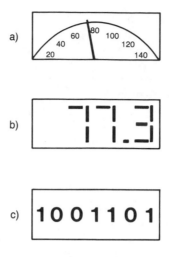

Figure 2.9    *Three types of speedometers: analog (a), digital with decimal read-out (b), and digital with binary readout (c).*

to 77.5 MPH or 77.6 MPH. No matter how many digits you have, unless you have an infinite number of them, you will never be able to display the analog speed of 77⅓ MPH exactly. Nevertheless, a digital readout is an inherently more precise way to measure an analog event.

To solve my speeding problem, I might use a microprocessor to limit my Porsche's top speed. (This is a strictly hypothetical argument, mind you.) Because electronic circuits mainly use binary numbers, I should also express my speed that way, necessitating a third speedometer, a binary type.

### Binary Numbers

Binary numbers are really no different from any others. All number systems employ a radix, also called a base, which defines the number of symbols the system uses. Most of us ten-fingered humans use the decimal system with, noncoincidentally, ten symbols, 0 through 9. From these basic symbols, a method called positional notation allows us to use them to express even very large numbers, such as the amount of the national debt.

In positional notation, each left-most symbol is a power of ten higher than the previous symbol. Thus the number 7085 represents $7 \times 10^3 + 0 \times 10^2 + 8 \times 10^1 + 5 \times 10^0$, or $7 \times 1000 + 0 \times 100 + 8 \times 10 + 5 \times 1$. The 7 is the most significant digit, while the 5 is the least significant.

Binary numbers operate similarly, except that the system is based on the power of two: 0 and 1 are used to represent the two (and only two) symbols in the system. Such a system makes perfect sense to an electrical machine: it can equate 1 with ON and 0 with OFF. Thus a voltage, or lack of it, represents the only two conditions it must deal with.

As in the decimal system, we employ positional notation to define numbers. Each left-most digit is a power of two higher than the previous digit. For example, the number 1001101 represents $1 \times 2^6 + 0 \times 2^5 + 0 \times 2^4 + 1 \times 2^3 + 1 \times 2^2 + 0 \times 2^1 + 1 \times 2^0$ or, in its decimal equivalents, $1 \times 64 + 0 \times 32 + 0 \times 16 + 1 \times 8 + 1 \times 4 + 0 \times 2 + 1 \times 1$, or 77. In this way, it can be seen that decimal words are interchangeable with binary words, which is illustrated in table 2.1. In any binary word, the left-most digit is called the most significant bit (MSB) and the right-most is called the least significant bit (LSB). Eight-bit words are called bytes. Most digital audio systems use at least 16-bit words to record, process, and reproduce audio signals. It is the precision of using numbers combined with the speed and reliability of circuits designed to process binary numbers that make digital systems well suited for working with information such as audio signals.

| Decimal | Binary |
|---------|--------|
| 0 | 0000 |
| 1 | 0001 |
| 2 | 0010 |
| 3 | 0011 |
| 4 | 0100 |
| 5 | 0101 |
| 6 | 0110 |
| 7 | 0111 |
| 8 | 1000 |
| 9 | 1001 |
| 10 | 1010 |
| 11 | 1011 |
| 12 | 1100 |
| 13 | 1101 |
| 14 | 1110 |
| 15 | 1111 |

Table 2.1  *Digital circuits prefer binary representation, rather than decimal.*

### Quantization Error

Numbers are great, but their discrete nature imposes a limitation. An analog waveform may be represented as a series of samples; the amplitude of each will yield a number which represents the analog value at that instant. By definition, an analog waveform has an infinite number of amplitude values, whereas in a digital representation we can choose only from a finite number of discrete values, or steps. The selected values will be only an approximation of the actual. Specifically, after sampling, the analog staircase signal must be approximated by the numerical value nearest to the analog value.

Quantization is the technique of approximating an analog amplitude to form a discrete number. In terms of the quantizing hardware, the number of allowable steps is determined by the length of the data word in bits. Just as the number of digits in our speedometer determined our resolution, the number of bits in our digitization equipment determines its resolution. Two bits would yield four ($2^2$) possible quantization values: 00, 01, 10, and 11. Eight bits would create $2^8$ or 256 steps (in binary form, ranging from 00000000 to 11111111). A 16-bit word would accommodate $2^{16}$ or 65,536 values (ranging from 0000000000000000 to 1111111111111111).

Word length determines the resolution of our digitizing system, and hence provides an important specification to measure the system's performance. Yet there will always be an error associated with quantization because the limited number of amplitude choices contained in the binary word can never completely map an infinite number of analog possibilities. Rarely will the chosen step be exactly at the analog value; usually it won't be quite exact. At worst, the analog level we desire to encode will be one half step away: that is, there will be an error of one half the least significant bit of the quantization word. For example, suppose the binary word 0010 corresponds to the analog step value of 2.0 V, and 0011 corresponds to 3.0 V, and the actual analog value at sample time is unfortunately 2.5 V. Since 0010½ isn't available, the system will round up to 0011 or down to 0010; either way, there will be an error of magnitude of ½ step.

Figure 2.10a shows how an input signal would be sampled, and the error created when the amplitude at sample time is quantized. Figure 2.10b shows the error at each sample time. Note that the error never exceeds a value of 1/2 step.

Digital hardware performance may be characterized by a ratio of the total number of steps covered by a quantization scheme to the maximum error. This ratio of maximum expressible amplitude to error determines the signal-to-error (S/E) ratio of the digitization system. For example, in a 16-bit system the ratio of maximum amplitude (65,536 steps) to error (0.5 of a step), would be 65,536/0.5 = 131,072. Every added bit doubles the number of possible values. The more bits the better, because they provide

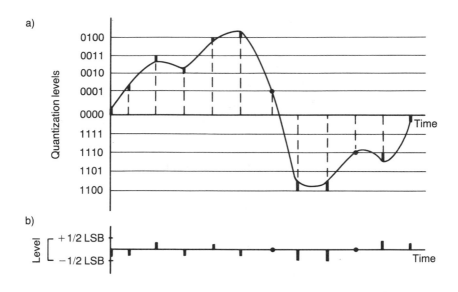

Figure 2.10    *When a signal is quantized (a), an error results (b). The magnitude of the error signal can never exceed 1/2 of a quantization step.*

more choices. So the steps are smaller and the magnitude of the error is smaller. In terms of decibels (dB), every added bit yields about a 6 dB increase in the system's S/E ratio because it reduces the quantization error by a factor of two. The S/E relationship can be conveniently expressed in terms of word length as S/E (dB) = $6.02n + 1.76$ where $n$ is the number of bits. Using this formula, a 16-bit system yields an S/E ratio of about 98 dB. This equation is discussed more fully in the references listed at the end of this chapter.

Quantization error may be understood as an analog signal whose amplitude cannot exceed one quantization interval (provided anomalies from the real world do not interfere). The difference between the original audio waveform and the regenerated waveform after digital-to-analog (D/A) conversion is due in part to quantization error. The error has a spectrum, or frequency response, which is a function of the original signal. Audibly, quantization error is a form of distortion; fortunately, with 16 bits it exists below the noise level in most analog systems. As we'll see, its effects can be reduced or eliminated in the recording chain with dither, a purposely introduced noise.

Quantization is affected by more than just word length; it is also a question of hardware design. There are many techniques available to accomplish quantization, and different strategies determine how the analog signal is matched to the steps. These algorithms influence the relative effects of quantization error. For example, a linear quantizer produces a relatively high error when low-level signals span only a few steps. A nonlinear system could be used to amplify low-level signals to utilize the fullest possible span of steps. However the resulting error is generally more benign in the linear quantizer, and more perceptible in the nonlinear system.

Sampling and quantization are the two fundamental design elements for an audio digitization system. In the case of the compact disc system, a sampling frequency of 44.1 kHz and a word length of 16 bits yields remarkable fidelity, comparable to the best analog systems.

## DITHER

Although a 16-bit system yields a theoretical signal-to-error ratio of 98 dB, it is disturbing to know that as the signal amplitude decreases the relative error increases. When signal level is on the order of one least-significant bit—that is, one quantization increment—errors could be audible under certain signal conditions. So quantization not only loses information, it creates some unexpected problems as well. Let's examine those problems and a remedy for quantization error as well.

### *Granulation Noise*

Digital signals are made up of discrete bits. This is a real blessing; it permits us to employ powerful digital methods for processing and storage. However, in quantization, the discrete nature of digital and the ensuing amplitude increments can create nonlinearity. Consider the example of a signal with amplitude on the order of one quantization step, such as the one in figure 2.11. The signal value crosses back and forth across the threshold, resulting in a square wave signal from the quantizer. At very low levels, quantization results in severe distortion. The quantization error floor is sometimes called "granulation noise" because it has been described as a gritty sound.

To make matters worse, the quantized square wave (like all square waves) is rich in odd harmonics, extending far beyond the half-sampling frequency. Thus aliasing, discussed previously, reappears *after* the anti-aliasing low-pass filter, because of the high-frequency content of the square wave. If the resulting harmonics are very close to a multiple of the sampling frequency, the beat tones drift through the frequency origin to produce a sound called "bird singing" or "birdies."

Quantization thus loses low-level information and can lead to aliasing and other effects. These effects occur at the low level of the quantization steps themselves. Thus, the amplitude of the distortion is also very low.

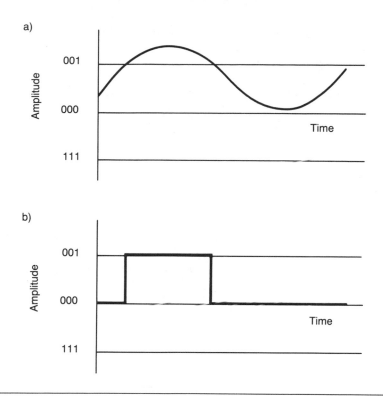

Figure 2.11    *Without dither, a low-level signal (a) will be quantized to create a square wave (b).*

Most high-amplitude audio signals mask the error effects. On the other hand, when the signal is low-level, it may not mask the distortion. Yet there is a solution.

### Resolution Below the LSB

Ideally, a digital audio conversion system must suppress any error it introduces. Obviously, the number of bits in the digitization word could be increased with a resultant decrease in error of about 6 dB per bit. This is difficult because of the cost of adding extra bits. An alternative, surprisingly, is to add a small amount of analog noise to the input signal; this noise is referred to as dither. It is important to note that this small amount of noise removes some quantization artifacts from a signal—it doesn't mask the artifacts, it actually removes them.

Let's reconsider our example of a signal with amplitude on the order of a quantization increment, but this time, let's add a dither signal; the result is modulation which preserves the information of the original signal. An undithered input sine wave results in the square wave output of figure 2.12a. With dithering, the duty cycle output of figure 2.12b results. When the duty cycle signal is averaged, the sine wave information emerges, as shown in figure 2.12c. The averaging illustrates how the ear will actually perceive the signal. It perceives the original signal and some added noise. This is far more desirable than the severely distorting waveform. From a more analytical standpoint, the spectrum of an undithered signal would yield harmonics from the quantized square wave. With dither, only the original fundamental waveform would be preserved with added noise. Thus dither changes the digital nature of the quantization error into noise, and the ear may then resolve signals with levels well below one quantization level.

That is an important conclusion: with dither, the resolution of a digitization system is below the least significant bit. By encoding the audio signal with dither, we may recover information, even though it might be smaller than the smallest increment of the quantizer. A dithered system thus behaves more like an analog system. A properly dithered signal will be audible beneath the noise floor (as low as 110 to 120 dB below maximum output level). Moreover, much of the distortion due to quantization is removed from the signal. The performance price? A degradation of about 1.5 dB in

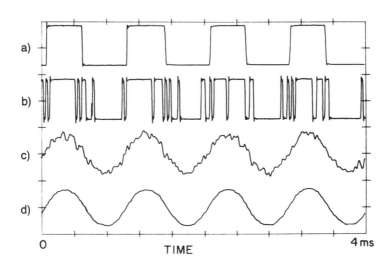

Figure 2.12 *An undithered sine wave will produce a quantized square wave (a). With dither, the amplitude of the sine wave is reflected in the quantized signal (b). This is clearly shown when the quantized signal is averaged (c). A longer average results in a smoother waveform (d). (From Vanderkooy and Lipshitz)*

the broadband S/E ratio of the digitization system, an increase which is negligible compared to the large S/E ratio inherent in the system. The paper by Vanderkooy and Lipshitz listed at the end of this chapter provides more information on dither.

What kind of noise is used for dither? Many types of dither signals, utilizing noise signals varying in their frequency content and amplitude, have been explored. These include Gaussian, rectangular, and triangular noise. The designer must determine which noise signal is best for a particular application. In some cases, a digital system might not even need a dither generator, because the residual analog noise in the input stages of the system itself can act as dither.

Some researchers have proposed digital dither generators, in which a pseudo random noise signal could be first injected to overcome quantization artifacts, and then later removed to prevent any degradation in S/E ratio.

Dither thus represents a unique and unlikely concept. The idea of adding analog noise to a digital system seems a little strange, but as we have seen, the outcome is lower distortion and consequently higher fidelity for the digital audio system.


## PULSE CODE MODULATION

Topics such as sampling and quantization form the basis of digital audio. All digital audio systems use these mechanisms to record and reproduce music. However, the methods by which they are utilized can vary tremendously. There are many ways to encode the digital data, with various system architectures to do the job. Pulse code modulation (PCM) is perhaps the most efficient high performance encoding method and forms the most popular digital audio system architecture. PCM is a modulation process in which an analog signal is expressed in digital form by means of binary coding. The vast majority of digital recordings are mastered on PCM digital audio recorders, and at the output of a CD player, the data returns to its PCM birthright at the digital-to-analog (D/A) converter.

### *Modulation*

Modulation is the process of encoding source information prior to transmission or storage. In general, a carrier signal forms the basis of the transmission channel, and the source information itself merely affects the carrier's parameters. For example, in amplitude modulation (AM) the carrier's *amplitude* varies relative to the information's amplitude at a rate relative to the information's frequency. In frequency modulation (FM) the carrier's *frequency* changes by an amount relative to the information's amplitude, and at a rate relative to the information's frequency. A radio receiver is given the task of demodulating, or removing, the carrier and outputting the original information. In AM and FM, both the modulation and the modulating signal are continuous; they are classified as wave parameter modulation schemes.

When the original information is digital, the nature of the modulation can be altered. A parameter of the transmitted pulses, or a code contained in the pulses, carries the information. For example, pulse amplitude modulation (PAM) uses pulse amplitude, pulse width modulation (PWM) uses pulse width, and pulse number modulation (PNM) uses a pulse count to encode the value of the information, as illustrated in figure 2.13.

PAM forms an intermediate waveform in digital audio systems; prior to analog-to-digital (A/D) conversion and following digital-to-analog (D/A) conversion, the audio signal exists as a staircase PAM waveform. PNM is plagued by bandwidth problems; a large number of pulses is required to encode a high resolution signal. For example if 65,536 steps were used to measure the signal's amplitude, then 65,536 pulses would be needed to record a full scale signal level.

### PCM

Pulse code modulation overcomes this bandwidth problem, yet retains a numerical coding of information for efficient transmission. In pulse code modulation (PCM) the digital waveform itself encodes the binary digits. Since the binary code itself is retained, the required bandwidth is much less. Its efficiency can be intuitively observed. For example, one can readily read the encoded data directly from the PCM waveform itself. In addition, the coded signal is fully compatible with digital circuits which are usually designed to operate with a binary code. Because of its efficient use of bandwidth and its compatibility with off-the-shelf circuitry, PCM has proven to be an expedient means of representing audio data for recording or reproduction. When it comes to storage on magnetic tape or optical disc, other forms of modulation may be more effective. There is one consistent drawback to PCM; like many other coding schemes, it requires a much wider bandwidth than the corresponding analog signal.

Pulse code modulation is efficient when confronting the essential problem of an audio digitization system: the conversion from analog to digital, and back again. When the analog audio signal is sampled, analog values form a PAM waveform. Quantization must document the instantaneous amplitude of the stairstep and generate a binary word for storage. Figure 2.14 shows how PCM directly creates the required binary code at the output of the A/D converter. Similarly, the D/A converter directly accepts PCM data and converts it to a PAM waveform. Additionally, PCM data is easily multiplexed—that is, several channels of data may be merged to form one channel.

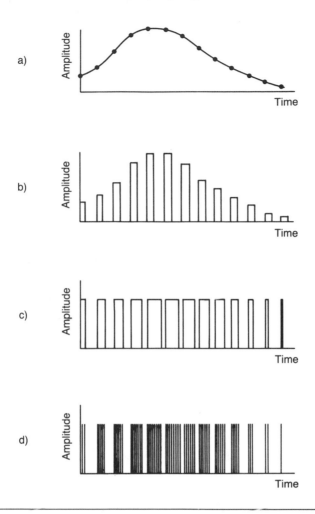

Figure 2.13    *An analog signal (a) may be represented through PAM (b), PWM (c), or PNM (d) pulse modulation.*

PCM is an effective modulation scheme. In its absence, at the very least, audio digitization systems would be more complex and costly.

## A DIGITIZATION SYSTEM

So far, we've examined the various theoretical underpinnings of digital audio, but one does not live by conceptualization alone; one also needs hardware. The time has come to look at a complete digitization system, focusing on a PCM hardware design.

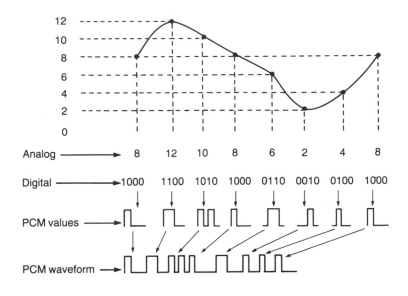

Figure 2.14   *With PCM, amplitude values are recorded directly in the binary waveform.*

### A PCM System

An audio digitization system is really nothing more than a kind of transducer which processes the audio for digital storage and then processes it again for reproduction. While that sounds simple, the hardware must be carefully engineered, for success in accomplishing its task (and the resulting quality of the reproduced audio) depends entirely on the quality of the system's design. Whoever said that all digital audio products sound alike never designed one or tried to manufacture it competitively (or listened very closely, either). Let's run through the trials and tribulations of the digitization chain.

A stereo PCM digitization scheme is shown in figure 2.15. The recording section consists of input amplifiers, a dither generator, input (antialiasing) low-pass filters, sample-and-hold circuits, analog-to-digital converters, a multiplexer, digital processing and modulation circuits, and a storage medium such as digital tape or optical disk. On the output side are demodulation and processing circuits, a demultiplexer, digital-to-analog converters, sample and hold (aperture) circuits, output (anti-imaging) low-pass filters, and output amplifiers. This hardware collection is the realization of our previous discussions. As we'll see, the output side forms the basis for the design of a compact disc player.

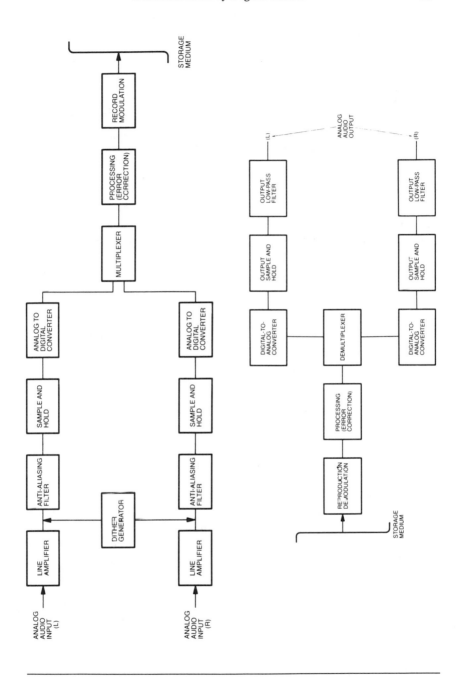

Figure 2.15 *The recording and reproduction sections of a PCM system. (Reproduced with permission of the publisher, Howard W. Sams & Co., Indianapolis,* Principles of Digital Audio, *by Ken C. Pohlmann,* © 1985.)

## Record Section

A digitization system typically begins with conversion from analog to digital. Of course, in some applications, this is unnecessary since the information begins in digital form. In the case of music, analog-to-digital conversion is usually required because sound usually begins as an acoustic analog waveform.

The input analog amplifiers must maintain the requirement of absolute quality in order not to compromise the fidelity of the ensuing digital system. The dither generator is a controlled noise circut. The analog signal is low-pass filtered by a very sharp cutoff filter to bandlimit the signal and its entire harmonic content to frequencies below the half-sampling frequency. A number of analog filter designs may be employed for this purpose; they all offer a flat pass-band, sharp cutoff, and attenuated stopband.

Unfortunately, analog filter designs also create phase shift problems in which the relative timing of different frequencies is varied. For example, low frequencies may arrive at the output of the filter before the high frequencies. Analog filters are also complex circuits, tricky to build, and prone to drift. As with the input amplifier, the input filter must be of high quality; any distortion or noise would be digitized along with the audio signal. Many designers are using digital oversampling filters at the output of the digitization system and sometimes at the input as well. We'll examine filters more carefully in Chapter Four.

The next circuit in the chain, the input sample-and-hold, samples discrete values of the input signal at a fixed periodic rate (the sampling rate) and holds each analog value while the analog-to-digital conversion takes place. This is required because a varying input might disrupt the analog-to-digital converter. A sample-and-hold circuit is essentially made of a capacitor and switch, such as the one in figure 2.16. The circuit tracks the signal until the sample command causes the switch to open, isolating the capacitor from the signal; the capacitor holds this analog voltage during conversion. The timing of the sample command must be carefully regulated to prevent jitter, the phenomenon of imprecise sample times. The capacitor must be carefully chosen to prevent any loss of voltage, known as droop.

Our signal now appears as a staircase, a hybrid analog signal ready for conversion to digital. The analog-to-digital (A/D) converter is the most critical and costly component in a digitization system. Consider that this circuit must resolve the held analog signal into as many as 65,536 steps, each with its own binary word, and it must accomplish this task in 10 or 20 microseconds. Fortunately, several circuits are available for this operation. For example, a successive-approximation-register (SAR) A/D converter contains a digital-to-analog converter and a comparator. The SAR

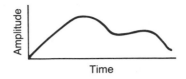

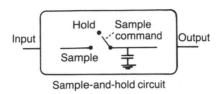

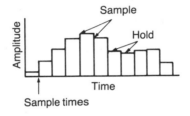

Figure 2.16 *A sample-and-hold circuit samples the audio signal to form a staircase waveform.*

tries a digital word, converts it, compares the analog result to the original input, and then corrects its approximation one bit at a time until the proper digital word has been determined and output. Thus a 16-bit SAR A/D converter must make 16 D/A conversions for each A/D conversion. Integrating A/D converters offer another design approach. A capacitor stores the input analog voltage, and then the timer counts as the voltage is discharged. The number of counts in the interval forms the output digital value. Whichever method is used, we accomplish our initial goal of quantizing the analog signal. The signal is now digital.

The output of the A/D converter is raw binary data ready to be processed as the designers see fit. However, a number of operations must occur. First, the A/D output is often parallel data in which all 16 bits of the data word appear at once on 16 lines; yet storage devices permit storage only of serial data, in which the bits appear one after another. Data is therefore converted from parallel to serial. In addition, the data for both left and right audio channels is multiplexed, or combined into one channel. Synchronization words, special non-audio bit patterns, are added to delineate the audio samples.

One of the system's most intriguing operations, error correction encoding, takes place at this point. In analog recording, an error is an error, and that's that. In digital we may provide for error detection and correction. The data stream, therefore, is provided with redundant information, extra data created from the original data to help detect and correct errors. We'll discuss error correction is more detail in Chapter Three. Finally, the data is modulated—that is, it is changed into a signal specifically suited for storage.

The storage medium itself is often the fixed or rotating head tape recorders, commonly found in the professional studio. Many recording engineers prefer fixed head designs for ease of editing and because of their familiarity with them from the analog days; multitrack recorders almost always use fixed heads. Alternatively, rotary head recorders, derived from video technology, are used and are more efficient because of their ability to store large amounts of data on a slowly moving tape. Increasingly, hard disk and optical disk recorders are entering the studio mainstream. No matter what happens in the studio (you're better off not knowing), the data is eventually transferred to the compact disc for consumer playback. Both CD players and the professional's recorder follow the reproduction side of our digitization chain.

### Reproduction Section

The initial reproduction circuits take care of many housekeeping functions, such as demodulation and demultiplexing. In this process, the data stream is recovered and is again put into parallel form. Our foresight in placing error detection and correction safeguards in the digital signal prior to storage pays off here. Errors introduced during playback are detected and corrected or concealed. This includes mechanical errors introduced by the recorder or player, such as transport wow and flutter, and media errors caused by media defects, dust, dirt, grape jelly, and fingerprints on the tape or disc.

Whereas analog-to-digital conversion is required only when the signal is originally analog, digital-to-analog conversion is always required, because our ears meaningfully respond only to analog waveforms. The digital-to-analog converter's task is the reverse of the analog-to-digital converter's, yet its operation is inherently simpler. Many D/A converter types will be discussed in more detail in Chapter Four. Whichever type is employed, the D/A produces an analog voltage corresponding to the digital samples.

The output values from the D/A are held by a sample-and-hold circuit. The sample-and-hold circuit (as noted before, sometimes called an aperture circuit) essentially consists of a switch that is timed to wait for the D/A conversion. When the D/A output voltage is stable and any glitches have passed, the switch passes the voltage, switching on and off at the original sampling rate. The output of the sample-and-hold is a pulse amplitude staircase signal.

However, the analog signal from the sample-and-hold circuit cannot be output directly. The de-sampled waveform contains an infinite spectrum of images of the original spectrum. Viewed in another way, the sharp edges of the staircase waveform represent ultrasonic frequencies not present in the original waveform. Although the images are above the highest audible frequencies, they must be removed because they could cause intermodulation distortion, among other problems. The staircase must be smoothed, or filtered, to remove the ultrasonic frequencies.

Reconstruction of the audio waveform is completed by the output low-pass (anti-imaging) filter. Specifically, the filter's response to the individual impulses in the PAM staircase add together to recreate the original waveform. The anti-imaging filter can be substantially identical to the anti-aliasing filter and performs the same cutoff function. The staircase function is smoothed, all the high frequency components of those sharp edges are removed, and the original analog waveform is recovered. In many designs, a digital oversampling filter is used. With oversampling, the number of samples is multiplied, and the images are thus extended in frequency, and a gentle analog filter can be used to remove them. Oversampling and waveform reconstruction will be discussed in more detail in Chapter Four.

The final part of our digitization system is the analog preamplifier, designed, one hopes, by analog designers, not digital specialists. Our PCM digitization and reconstruction system is complete.

### Alternative Systems

The architecture of a fixed, linear PCM system comprises the classic audio digitization design. However, in the interests of economy of either the cost or the data rate, the fixed, linear design may be modified. For example, a compander could be used. The compander changes the amplitude dynamics of the signal; its measurement during digitization is thus made nonlinear. Using techniques similar to those in analog noise reduction circuits, the signal may be compressed prior to the PCM A/D and expanded after the D/A to improve the S/N ratio of a lower-bit word system. In essence, low-level signals are measured with small increments, while high-level signals use large increments.

In other applications, such as satellite transmission, data reduction is critical because higher transmitted data rates add up to lower cost. A block floating point design might be the most efficient. A 16-bit A/D converter may be used to convert a memory block of samples. Then a calculation is made to determine the largest value in the block. Based on this value, all the words in the block are digitally attenuated by a calculated scale factor. Usually, the number of bits output is much lower than the number of bits originally in the converted block. The scale factor must accompany the data block for proper rescaling during D/A conversion. Because only one scaling factor is required for an entire block, and the number of bits in the block has been reduced, data reduction is accomplished.

No matter which method is employed, a complete digital audio system isn't really all that difficult, at least in block diagram form. However, we haven't nearly exhausted the mysteries and amazing facts underlying the compact disc, as the remaining pages attest.

**FOR FURTHER READING**

Blesser, B. "Digitization of Audio." *Journal of the Audio Engineering Society* 26(10):739–71, October, 1978.

Blesser, B., and B. Locanthi. "The Application of Narrow-Band Dither Operating at the Nyquist Frequency in Digital Systems to Provide Improved Signal-to-Noise Ratio over Conventional Dithering." *Journal of the Audio Engineering Society* 35(6):446–54, June, 1987.

Blesser, B., B. Locanthi, and T. G. Stockham, Jr., eds. *Digital Audio.* New York: Audio Engineering Society, 1983.

Hnatek, E. R. *A User's Handbook of D/A and D/A Converters.* New York: Wiley, 1976.

Mathews, Max V. *The Technology of Computer Music.* Cambridge: MIT Press, 1969.

Nakajima, Heitaro, Toshitada Doi, Jyoji Fukuda, and Akira Iga. *Digital Audio.* Blue Ridge Summit, Penn.: Tab, 1983.

Nyquist, H. "Certain Topics in Telegraph Transmission Theory." *Transactions of the American Institute of Electrical Engineers* 47(2):617–44, April, 1928.

Pohlmann, Ken C. *Principles of Digital Audio.* Indianapolis: Sams, 1989.

Vanderkooy, John, and Stanley Lipshitz. "Resolution Below the Least Significant Bit in Digital Audio Systems with Dither." *Journal of the Audio Engineering Society* 32(3):106–13, March, 1984. Correction, *Journal of the Audio Engineering Society* 32(11):889, November, 1984.

Yoshikawa, S. "An Introduction to Digital Audio." In *Proceedings of the AES Third International Conference.* New York: Audio Engineering Society, 1985.

# Chapter Three

# The Compact Disc System

## INTRODUCTION

Storing audio information places great demands on a digital medium. A 60-minute musical selection, recorded in stereo with PCM (pulse code modulation) at a sampling rate of 44.1 kHz and with 16-bit quantization, generates over 5 billion bits. Error correction, synchronization, and modulation are required for successful storage. The total capacity required is over 15 billion bits (that's 15 thousand million). In addition, a commercially popular music storage medium requires random access, small size, convenience of use, robustness, low cost, and ease of replication. Clearly, digital audio's requirements are considerable.

The compact disc format was developed to meet these demands. A CD audio disc holds a specification-defined maximum of 74 minutes (variations can increase this to 80 minutes or more) of high fidelity music on a highly robust and economically manufactured disc. A CD player provides access to any part of the audio program within a second or less, in addition to having many user-convenience features. The format is well suited to audio storage demands.

The magnitude of the challenge of digital audio storage and the magnitude of the achievement of the compact disc have resulted in a storage medium of unprecedented capacity, durability, and flexibility. Thus the compact disc is highly suitable for many non-audio applications. As a result, a number of alternative CD formats have been developed. However, all the CD incarnations, which will be discussed in Chapter Six, utilize the same basic CD specifications that are used in audio CDs. To avoid confusion, the audio CD system is sometimes called CD-DA, for Compact Disc-Digital Audio, or simply the CD-Audio format.

## SYSTEM OVERVIEW

Music input to a digital recording and reproduction chain passes through the recording side of a PCM system, as described in Chapter Two. The master recording is stored in digital form on magnetic tape or optical disk. After recording, mixing, and editing, the tape is ready to be reproduced via the compact disc. The disc manufacturing facility converts the master tape to a master disc and replicates the disc to produce many CD copies. A CD player functions as the reproduction side of the PCM system, outputting the originally recorded music.

When digital technology is used for all the intermediate steps, a sophisticated chain of events transpires—that is, the music is converted to binary code when it enters the recording studio and stays in binary code throughout the chain, and is converted back to analog form as it leaves the CD player.

Indeed, many CD players have digital outputs so data is preserved in that form until it reaches the power amplifier. In other words, a compact disc contains the same audio information, bit for bit, that was recorded in the studio. To a large degree, you are hearing exactly what was recorded by the engineer. This, of course, is what music recording is all about.

Specifications for the compact disc system are shown in table 3.1. These parameters were jointly developed by Philips and Sony, and are defined in the standards document known as the *Red Book*. The CD standard is also contained in the IEC (International Electrotechnical Commission) standard BNN15-83-095, "Compact Disc Digital Audio System." Disc and player manufacturers must obtain a compact disc license to utilize these specifications. Disc dimensions are defined in the standard, as are pit dimensions, the physical formations which encode data. Although the disc itself may be made of any transparent material with a refraction index of 1.55, polycarbonate plastic is generally used.

The optical system that reads data from the disc uses a laser beam with a 780 nanometer wavelength. Other optical properties are defined in the CD standard as well. The basic specifications pertinent to player design are contained in the signal format specifications. Sampling frequency, quantization word length, data rate, error correction code, and modulation scheme are all defined in the CD standard (and discussed in detail in the pages to follow). Player manufacturers have considerable freedom in the actual design of their players; this accounts for the wide variety in player features and quality. Similarly, disc manufacturers enjoy a certain degree of latitude in tolerance.

## OPTICAL STORAGE

The physical characteristics of the compact disc are shown in figure 3.1. Disc diameter is 120 millimeters, hole diameter is 15 millimeters, and

**DISC**

| | |
|---|---|
| Playing time: | 74 minutes, 33 seconds maximum |
| Rotation: | Counter-clockwise when viewed from readout surface |
| Rotational speed: | 1.2–1.4 m/sec. |
| Track pitch: | 1.6 μm |
| Diameter: | 120 mm |
| Thickness: | 1.2 mm |
| Center hole diameter: | 15 mm |
| Recording area: | 46 mm–117 mm |
| Signal area: | 50 mm–116 mm |
| Material: | Any transparent material with 1.55 refraction index, such as polycarbonate |
| Minimum pit length: | 0.833 μm (1.2 m/sec.) to 0.972 μm (1.4 m/sec.) |
| Maximum pit length: | 3.05 μm (1.2 m/sec.) to 3.56 μm (1.4 m/sec.) |
| Pit depth: | Approx. 0.11 μm |
| Pit width: | Approx. 0.5 μm |

**OPTICAL SYSTEM**

| | |
|---|---|
| Standard wavelength: | $\lambda = 780$ nm (7,800Å) |
| Focal depth: | $\pm 2$ μm |

($\lambda/NA \leqq 1.75$ μm, $NA$: Numerical Aperture)

**SIGNAL FORMAT**

| | |
|---|---|
| Number of channels: | 2 channels (4-channel recording possible) |
| Quantization: | 16-bit linear quantization |
| Quantizing timing: | Concurrent for all channels |
| Sampling frequency: | 44.1 kHz |
| Channel bit rate: | 4.3218 Mb/sec. |
| Data bit rate: | 2.0338 Mb/sec. |
| Data-to-channel bit ratio: | 8:17 |
| Error correction code: | CIRC (with 25% redundancy) |
| Modulation system: | EFM |

Table 3.1   *Specification table for the compact disc system.*

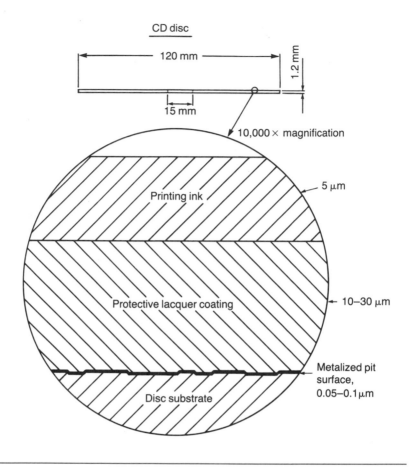

Figure 3.1 *Scale drawing of CD data surface.*

thickness is 1.2 millimeters. The innermost part of the disc does not hold data; it provides a clamping area for the player to hold the disc firmly to the spindle motor shaft. Data is recorded on an area 35.5 millimeters wide. A lead-in area rings the innermost data area, and a lead-out area rings the outermost area. The lead-in and lead-out areas contain non-audio data used to control the player. On many discs, a change in appearance in the reflective data surface marks the end of the musical information.

A transparent plastic substrate forms most of a disc's 1.2 millimeter thickness. Data is physically contained in pits which are impressed along its top surface and are covered with a very thin (50 to 100 nanometers) metal (e.g., aluminum, silver, or gold) layer. Another thin (10 to 30 micrometers) plastic layer protects the metalized pit surface, on top of which the identifying label (5 micrometers) is printed. A laser beam is used to read the data. It is applied from below and passes through the transparent substrate and back again. The beam is focused on the metalized data surface embedded inside the disc. Since data on a disc is read by a light beam, playing a CD causes no more wear to the recording than your reading causes to the words printed on this page.

### The Pit Track

The physical method of accomplishing data storage in pits on a flat surface is not directly visible to the naked eye. You would need a scanning electron microscope (such as the one used to take figure 3.2) to get a good look at the pits. The pits are amazingly small, much smaller than we bulky humans can appreciate. For example, a pit is about 0.5 micrometers wide, or about 700 times smaller than a pin prick.

A disc contains a track of pits arranged in a continuous spiral running from the inner circumference to the outer. It is advantageous to start the music on the inside because the outer diameter of a disc, in some manufacturing processes, is more generally prone to manufacturing defects. CDs

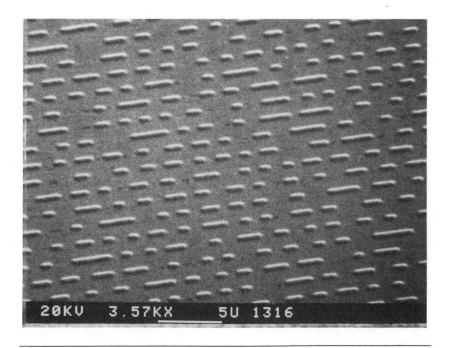

Figure 3.2   *Compact disc pit surface (photo: University of Miami).*

with shorter playing time thus provide a greater manufacturing yield. In addition, by starting from the inside, adoption of smaller diameter discs (such as 8 centimeter CD-3 discs) or larger diameter discs (such as 20 and 30 centimeter CD-Video discs) is facilitated.

Figure 3.3 diagrams the track pitch, the distance between successive tracks, which is 1.6 micrometers (that's about 600 tracks to a millimeter). There are 22,188 revolutions across the disc's signal surface of 35.5 millimeters. A pit track might contain 3 billion pits. Unspiraled, the track would stretch about 3½ miles. The construction of the CD is diffraction-limited—that is, the wave nature of light would not permit smaller formations. The track pitch acts as a diffraction grating, producing a rainbow of colors. In fact, CD pits are among the smallest of all manufactured formations.

Examination of a pit track would reveal that the linear dimensions of the track are the same at the beginning of its spiral as at the end. This means that a CD must rotate with CLV (constant linear velocity), a condition in which a uniform relative velocity is maintained between the disc and the pickup.

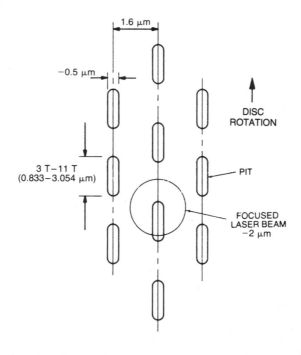

Figure 3.3    *Track pitch is 1.6 micrometers. Data is read through an intensity-modulated laser beam.*

To accomplish this, the rotation speed of a compact disc varies depending on the position of the pickup. Because each outer track revolution contains more pits than each inner track revolution, the disc must be slowed down as it plays in order to maintain a constant rate of data. The disc rotates at a speed of 500 rpm when the pickup is reading the inner circumference, and as the pickup moves outward, the rotational speed gradually decreases to 200 rpm. Thus a constant linear velocity is maintained. In other words, all of the pits are read at the same speed, regardless of the circumference of that part of the spiral. The trick is a CLV servo system; the player constantly reads frame synchronization words from the data and adjusts the disc speed to keep the data rate constant.

The compact disc's CLV system differs significantly from LPs. A turntable's motor rotates an LP at a CAV (constant angular velocity) of 33⅓ rpm. As a result, outer grooves have a greater apparent velocity than inner grooves. One ramification of this is that the high-frequency reponse of inner grooves is remarkably inferior to that of outer grooves. If the CD used CAV, pits on the outside diameter of the disc would have to be longer than those on the inner diameter. This would decrease data density and decrease playing time.

Although the CLV of any particular compact disc is fixed, the CLVs used on different discs can range from 1.2 to 1.4 meters/second. In general, discs with playing times of less than 60 minutes are recorded at 1.4 meters/second, while discs with longer playing times use a slower velocity, to a minimum of 1.2 meters/second. The CD player is indifferent to the actual CLV; it automatically regulates the disc rotational speed to maintain a constant bit rate of 4.3218 MHz.

### Data Readout

The fact that the laser beam travels through the disc substrate provides one of the most significant assets of the CD system. When light passes from one medium to another with a different index of refraction, its wavelength changes and it bends. For example, drop a pencil in half a glass of water; the pencil appears to be broken because the air/water boundary has bent the light. The velocity of light decreases when it passes from air to water.

Figure 3.4 shows that a pickup's laser beam responds similarly. The plastic substrate has refractive index of 1.55 (as opposed to 1.0 for air); the velocity of light slows from $3 \times 10^5$ kilometers/second to $1.9 \times 10^5$ kilometers/second. When the velocity of light slows, the beam is bent, and focusing occurs. Because of the refractive index, the thickness of the disc, and the numerical aperture of the laser's lens, the size of the laser beam on the disc surface is approximately 800 micrometers, but is focused to approximately 1.7 micrometers at the pit surface. The laser beam is thus focused to a point slightly larger than a pit width. Moreover, the effects of

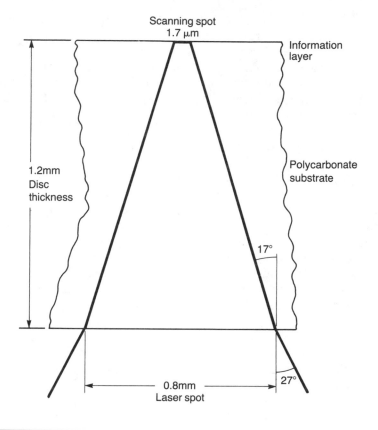

Figure 3.4   *The refractive index of the disc substrate contributes to the focusing of the laser beam.*

any dust or scratches on the substrate's outer surface are minimized because their size (and importance) at the data surface are effectively reduced along with the laser beam. Specifically, any obstruction less than 0.5 millimeters becomes insignificant and causes no error in the readout.

The entire pit surface, as noted, is metalized. The reflective flat surface, called land, causes almost ninety percent of the laser light to be reflected back into the pickup. When viewed from the laser's perspective (underneath), the pits appear as bumps. The height of each bump is between 0.11 and 0.13 micrometer. This dimension is slightly smaller than a carefully chosen dimension: the laser beam's wavelength in air is 780 nanometers (some players use 790 nanometers). Inside the polycarbonate substrate, with a refractive index of 1.55, the laser's wavelength is about 500 nanometers. The height of the bumps is thus approximately 1/4 of the laser's wavelength in the substrate.

Assume the height is exactly 1/4 the laser's wavelength. Light striking land thus travels a distance 1/2 wavelength (1/4 + 1/4) further than light striking a bump. This creates a phase difference of 1/2 wavelength between the part of the beam reflected from the bump and the part reflected from the surrounding land, as shown in figure 3.5. The phase difference causes the two parts of the beam to destructively interfere with and cancel each other, forming a diffraction pattern. In short, a bump disperses light, reducing the intensity of the reflected light.

In theory, when the beam strikes an area between pits, virtually all of its light is reflected, and when it strikes a pit, virtually all of its light is cancelled, so that virtually none is reflected. In practice, the laser spot is larger than is required for complete cancellation between pit and land reflections, and pits are made slightly shallower than the theoretical figure of 1/4 wavelength; this yields a better tracking signal, among other things. About 25 percent of the power of the incident light is reflected from a long bump. In any case, the presence of pits and land is thus read by the laser beam; specifically, the disc surface modulates the intensity of the light beam. Thus the data physically encoded on the disc can be recovered by the laser and later converted to an electrical signal.

So much for the physically obvious, whether visible to the naked eye or not. Not obvious at all is the format by which the data is physically encoded

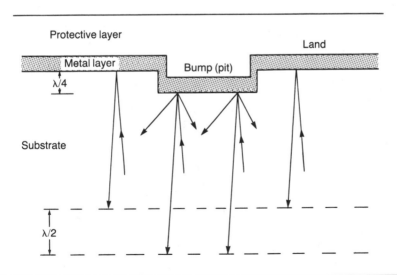

Figure 3.5 *A bump (pit) height causes a 1/2 wavelength path difference relative to land.*

on the disc. For example, contrary to what one might expect, the pits and intervening reflective land on the CD surface do not directly designate 1's and 0's. Rather, each pit *edge,* whether leading or trailing, is a 1 and all areas in between, whether inside or outside a pit, are 0's. This is a much more efficient storage technique than coding the binary bits directly with pits.

Still less obvious are the curiously varying lengths of the pits. The pit and the reflective land lengths vary incrementally, with nine different pit and land lengths. As we shall see, combinations of these varying dimensions physically encode the data.

## ERROR CORRECTION

Error correction is one of the great opportunities—and obligations—of digital audio storage media such as the compact disc. It is a great opportunity because it offers something never before possible with analog media—the chance to correct your mistakes. When you scratch a long playing record, the grooves are irrevocably damaged, along with the information contained in them. Forever after, there will be a click or pop when the damaged part of the groove passes underneath the phonograph needle.

But when you scratch a CD, the nature of the data on the disc and the player's design offer you a second chance. Specifically, the data on the disc has been specially encoded with an error correction code, and your player uses the code to correct for damaged data. Thus it delivers the original undamaged variety instead, performing its error correction every time the disc is played.

To illustrate a fundamental aspect of error correction, consider the two messages below:

1. Please turn to page 345 in your hymnals.
2. Hey gang! Let's party! Hey gang! Let's party!

Assume the first message represents the information in an LP groove, and the second is the data in a CD pit track. Now, place one of your fingers vertically across this page, representing a scratch. You'll observe that part of the first message is irrevocably gone, whereas the second message is intact, because it can be reconstructed. Specifically, we have used redundant data to protect the message. By comparing the redundant messages, we can overcome the effect of the error. Note that we haven't prevented the error; we have simply insured against its effect. Clever, eh?

Of course, even the most clever of ideas has its limitations. As you place more fingers over the page, it becomes more difficult to reconstruct the digital message successfully. Thus the severity of the error plays an important role; our ability to correct errors has limitations. Furthermore, if you place your finger horizontally across the page, you might completely obscure the entire line, destroying both the message and its redundancy. The nature of the error thus plays a part too. Finally, we should note that error correction exacts a cost; in this case, the message coded with error correction requires twice the storage space.

On the other hand, error correction is an obligation. Digital audio on a compact disc might require storage of 15 billion bits. With such great data density, even the smallest speck of dust would wipe out a considerable number of bits, as shown in figure 3.6. In reality the type of error correction utilized would have to be a great deal more sophisticated than a simple redundancy scheme. Even one bad bit could wreak havoc. For example, if the digital word 0000000000000000 (representing silence) was misread as 1000000000000000 (representing a pretty loud level), a click some 90 dB above the silence would result.

### Detection

Before error correction takes place, the errors must be detected. While this might sound obvious, the problem can be difficult. If presented with a data word, could you tell whether or not an error had occurred? For example, does 1100101000011110 contain an error? Unless you are psychic, there is no way to tell. The message could be sent twice: 1100101000011110 1100101100011110, and close examination would reveal a difference between them. Obviously, both cannot be correct, but which one is the right one? The message could be sent three times: 1100101000011110 1100101100011110 1100101000011110, and you might have a good suspicion of which one was correct, but would you be sure? What if the message were sent three times, and they were all different?

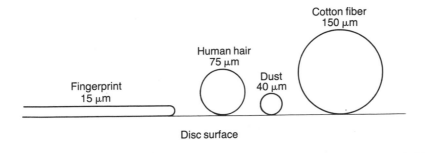

Figure 3.6  *Even miniscule obstructions such as dust are large compared to the 1/2 micrometer-wide data pits.*

While simple repetition is an inefficient way of going about errror detection, a more enlightened variation, data redundancy, is the essence of error correction. Data redundancy is extra information derived from the original information; hence it is redundant. In general, the greater the redundancy, the better the error correction. As we have seen, redundancy adds to storage overhead and must be optimized in a practical system; this leads to the development of elaborate error correction codes which make very efficient use of redundancy by coding the information in certain ways.

### Correction

In practice, the redundancy contained in correction codes often takes the form of a parity bit added to every data word. The parity bit is chosen so the number of 1s or 0s in the group (data word plus parity bit) is even or odd. For example, a parity bit may be formed with this rule: if the number of 1s in the data word is even (or zero), the parity bit is made 0; if the number of 1s is odd, the parity bit is made 1. The total number of 1s will always be an even number (or zero); this is called even parity. By the same token, odd parity could be used.

This scheme allows for error detection of received data: any word with an odd number of 1s must be invalid. Odd parity can detect one-bit errors in data (actually, it detects all errors involving an odd number of bits). However, if two or any even number of bits are bad, the scheme fails to detect the error, and a bad parity bit would cause good data to be flagged as erroneous. Moreover, the scheme cannot ascertain which bit is bad. Thus it cannot correct errors. Clearly, a more sophisticated scheme is needed.

For correction, in essence, more parity bits are required to solve the problem, and the algorithm used to select the parity bits determines the performance of the error correction code. For example, in some codes the data is divided into blocks, and parity values are added to each block. Consider the example in figure 3.7. In addition to the twelve data values in 3.7a, nine extra parity values are created and appended to the original data block. They are placed at the end of each row and column, and form the sum of that row and column, as shown in 3.7b. Note that a parity value is also included for the parity row and column. If an error occurs in any data (or parity) value, the error can be easily located, and the correct value can be easily calculated, using the other data present.

For example, suppose that the data block in Figure 3.7c was received. As we recalculate each parity value at the receiving end and check it against each transmitted parity value, we observe a disagreement. In fact, there is a disagreement in both a row and a column parity value. The intersection of the row and column points to the error. Furthermore, we can now substitute the correct value, derived from the transmitted parity values. The data in the block is thus substantially more reliable. Of course,

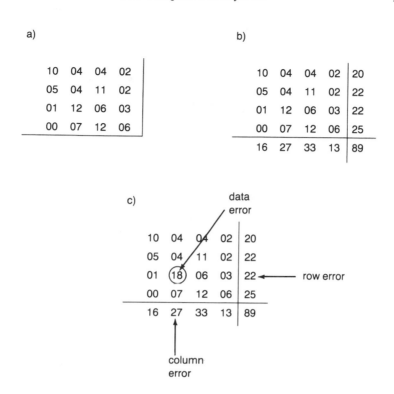

Figure 3.7    *A data block (a) may have parity values attached on each row and column (b). In the event of an error (c), parity may be used to correct the error.*

instead of 12 values, 20 are now required for the error code. In practice, a code may take the form shown in figure 3.8. Several parity bits (a) are generated from combinations of input data bits. Transmitted data is parity-tested, and odd parity indicates an error. Using the results of the parity check, a logic table may be used to determine which bit is incorrect. If data 0011 is received as 0111 (c), parity indicates an error in bit 2.

Numerous error correction codes have been devised. For example, Hamming codes derive multiple parity bits from combinations of the data bits. Simple Hamming codes can be constructed which will detect two errors and correct one error. Similarly, Reed-Solomon codes can detect and correct large numbers of errors. Using codes such as Reed-Solomon, a digital audio system can detect and correct errors, and supply information that is as good as new. As we will see, the compact disc system uses a Reed-Solomon error correction code as part of its defense against errors.

However, as we have seen, the performance of the error correction system depends on the nature of the error. For example, what if a large error

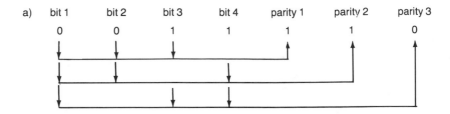

a)

| bit 1 | bit 2 | bit 3 | bit 4 | parity 1 | parity 2 | parity 3 |
|-------|-------|-------|-------|----------|----------|----------|
| 0 | 0 | 1 | 1 | 1 | 1 | 0 |

b)

| bit 1, bit 2<br>bit 3, parity 1 | bit 1, bit 2<br>bit 4, parity 2 | bit 1, bit 3<br>bit 4, parity 3 | location<br>of error |
|---|---|---|---|
| even | even | even | none |
| odd | even | even | parity 1 |
| even | odd | even | parity 2 |
| even | even | odd | parity 3 |
| even | odd | odd | bit 4 |
| odd | even | odd | bit 3 |
| odd | odd | even | bit 2 |
| odd | odd | odd | bit 1 |

c)

| bit 1 = 0 | bit 1 = 0 | bit 1 = 0 |
|---|---|---|
| bit 2 = 1 | bit 2 = 1 | bit 3 = 1 |
| bit 3 = 1 | bit 4 = 1 | bit 4 = 1 |
| parity 1 = 1 | parity 2 = 1 | parity 3 = 0 |
| odd | odd | even |

**Figure 3.8**  *An error correction code uses combinations of data bits to form multiple parity bits.*

obliterated both the data and its parity? There would be nothing left to reconstruct the message. It is thus important to understand the nature of the errors and devise protection to fit their nature. Errors can occur in large groups, called burst errors, or in isolated instances, called random errors. The compact disc must guard against both kinds; for example, a badly formed pit could cause a random error, whereas a dust particle could cause a burst error. Clearly, burst errors are the most troubling. A good error correction code uses parity in addition to other processing, such as interleaving.

## Interleaving

Interleaving is employed to guard against the very likely occurrence of burst errors. Interleaving might be thought of as shuffling a deck of cards; data symbols are redistributed in the bit stream prior to recording so that consecutive words are never adjacent on the medium. An error occurring in the medium (such as a dust particle on the disc) might prevent the successful reading of a number of consecutive values. However, upon de-interleaving the shuffled words are placed back in their original and rightful position in the stream, and the errors are scattered in time. Thus isolated, they are much easier to correct. Interleaving is particularly useful for long burst errors; consecutive errors are scattered by de-interleaving, becoming more like random errors which are more easily corrected. An interleaving example is shown in figure 3.9. Interleaving appears complicated, but it can be accomplished by simply delaying the data words by

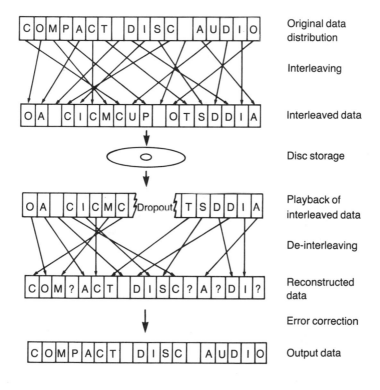

Figure 3.9    *When interleaved data is de-interleaved, consecutive errors are scattered, making correction easier.*

differing amounts prior to recording. Delaying the data words again (in a complementary manner) upon playback completes the technique.

Cross interleaving carries the idea one step further. Data is interleaved numerous times, over both short and long time intervals. This provides correctability for larger errors. As we shall see, the CD system uses the Cross Interleave Reed-Solomon Code (CIRC) for error protection. It employs parity checking to correct random errors and cross interleaving to permit parity to correct burst errors.

### Concealment

Although correction of massive errors is possible, it would be impractical to implement. In real-life digital audio systems, some errors overwhelm the error correction scheme. These errors are flagged by the correction circuits and passed on to error concealment circuits.

Without concealment, erroneous data that escaped error correction could result in an audible click. Error concealment systems employ interpolation and muting circuits following the CIRC decoder. Although an important part of error protection, they are unrelated to the CIRC. Specifically, they attempt to handle errors too massive for CIRC correction. Using error flags from the CIRC decoder, the player's concealment circuits determine whether to output the data directly, to interpolate it, or to mute.

Interpolation is the technique of using valid data surrounding an error as a basis of forming an approximation of the erroneous data. These values are used to calculate a new value to substitute for the error. Because of the high correlation between music samples, an uncorrected error can be made virtually inaudible by synthesizing new data from surrounding data. Although clicks are avoided, a momentary increase in distortion is produced.

Numerous interpolation schemes are used, with different performance levels. In its simplest form, zero-order interpolation holds the previous value and repeats it to cover the missing or incorrect word. In first-order interpolation, the erroneous word is replaced with a word derived from the mean value of the previous and subsequent words.

In worst case scenerios, where the error is so massive that even interpolation would fail, we choose to mute the audio signal. The brief silence is preferable to the burst of digital noise, usually heard as a click. By attenuating the signal before and after the mute, even these catastrophic errors are often made inaudible to most listeners.

However, the digital audio signal cannot be muted by switching the bit stream to zero; this could result in an audible click. Muting methods vary from player to player. For example, the signal may be faded down by multiplying the samples by descending coefficients, usually taken from a half cycle of a cosine waveform. The fade-out must begin prior to the bad data; this is accommodated by feeding the signal through a delay before the muting circuit. The mute signal thus arrives before the bad data. Following the bad data, a fade-in is similarly accomplished. Smooth mutes are surprisingly inaudible.

## CROSS INTERLEAVE REED-SOLOMON CODE (CIRC)

As we have seen, error correction is essential to the success of digital audio. Without it, any digital recording on tape or disc would sound like a badly scratched LP at best, or at worst, be simply unplayable. In fact, without error correction, digital audio would be an impossibility.

The raw error rate from a CD is around $10^{-5}$ to $10^{-6}$, or about one error for every 0.1 to 1.0 million bits. This is impressive storage capability, but considering that a disc will output over 4 million bits per second, the need for error correction is obvious. With error correction, perhaps 200 errors per second will be completely corrected. To achieve such results, the CD employs the cornerstones of error correction: interleaving to distribute errors, and parity to correct them. The particular algorithm used for error correction in the compact disc system is, as mentioned earlier, the Cross Interleave Reed-Solomon Code (CIRC). The CIRC circuit uses two correction codes for additional correcting capability and three interleaving stages to encode data before it is placed on a disc. Similarly, CIRC performs error correction while decoding the data during playback.

### Reed-Solomon Codes

The Reed-Solomon code used in CIRC is a highly efficient error correcting code. It is particularly well suited for the compact disc system because its decoding requirements are relatively simple. To illustrate the operation of CIRC, suppose that *A, B, C,* and *D* are four data words, and *P* and *Q* are two parity words. The $\oplus$ symbol denotes modulo 2 addition (EX OR), and the alphas are weighting factors. The data words are placed into two simultaneous equations:

$$A \oplus B \oplus C \oplus D \oplus P \oplus Q = 0$$
$$\alpha^6 A \oplus \alpha^5 B \oplus \alpha^4 C \oplus \alpha^3 D \oplus \alpha^2 P \oplus \alpha Q = 0$$

Solving for P and Q, we have

$$P = \alpha A \oplus \alpha^2 B \oplus \alpha^5 C \oplus \alpha^3 D$$
$$Q = \alpha^3 A \oplus \alpha^6 B \oplus \alpha^4 C \oplus \alpha D$$

where we assume that

$$\alpha = 010$$
$$\alpha^2 = 100$$
$$\alpha^3 = 011$$
$$\alpha^4 = 110$$
$$\alpha^5 = 111$$
$$\alpha^6 = 101$$
$$1 = \alpha^7 = 001$$
$$0 = 000$$

Table 3.2 shows some sample values for $A$, $B$, $C$, $D$, $P$, and $Q$. To detect errors in the received data, two syndromes, or error patterns, are calculated by these decoding equations:

$$
\begin{aligned}
S_1 &= A' \oplus B' \oplus C' \oplus D' \oplus P' \oplus Q' \\
&= E_A \oplus E_B \oplus E_C \oplus E_D \oplus E_P \oplus E_Q \\
S_2 &= \alpha^6 A' \oplus \alpha^5 B' \oplus \alpha^4 C' \oplus \alpha^3 D' \oplus \alpha^2 P' \oplus \alpha Q' \\
&= \alpha^6 E_A \oplus \alpha^5 E_B \oplus \alpha^4 E_C \oplus \alpha^3 E_D \oplus \alpha^2 E_P \oplus \alpha E_Q
\end{aligned}
$$

where $A'$ through $Q'$ are the reproduced words, $E_A$ through $E_Q$ are the errors of each word, and the alphas (along with 1 and 0) are the weighting constants. If there is no error, then $S_1 = S_2 = 0$. If the word $A$ is erroneous, $S_1 = E_A$ and $S_2 = \alpha^6 S_1$. In other words, an error results in non-zero syndromes, and the value of the erroneous words can be determined by the difference of the weighting between $S_1$ and $S_2$.

As noted previously, CIRC employs cross interleaving, the separation of two error correction codes by an interleaving stage. Thus one code can check the accuracy of the other code. Another important aspect about cross interleaving is that error correction is enhanced, but the amount of redundancy is not increased. An example of cross interleaving and the way it facilitates parity checking is shown in figure 3.10. S represents data val-

**Recorded data**

| Information words | | Parity words | |
|---|---|---|---|
| A | 0 0 1 | P | 1 1 1 |
| B | 1 0 1 | Q | 1 1 0 |
| C | 0 1 1 | | |
| D | 1 0 0 | | |

Table 3.2    *Sample values and calculated parity words.*

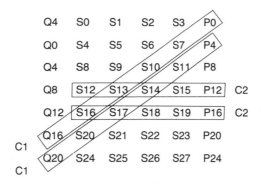

<br />

Figure 3.10    *Cross interleaving permits more efficient correction of errors by decoders.*

ues (called symbols), P and Q are parity values, and C1 and C2 are correction decoders capable of correcting one and two symbols respectively. If S13 is erroneous, C1Q16 corrects it. If S13 and S14 are erroneous, C1Q16 and C1Q20 correct them. If S13 and S16 are erroneous, C2P12 and C2P16 correct them. If S13, S14, S16 and S17 are erroneous, C2P12 and C2P16 correct them by using C1's error detection pointers. If there are more errors on the P12 and P16 strings, correction becomes impossible. CIRC uses cross interleaving similarly; however, the C1 and C2 decoders are more powerful.

### CIRC Encoding

The complete CIRC encoding scheme is shown in figure 3.11. With this encoding algorithm, bits from the audio signal are cross-interleaved, and two encoding stages generate parity symbols, or data values. Error correction encoding begins with the first stage of interleaving, which is designed to assist interpolation. Twenty-four 8-bit symbols are applied to the CIRC encoder. A delay of two symbols is placed between even and odd samples: that is, even samples are delayed by two blocks. Interpolation can be accomplished in the case where two uncorrectable blocks occur. Next, the symbols are scrambled so as to separate even and odd numbered data words. This process facilitates concealment.

The C2 encoder accepts the 24-byte parallel word and produces 4 bytes of Q parity. Q parity is designed to correct one erroneous symbol or up to

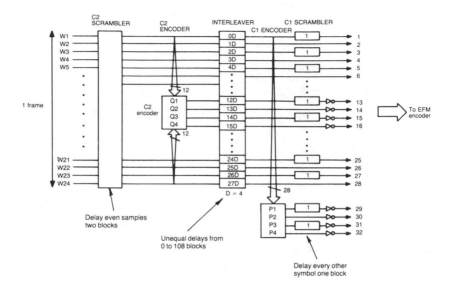

Figure 3.11    *CIRC encoding.*

four erasures in one word. An erasure is a word that has been erased by the decoders because detection has ascertained its value is unreliable. The parity symbols are placed in the center of the block to increase the odd/even distance. This enhances interpolation in the case of burst errors.

Cross interleaving follows the C2 encoder. The 28 bytes are delayed by differing periods, which are integer multiples of four blocks. As a result of this convolutional interleave, each C2 word is stored in 28 different blocks, distributed over 109 blocks. In mathematical terms, we have crossed a data array in two directions.

The C1 encoder accepts a 28-byte word (from 28 different C2 words) and produces four more bytes of P parity. The C1 encoder is used to correct single symbol errors, and detect and flag double and triple errors for Q correction.

A last interleave stage introduces a fixed delay of one symbol to alternate symbols. This odd/even delay spreads the output words over two data blocks. This prevents random errors from disrupting more than one symbol in one word, even if two adjacent symbols in one block are erroneous. Finally, the P and Q parity symbols are inverted to provide non-zero P and Q symbols with zero data. This assists data readout during areas with muted audio program. Thirty-two 8-bit symbols leave the CIRC encoder.

## CIRC Decoding

Upon playback, following demodulation, data is sent to a CIRC decoder for de-interleaving, error detection, and correction. The CIRC decoding process reverses many of the processing steps accomplished during encoding; the complete CIRC decoding process is shown in figure 3.12. It utilizes parity from two Reed-Solomon decoders, and de-interleaving. The first decoder, C1, is designed to correct random errors and to detect burst errors. It puts a flag on all burst errors to alert the second decoder, C2. Given this prior knowledge, and help from de-interleaving, C2 is able to correct burst errors, as well as random errors that C1 was unable to correct.

During reproduction, the CIRC decoder accepts one frame of 32 8-bit symbols: 24 are audio symbols, and 8 are parity symbols. Odd numbered symbols are delayed, and parity symbols are inverted. The delay lines have a delay equal to the duration of one symbol. Thus information of even numbered symbols of a frame is de-cross-interleaved with that of the odd numbered symbols on the next frame. This de-interleaving places the even and odd numbered audio symbols back into their original order by re-arranging their order as read from the disc. Any sequence of errors on the disc is thus distributed among valid data.

In the C1 decoder, errors are detected and corrected by the four P parity symbols; short duration random errors are corrected, and longer burst errors are passed along. Specifically, the C1 decoder can correct a symbol error in every word of 32 symbols. If there is more than one erroneous symbol, then all 28 data symbols are marked with an erasure flag and passed on. Valid symbols, those adhering to the encoding rules of C1, are passed along unprocessed.

The delays between the decoders are of unequal length and longer than those at the input to the C1 decoder; this convolutional interleaving enables the C2 decoder to correct longer burst errors. Because the word arriving at C2 contains symbols from C1 decoded at different times, symbols marked with an erasure flag are now distributed among valid symbols. This helps the C2 decoder correct burst errors. Symbols without a flag are assumed error free and passed through unprocessed. In the C2 decoder errors are corrected by the four Q parity symbols. C2 can detect and correct single symbol errors, correcting up to four symbols, if flagged (in some implementations, only two symbols can be corrected). Burst errors and errors which might have occurred in the encoding process itself (rather than in the medium) are corrected. In addition, C2 can correct symbols miscorrected by C1 decoding. When C2 cannot accomplish correction because more than four symbols are flagged, 24 data symbols are flagged as uncorrected and passed on for interpolation. Final de-scrambling and delay is performed, to assist interpolation.

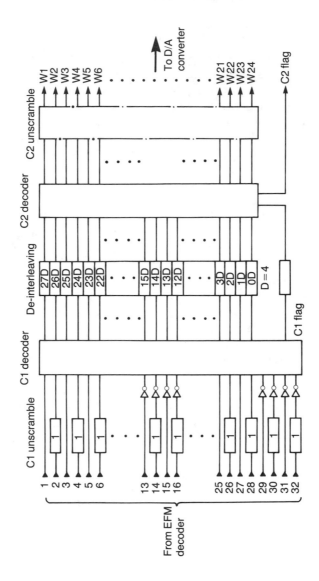

Figure 3.12     *CIRC decoding.*

The use of two correction decoders and cross interleaving helps tackle a particularly difficult error scenario. Interleaving distributes burst errors, perhaps caused by surface contamination, over different words for easier correction. Nevertheless, correction is difficult when a burst error coincides with a random error introduced perhaps by a manufacturing defect. In the CD standard, random errors are defined to be single symbol errors, or no more than 17T (time periods) in length. Any longer errors are burst errors. EFM coding (explained later in this chapter) guarantees that a random error will never corrupt more than two symbols, and the even/odd interleave guarantees that a two-symbol random error will always appear as a single error in two different C1 words after de-interleaving. Random errors are thus always correctable, and the C2 decoder retains its burst error correction capability.

### CIRC Performance

It should be noted that CD players are not created equal in terms of error correction. Any CD player's error correction ability is limited to the success of the strategy chosen to decode the CIRC code on the disc. For example, for more efficient correction, decoding could be repeated alternatively, in the form C1, C2, C1, C2.

A measure of the overall correction performance is the number of interpolated sample values for a given bit error rate (BER) in a given time. The lower the interpolation rate for a given BER value is, the better the system's random error correction quality will be. Alternatively, BLER (block error rate) measures blocks containing errors. An assessment of system performance must also account for uncorrected errors that pass through the error correction circuitry. These errors may result in an audible click on the output. Table 3.3 summarizes the specifications of the CIRC system.

| Aspect | Specification |
|---|---|
| Maximum *completely* correctable burst length | ≈ 4000 data bits (i.e. ≈ 2.5 mm track length on the disc) |
| Maximum interpolatable burst length in the *worst* case | ≈ 12,300 data bits (i.e. ≈ 7.7 mm track length) |
| Sample interpolation rate | One sample every 10 hours at BER = $10^{-4}$; 1000 samples per minute at BER = $10^{-3}$ |
| Undetected error samples (clicks) | Less than one every 750 hours at BER = $10^{-3}$; negligible at BER ≤ $10^{-4}$ |

Table 3.3   *Performance specifications of CIRC.*

In theory, CIRC detects and completely corrects burst errors of up to 4000 bad bits, or a period of 1.9 milliseconds, or a physical defect 2.5 millimeters long. Interpolation can conceal errors of up to 12,300 bad bits, corresponding to a physical defect of 7.7 millimeters. Looked at in another way, the raw error rate (before correction) from a compact disc may range from $10^{-5}$ to $10^{-6}$, or one error in every $10^5$ to $10^6$ bits. After CIRC, in theory, the error rate is between $10^{-10}$ and $10^{-11}$, or about one uncorrected error in every 10 or 100 billion bits.

However, the quality of the error correcting performance varies from player to player. Depending on the CIRC decoding strategy used, the theoretical probability of an error occurring can vary from quite often to almost never. Three different CIRC decoding strategies are shown in figure 3.13, and their random error correction performance is shown in figure 3.14. Although the simplest strategy, number 1 (in figure 3.13), is satisfactory for most applications, strategy 3 is clearly much better. In the example, other strategies were developed by interchanging the C1 and C2 decoders of strategies 2 and 3. Strategy (2,3) uses the C1 decoder from strategy 2 and the C2 decoder from strategy 3. This illustrates the effect of different error conditions on the success of the correction strategy. For example, strategy 3 is superior to strategy 2 primarily because of its ability to correct two independent errors at the C1 decoder. Thus for correcting burst errors, strategy 3's superiority could be drastically reduced.

In short, it is difficult for designers to evaluate error correction performance prior to real use. Figure 3.15 shows an example of error correction performance on three discs. The clean disc represents normal conditions (with a block error rate of $3.3 \times 10^{-4}$). On the disc with the fingerprint, the smudge covers the entire disc. The block error rate is $5.6 \times 10^{-4}$. To create the scratches, the disc was rubbed on a wooden table for approximately one minute. This created a block error rate of $4.5 \times 10^{-3}$. In practice, for CDs that are in reasonably good shape, you might find one uncorrected error per disc, to be dealt with by error concealment methods.

## DATA ENCODING

Compact disc encoding is the process of placing audio data in a format suitable for storage on the disc. A frame structure provides such a format. The frame furnishes a means to distinguish the data types: audio data and its parity, synchronization word, and subcode. The information contained in a CD frame (prior to modulation) contains a 27-bit synchronization word, 8-bit subcode, 192 data bits, and 64 parity bits. CD frames are assembled when the master disc is encoded. Assembly of the frame involves several

1) *Strategy 1 (Simple Correction Strategy)*

$C_1$ Decoder
  *if* single- or zero-error syndrome
  *then* modify at most one symbol
    accordingly
  *else* assign erasure flags to all symbols
    of the received word

$C_2$ Decoder
  *if* single- or zero-error syndrome
  *then* modify at most one symbol
    accordingly
  *else if* $f > 1$
    *then* copy $C_2$ erasure flags
      from $C_1$ erasure flags
    *else if* $f \leq 1$
      *then* assign erasure flags to
        all symbols of the
        the received word

2) *Strategy 2 (Middle Correction Strategy)*

$C_1$ Decoder
  *if* single- or zero-error syndrome
  *then* modify at most one symbol
    accordingly
  *else* assign erasure flags to all symbols
    of the received word

$C_2$ Decoder
  *if* single- or zero-error syndrome
  *then* modify at most one symbol
    accordingly
  *else if* $f > 2$
    *then* copy $C_2$ erasure flags
      from $C_1$ erasure flags
    *else if* $f = 2$
      *then* try two-erasure decoding
      *else if* $f < 2$ or *if* two-erasure
        decoding fails

        *then* assign erasure flags
          to all symbols of the
          received word

3) *Strategy 3 (Superstrategy)*

$C_1$ Decoder
  *if* single- or zero-error syndrome
  *then* modify at most one symbol
    accordingly
  *else if* double-error syndrome
    *then* modify two symbols
      accordingly assign erasure
      flags to all symbols of the
      received word
    *else* assign erasure flags to all
      symbols of the received word

$C_2$ Decoder
  *if* single- or zero-error syndrome
  *then* modify at most one symbol
    accordingly
  *else if* $f \leq 4$
    *then if* double-error syndrome
      and $L_c = 2$
      *then* modify two symbols
        accordingly
      *else if* {double-error syndrome
        and $[(L_c = 1$ and $f \leq 3)$
        or $(L_c = 0$ and $f \leq 2)]\}$
        or $(f \leq 2$ and not double-
        error syndrome)
      *then* assign erasure flags
        to all symbols of the
        received word
      *else* copy $C_2$ erasure flags
        from $C_1$ erasure flags
    *else* copy $C_2$ erasure flags from
      $C_1$ erasure flags

Figure 3.13   *CD players employ different CIRC decoding strategies. Three strategies are shown here. The lowercase* f *is the number of erasure flags input into the* $C_2$ *decoder.* $L_C$ *is the number of erasure flags agreeing with the error locations calculated from the syndrome. (From Vries and Odaka)*

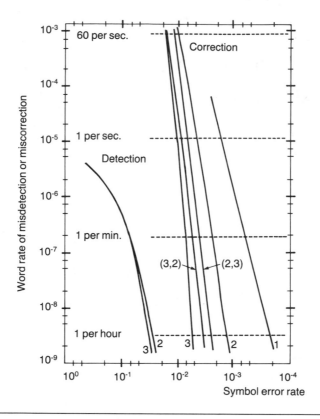

Figure 3.14 *Performance curves for three decoding strategies for random errors. (From Vries and Odaka)*

processing steps, as well as modulation and the addition of merging bits. The complete encoding sequence is shown in figure 3.16.

Encoding begins with the audio data. Six 32-bit PCM audio sampling periods (alternating from 16-bit left and right channels) are grouped in a frame, the left channel preceding the right. Each 32-bit sampling period is divided to yield four 8-bit audio symbols. (The original 16-bit number is called a word, and it is split into two 8-bit symbols.)

After grouping audio data into symbols, error correction encoding takes place. The CD system, of course, employs the Cross Interleave Reed-Solomon Code (CIRC). As we've seen, it uses a combination of interleaving and parity to make the data more robust against errors encountered during storage.

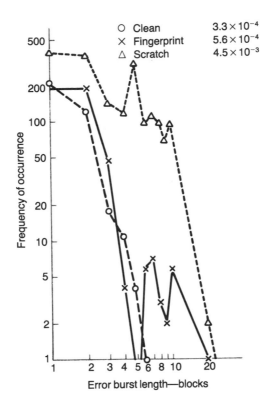

Figure 3.15    *Examples of error correction performance for damaged discs.*
*(From Doi)*

### Subcode

Following CIRC encoding, an 8-bit subcode symbol is added to each frame. The eight subcode bits are designated as P,Q,R,S,T,U,V, and W, sometimes referred to as the PQ code. The CD player collects subcode symbols from 98 consecutive frames to form a subcode block, with eight 98-bit words. Only the P and Q bits are used in audio CDs. Included is information specifying the total number of selections on the disc, their beginning and ending points and timings, the index points within a selection, the program lead-in and lead-out points, and updated information on the pickup's position as the disc is played. The other six bits (R,S,T,U,V, and W) are available for encoding other information on audio CDs. Subcode is discussed in more detail in Chapter Four.

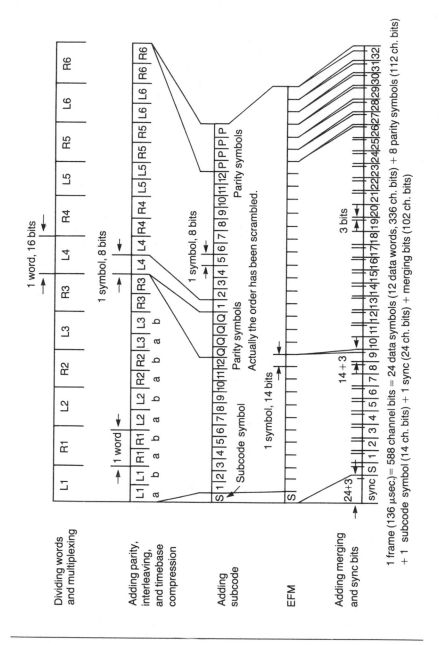

Figure 3.16   *Complete CD encoding process.*

## EFM Modulation

After the audio, parity, and subcode data are assembled, the bit stream is modulated using eight-to-fourteen modulation (EFM). Blocks of 8 data bits are translated into blocks of 14 bits, known as channel bits, using a ROM dictionary which assigns an arbitrary and unambiguous word of 14 bits to each 8-bit word; a part of the lookup table is shown in table 3.4.

By choosing the right 14-bit words, the bit patterns with a low number (and known rate) of transitions between 0 and 1, greater data density can be achieved. It would be inefficient to store the 8-bit symbols directly on the disc; the large number of 0/1 transitions would demand many pits. The 8 data bits require $2^8$ or 256 different code patterns. However, the 14-bit channel word can offer 16,384 combinations. In addition, 8-bit symbols have many similar patterns; for example, if one bit were wrong, 00001011 would be confused with 10001011. With 14-bit words, more unique patterns can be selected. EFM thus provides a kind of error correction.

To achieve pits of controlled length, only those combinations are selected in which more than two but less than ten 0s appear continuously. Only 267 combinations satisfy these criteria. With these patterns, the minimum inversion width of the signal is limited by the recording density, and the maximum inversion width is limited by the clock bit extraction. The conversion is thus a compromise between several conditions. Because only 256 patterns are needed, 11 of the 267 patterns are discarded (two of them are used for subcode synchronization words).

| Data bits | Channel bits |
|-----------|--------------|
| 00000000  | 01001000100000 |
| 00000001  | 10000100000000 |
| 00000010  | 10010000100000 |
| 00000011  | 10001000100000 |
| 00000100  | 01000100000000 |
| 00000101  | 00000100010000 |
| 00000110  | 00010000100000 |
| 00000111  | 00100100000000 |
| 00001000  | 01001001000000 |
| 00001001  | 10000001000000 |
| 00001010  | 10010001000000 |

Table 3.4    *In EFM, each 8-bit word is translated to a 14-bit word, selected for its specific bit pattern.*

## Merging Bits

Blocks of 14 bits are linked by 3 merging bits. Two merging bits (always 0s) are required to prevent the possibility of successive 1's between serial words (a violation of the coding scheme). The additional merging bit (either a 1 or a 0, depending on the preceding and succeeding patterns) is added to each code pattern to aid in clock synchronization and to suppress the signal's low-frequency component.

The signal's low-frequency component is suppressed by selecting merging bits which maintain the signal's average digital sum value at zero, as shown in figure 3.17. The digital sum value is determined by assigning $+1$ and $-1$ to the high-level (1) and low-level (0) amplitudes respectively. The merging bits may take either state; the processor selects a 1 or 0 to reduce the overall digital sum value. In figure 3.17a two consecutive EFM patterns result in a digital sum value offset. With a transition introduced into the merging bits, the digital sum value is reduced. Note that the data content itself is not affected. The ratio of high to low bits before and after modulation is 8:17. During demodulation, only the 14 data bits will be processed; the 3 merging bits are discarded.

## Pit Length

At this stage of the encoding, the signal exists as a non-return-to-zero (NRZ) signal. This is a form commonly employed for processing digital data in which the signal level is high at 1 and low at 0. After EFM modulation, the signal is converted to non-return-to-zero-inverted (NRZI) form. In this form, the signal inverts at the center of each 1. NRZ and NRZI are reviewed in figure 3.18. NRZI gives the waveform fewer transitions and thus simplifies the pit structure on the disc.

The resultant channel stream produces pits and lands which are at least three channel bits and no more than eleven channel bits long. The $3T$ pit is thus the highest frequency signal (720 kHz) while the $11T$ pit is the lowest (196 kHz). $T$ signifies one period. Pit lengths thus vary from 0.833 to 3.054 micrometers at 1.2 meter per second, and from 0.972 to 3.56 micrometers at 1.4 meters per second. It is the combination of these varying dimensions which physically encode the data. The selection of EFM bit patterns defines the physical relationship of the pit dimensions. The pit and intervening reflective land on the CD surface do not directly designate 1s and 0s. Rather, as shown in figure 3.19, each pit edge, whether leading or trailing, is a 1 and all increments in between, whether inside or outside a pit, are 0s. This is a much more efficient storage technique than coding the binary bits directly with pits.

With EFM there are more bits to accommodate, but with modulation the highest frequency in the output signal is decreased; therefore, a lower

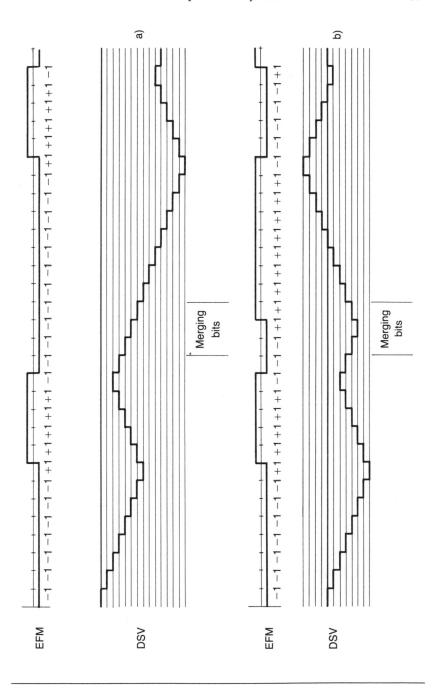

Figure 3.17 *If merging bits were not used (a), the DSV would accumulate an offset. With merging bits (b) that DC component is controlled.*

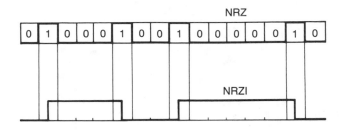

Figure 3.18 *After modulation, the signal is converted from NRZ to NRZI form.*

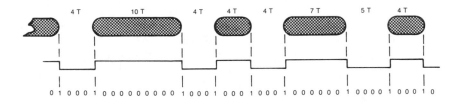

Figure 3.19 *Pit edges encode logical 1 channel bits.*

track velocity can be utilized, which results in longer playing time. This is a very efficient encoding method because the number of bits transmitted, divided by the number of transitions needed on the medium to convey them, is high.

### Frame Assembly

The individual frames in the resulting EFM bit stream must be delineated. Thus a synchronization pattern is added prior to each frame. This is necessary to make the bit stream self-clocking; that is, no modulation clock is needed to maintain an accurate readout rate. The synchronization word is uniquely distinguishable from any other possible data configuration; it is 3 transitions separated by $11T$. Specifically, the 24-bit synchronization word is 100000000001000000000010 plus 3 merging bits.

The total number of channel bits per frame after encoding is 588, comprising the following: 24 synchronization bits, 336 ($12 \times 2 \times 14$) data bits, 112 ($4 \times 2 \times 14$) error correction bits, 14 subcode bits, and 102 ($34 \times 3$) merging bits, as shown in figure 3.20. When the data manipulation is com-

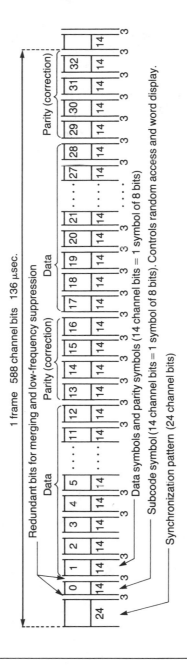

Figure 3.20    *Summary of frame format.*

| 1 sample: | 1 word: 16 bits, 2 symbols | Sample rate: | 44.1k samples/sec/channel |
|---|---|---|---|
| 1 data or parity symbol: | 14 bits (8 bits before EFM) | Data bit rate: | 1.4M bits/sec |
| 1 subcoding symbol: | 14 bits (Note that meaningful information is on the accumulated 98 frames.) | Frame rate: | 7.35k frames/sec (75 subcode-frames/sec) |
| | | Control bit rate: | 58.8k bits/sec |
| 1 sync signal: | 24 channel bits | Transfer rate: | 2.03M bits/sec before EFM |
| 1 frame | 6 samples/channel: 12 data words | Bit rate: (clock frequency): | 4.3218M bits/sec |

Table 3.5    *Data formats and data rates.*

pleted, the original audio bit rate of 1.41 million bits per second has been augmented to 4.3218 million bits per second. CD data format and rates are summarized in table 3.5.

It is important to remember that the only information in a CD signal is the position in time of the pit transitions. In other words, all data is represented as timing patterns. This means that there are more data bits recorded than there are transitions on the disc. (Specifically, there are 24 data bits for every 17 disc transitions). That's efficiency.

## DATA DECODING

The pits on the CD data surface, as we have seen, are the physical manifestation of complicated data encoding, including multiplexing, interleaving, parity, error protection, and EFM, all of which take place at the lathe when the master disc is cut. The decoding of these bits requires complex signal processing. The player must demodulate the data, de-interleave it and correct data errors, while observing the data format originally encoded on the master disc. The complexity of the task accounts for the design differences between players, but the overall scheme remains similar.

### *EFM Demodulation*

When the laser beam is reflected at the disc surface during playback, the varying intensity of the returned beam is detected by a photodiode sensor. It is the voltage from the sensor which is ultimately transformed into the analog audio signal output from the player. However, the encoded data from the pickup must first be decoded. The signal encoded on the disc utilized eight-to-fourteen modulation (EFM), which specified that the signal be comprised of not less than two 0's or more than ten 0's between logical transitions (pit edges). This results in pit lengths expressed in a variety of combinational patterns from a pit length 3 units long to a pit length 11 units long; this sets the frequency limits of the EFM signal read from the disc. As we've seen, this range is sometimes referred to as a $3T$–$11T$ signal with $T$ referring to the period of one bit. The audio output is ultimately derived from the lengths (read as timing intervals) of the data pits and lands.

The photodiode and its processing circuits produce a signal resembling a high frequency sine wave called the EFM signal. Because of its high frequency, it is sometimes referred to as an RF (radio frequency) signal. Figure 3.21 shows the RF signal from a series of pits. A collection of data periods is often called the eye pattern. (The diamond-shaped area in the middle of the pattern, along the axis, looks like an eye, if you've got a lively imagination.) An eye pattern is shown in figure 3.22.

Figure 3.21    *Data pits are used to produce a representative RF signal.*

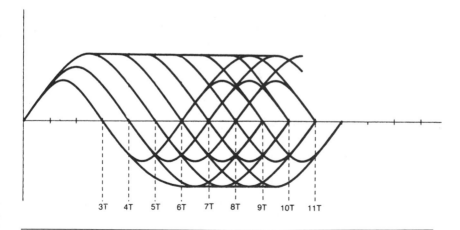

Figure 3.22    *A collection of RF signals forms the eye pattern.*

The varying periods of these sine waves ($3T$, $4T$, etc.) reflect the periods of time required to read the disc pits. The eye pattern is thus an electrical equivalent of the disc's data. The digital data can always be recovered from the eye pattern if it can be determined when the signal crosses the zero axis relative to the $3T$–$11T$ time patterns. Whenever a player is tracking data, the eye pattern is present, and the quality of the signal may be observed from the pattern. For example, a skewed disc would result in a distorted eye pattern.

The zero-crossings of the eye pattern contain the sole information content of the EFM signal. Because pit walls are not vertical, the resulting signal is not square. In addition, pits can be longer or shorter than the actual pulse width of the recorded EFM signal, depending on cutting conditions. This causes the RF signal to be asymmetrical to the DC level. Figure 3.23 shows a threshold control circuit which adjusts the threshold level, elimi-

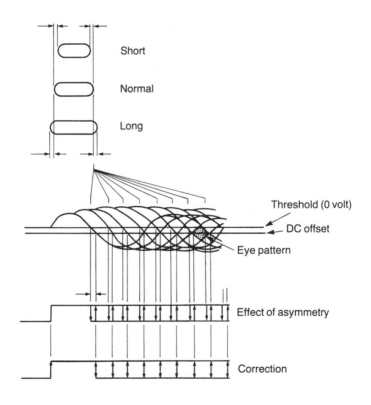

Figure 3.23    *A threshold control circuit eliminates DC offset, due to asymmetry in pit length, in the RF signal.*

nating DC offset in order to achieve correct pulse width. The resulting binary waveform now has a more normal digital appearance; the varying widths of the waveforms still contain the EFM information.

Because the eye pattern at the photodiodes has a very small amplitude, it must be boosted by a preamplifier. An equalization network or transversal filter must be used to ensure that the smallest signal duration (high frequency) $3T$ is equal in amplitude with the longest duration (low frequency) $11T$. The filter must compensate for the fact that shorter period signals ($3T$, $4T$, $5T$, etc.) are lower in amplitude than the others. The overall signal is processed through an automatic gain control circuit; no matter what the reflectivity of the CD (within certain tolerances), this circuit optimally adjusts the level of the eye pattern.

Although the EFM signal is comprised of a varying sinusoidal waveform, it is truly digital; it undergoes processing to convert it into a series of square waves more easily accepted by the digital circuits to follow. This does not affect the encoded data, since it is the width of the EFM periods which holds the information of interest. Following the conversion of the eye pattern to square waves, the NRZI (non-return to zero inverted) signal is returned to NRZ (non-return to zero), the representation in which a high level is a 1, and a low level is a 0.

The transitions are used to phase-lock a separator clock with period $T$. This clock identifies the number of $T$ periods between transitions and thus distinguishes between the $17T$ symbols (each of the 33 symbols of a data frame is $17T$ long). Thanks to our pains in the encoding process, the data off the disc is thus self-clocking. The pulse generator has a slope-sensing window of one period ($1T$) for correctly reading a signal with any jitter or time base error.

The first piece of data to be extracted from the NRZ signal is the synchronization word, three transitions separated by $11T$ periods. The start of each data frame can thus be identified. This synchronization information is used to synchronize the 33 symbols of channel information in each frame, and a synchronization pulse is generated to aid in locating the zero crossing of the EFM pattern and to generate a transition at these points to produce a binary signal. The $3T$ merging bits have served their purpose of preventing EFM code violations and suppressing DC. They are separated from the $17T$ symbols, leaving $14T$ symbols.

Because the circuit which controls the disc's precise rotational speed has a limited range, disc speed must be controlled approximately. This is often accomplished by examining the durations of transitions in the EFM signal. The $3T$–$11T$ range means that transitions cannot occur faster than approximately 0.66 microseconds or slower than 2.44 microseconds. When first starting to play a disc, or after jumping to a different track radius (with a different track speed), a correction signal is generated to bring the disc rotation to within the capture range of the timebase corrector (explained below) for precise regulation. This is one reason why C1 and C2 parity bytes are inverted in the CIRC encoder; 1s are placed in the bit stream when the data is muted with all 0s. Thus minimum and maximum pits lengths are recorded during the disc lead-in where the player must quickly regulate disc speed.

The EFM signal is now demodulated so that every 14-bit EFM word again becomes 8 bits. Depending on player design, demodulation is effected either by logic circuitry or a lookup table, which is a list stored in memory that uses the recorded data to refer to the original patterns of 8 bits.

The data stream now contains audio samples, redundancy, and subcode. The EFM demodulator sends subcode data to the display circuit to convey timing and other information to the player front panel. Other control signals contained in the subcode are used, among other things, to alert the player's control microcomputer to the exact location of the pickup.

### Timebase Correction

A buffer is used to remove the effect of disc rotational irregularities; it is sometimes called a timebase corrector. A RAM (random access memory) is commonly used. Data input to the buffer may be irregular, but the buffer output is precisely controlled by a crystal clock.

Timebase correction can be performed with about 16K of storage, and de-interleaving may be accomplished with the same memory. Timebase correction clocking ensures that the data is output at a constant rate despite any variations in the data stream entering the signal processing circuits. Such variations are introduced by the disc's rotating speed. Timebase correction clocking thus eliminates one of the inherent problems of analog systems, speed variations called wow and flutter. In addition to preventing mechanical error, care is taken with the decoded data to ensure that no timing variations are introduced into the bit stream itself.

Error conditions such as buffer overflow or underflow exceed the limits of the system. To prevent these, the buffer's level is constantly monitored by examining the write address. This information is supplied to the circuit which controls the speed of the disc motor and hence the bit rate entering the player. Alternatively, the data separator clock, counting samples from the disc, can be compared to a fixed reference in order to generate a rotation control voltage. Whichever method is used, it is interesting to note that the actual disc speed is unimportant; the player will rotate the disc at any speed necessary to achieve the proper data rate. As a result, CDs may be mastered with a linear track velocity between 1.2 and 1.4 meters/second: however, the velocity will be constant on a given disc.

### Output Processing

Following demodulation, interleaved audio and parity data are routed to the CIRC error correction circuit for de-interleaving, error detection and correction. Interpolation and muting circuits, previously discussed, follow the CIRC decoder. Using error flags from the decoder, the player's signal processing circuits determine whether to output data directly, to interpolate it, or to mute the sound. Interpolation and muting performance may also differ from player to player.

Following error correction, the left and right audio channels must be demultiplexed, and their respective samples joined together in the same sequence and at the same rate in which they were recorded.

After these signal processing chores are accomplished, the data has been restored to its original state: 16-bit samples of digital audio information. In other words, the audio data has been reconstituted to the player's best ability. After a quick trip through D/A converters and low-pass analog filters, or oversampling filters which precede D/A conversion, the analog signals are output.

The compact disc bit stream is thus a little trickier than one might assume. In the interest of density and robustness, the data must undergo sophisticated processing during both encoding and decoding. All the more reason to appreciate the sound a CD player delivers. Next time you listen to Schubert's *Trout Quintet,* remember the bit stream it came from.

### FOR FURTHER READING

Berlekamp, Elwyn R. *Algebraic Coding Theory.* New York: McGraw-Hill, 1968, and Laguna Hills, Calif.: Aegean Press, 1983.

————. "Error Correcting Codes for Digital Audio." In Blesser, B., B. Locanthi, and T. G. Stockham, Jr., eds. *Digital Audio.* New York: Audio Engineering Society, 1983.

Carasso, M. G., J. B. H. Peck, and J. P. Sinjou. "The Compact Disc Digital Audio System." *Philips Technical Review* 40(6):151–55, 1982.

Doi, Toshitada. "Error Correction for Digital Audio Recordings." In Blesser, B., B. Locanthi, and T. G. Stockham, Jr., eds. *Digital Audio.* New York: Audio Engineering Society, 1983.

Hamming, R. W. *Coding and Information Theory.* Englewood Cliffs, N. J.: Prentice-Hall, 1980.

Heemskerk, J. P. J., and Kees A. Schouhamer-Immink. "Compact Disc System Aspects and Modulation." *Philips Technical Review* 40(6):157–64, 1982.

Hoeve, H., H. H. J. Timmermans, and Lodewijk B. Vries. "Error Correction and Concealment in the Compact Disc System." *Philips Technical Review* 40(6):116–73, 1982.

IEC (International Electrotechnical Commission). "Compact Disc Digital Audio System." Standard BNN15-83-095.

Lin, S. *An Introduction to Error-Correcting Codes*. Englewood Cliffs, N. J.: Prentice-Hall, 1970.

Ogawa, Hiroshi, and Kees A. Schouhamer-Immink. "EFM—The Modulation Method for the Compact Disc Digital Audio System." In Blesser, B., B. Locanthi, and T. G. Stockham, Jr., eds. *Digital Audio*. New York: Audio Engineering Society, 1983.

Peterson, W. W. "Error-Correcting Codes." *Scientific American* 206(2):96–108, February, 1962.

Reed, I. S., and G. Solomon. "Polynomial Codes Over Certain Finite Fields." *J. Soc. Indust. Appl. Math.* 8:300–304, 1960.

Shenton, D., E. Debenedictis, and B. Locanthi. "Improved Reed-Solomon Decoding Using Multiple-Pass Decoding." *Journal of the Audio Engineering Society* 33(11):878–87, November, 1985.

Vries, Lodewijk B., and Kentaro Odaka. "CIRC—The Error Correcting Code for the Compact Disc Digital Audio System." In Blesser, B., B. Locanthi, and T. G. Stockham, Jr., eds. *Digital Audio*. New York: Audio Engineering Society, 1983.

Watkinson, J. R. "Inside CD, Part 1." *Hi Fi News and Record Review* 31(11):31–37, November, 1986.

———. "Inside CD, Part 3." *Hi Fi News and Record Review* 32(1):37–39, January, 1987.

# Chapter Four

# CD Player Design

## INTRODUCTION

A compact disc player is perhaps the most sophisticated and electronically complex piece of home entertainment equipment to ever reach the consumer. Yet even the most advanced products often have humble origins. For example, when Sony set out to design the first portable CD player, chief engineer Kozo Ohsone made a block of wood about 5 inches square and 1 1/2 inches high and presented it to the design team, informing them that the portable player would be that size. To make sure that none of the wily engineers tried replacing it with a bigger block, he signed his name on the bottom.

## PLAYER OVERVIEW

A compact disc player contains two primary systems: the audio data processing system, and the servo and control system. A complete player block diagram is shown in figure 4.1. The data path directs the modulated light from the pickup through a series of processing circuits, ultimately yielding a stereo analog signal. The data path consists of elements such as the data separator, the buffer, the de-interleaving RAM, the error correction and concealment circuits, the oversampling filter, the D/A converters, and the output filters. The servo, control, and display system must direct the mechanical operation of the player, including spindle drive, auto-tracking, auto-focus, and the user interface to the player's controls and displays.

A CD player employs a readout system using a semiconductor laser. A non-contact means is required to read data, maintain the laser beam's focus, and track the pit spiral. The result is a highly sophisticated pickup, utilizing complex optical devices within servo loops. The servos use electrical signals from the pickup to control motors to mechanically adjust the pickup's position horizontally and vertically, relative to the disc surface.

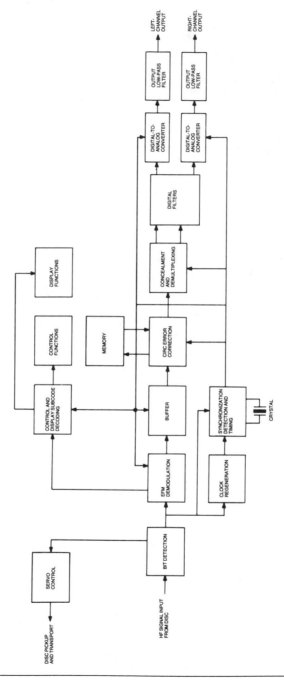

Figure 4.1    *Block diagram of a CD player showing audio path, as well as servo and control functions.*

A spindle motor is used to rotate the disc with constant linear velocity. Thus the disc must vary its speed depending on where the pickup is located underneath the surface. In another servo loop, information from the data itself is used to determine the correct rotating speed and maintain the proper data output rate.

A microprocessor monitors user controls and their interface to the player's circuitry. Various modes of player operation are controlled by software. Subcode data plays an important role in directing the pickup to the proper disc location. For example, a time code is used to locate the start of any track.

Once the data is recovered from the disc, the player must decode the audio information to reconstruct the audio signal. The EFM data is demodulated, errors are detected and corrected by decoding the error correction algorithm, and the audibility of gross errors is minimized through interpolation and muting. The digital data must be converted to a stereo analog signal. This requires one or two D/A converters, and low-pass filters. The latter requirement can be taken care of either in the analog domain or the digital domain.

Present in the audio output stages of every player is an audio de-emphasis circuit. Some CDs are encoded with audio pre-emphasis in which high frequencies on the master tape are boosted slightly (50/15 microsecond characteristic). Upon playback, the disc's high frequencies are inversely attenuated; the result is a slight improvement in signal-to-noise ratio. CD tracks that are encoded with pre-emphasis are so denoted by an appropriate flag in the subcode; the player automatically reads the pre-emphasis flag and switches in the de-emphasis circuit when required.

A final output circuit is nothing more than a buffer to the outside world. It ensures that the player's line level output is appropriate to drive external amplifiers with a minimum amount of analog distortion.

It is interesting to note that the various subsystems in a CD player are closely interrelated with a tightly interlocked timing relationship, as shown in figure 4.2. A few key numbers unlock the relationship: the audio data rate is 176.4 kbytes per second (44.1 kHz sampling of four 8-bit words). Because there are 24 audio bytes in a frame, the frame rate is 7350 Hz (176.4/24). Because there are 588 $T$ periods in a frame, the master clock $T$ is 4.3218 MHz (7350 × 588). A total of 98 frames are needed to form one subcode block so the subcode rate is 75 Hz (7350/98). Similarly, minimum and maximum recorded frequencies, EFM rate, and the subcode rate can be derived.

The remainder of this chapter examines all of these topics in more detail, focusing on the laser pickup, output circuitries—such as D/A converters—and low-pass filters. Chapter Three examined intermediate signal processing.

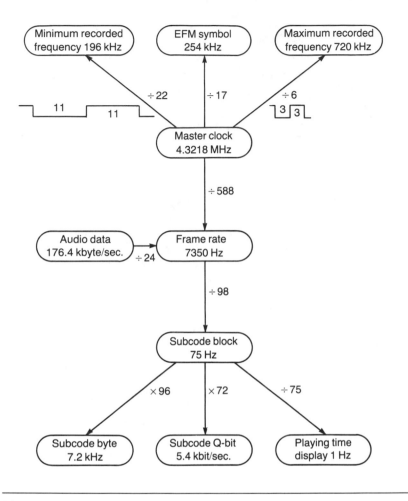

Figure 4.2    *Timing interrelationships in CD player design.*

## PICKUP DESIGN

The compact disc is certainly one of the most advanced storage media available. One reason is its optical pickup. A disc might contain three billion pits precisely arranged on a spiral track. The optical pickup must focus on, track, and read that data spiral. The entire lens assembly, a combination of the laser source and the reader, must be small enough to glide laterally beneath the disc, moving in response to tracking information and user random-access programming. Furthermore, the pickup must maintain focusing and tracking even under adverse playing conditions, such as the playback of a dirty disc or impact and vibration. It is perhaps the difficulty of this task that has encouraged considerable engineering diversity in optical pickup design and the best way to retrieve data from CDs.

### *Auto-Tracking*

Intensity-modulated laser light carries the data, and nothing (except light) touches the medium surface. This poses an interesting engineering problem. How do we track a spiral pit track if there is no groove to guide the pickup? The answer, of course, is the auto-tracking system found in all CD players.

The spiral pit track on a compact disc, running from a center circle nearly to the outer edge, makes 30 revolutions within the width of an LP microgroove. A disc that is off center might exhibit track eccentricity of as much as 300 micrometers, which is the equivalent of 60 pit tracks. In addition, vibration can challenge the pickup's ability to track within a ±0.1 micrometer tolerance. Engineers have devised four methods for tracking the pit spiral: (1) one-beam push-pull, (2) one-beam differential phase detection, (3) one-beam high frequency wobble, and (4) three-beam.

### *Auto-Focusing*

With pits flying past at about 600,000 pits per second, the optical pickup has its work cut out for it. Moreover, even the flattest disc isn't perfectly flat; the disc specifications acknowledge this by allowing for a vertical deflection of ±600 micrometers. Meanwhile, the laser beam must stay focused within a ±2 micrometer tolerance. Otherwise, the phase interference between the directed and reflected light is lost along with the audio data, as well as the tracking information, and, ironically, the focusing information. The objective lens must therefore be able to refocus as the disc surface deviates vertically. A servo-driven auto-focus system manages this, utilizing control electronics and a servo motor to drive the objective lens. Three techniques are available for generating a focusing signal: (1) a cylindrical lens using astigmatism, (2) a knife edge using Foucault focusing, and (3) critical angle focusing.

Any pickup must, of course, perform both tracking and focusing simultaneously. Thus a completed design would utilize a combination of these techniques. Fortunately, concerned audiophiles are spared the task of analyzing all the permutations. When the focusing and tracking mechanisms are combined, two pickup designs stand out from the rest: (1) one-beam push-pull tracking with Foucault focusing and (2) three-beam tracking with astigmatic focusing.

These designs have been commercialized, with each manufacturer choosing its preference: one-beam or three-beam pickups. One-beam pickups are usually mounted on the end of a pivoting arm which swings the pickup across the disc in an arc. Three-beam pickups are always mounted on a sled which slides linearly across the disc. Let's consider both types of pickups, beginning with the three-beam design.

### Three-Beam Optical Design

Although design particulars vary among manufacturers, three-beam pickups are generally similar in function. Figure 4.3 illustrates the optical path of a three-beam pickup. A one-beam pickup uses a similar optical path.

To achieve sharp focus on the data surface and proper intensity modulation from the pit height, it is necessary to use a laser as the light source. Laser is an acronym for *light amplification by stimulated emission of radiation*. A laser uses an optical resonator to stimulate atoms to a higher energy level that induces them to radiate in phase. Laser light differs significantly from white, visible light. A light bulb, for example, radiates all the frequencies of the spectrum at all different phases. A laser light is monochromatic (composed of a single frequency), and is coherent in phase. Phase coherency is vital, of course, to implement phase cancellation in the beam produced by disc pits so that disc data can be read. CD pickups use an aluminum gallium arsenide (AlGaAs) semiconductor laser with, for example, a 0.5 milliwatt optical output radiating a coherent-phase laser beam with a 780 nanometer wavelength (some manufacturers use 790 nanometers). The beam is thus comprised of near-infrared light.

The laser diode is placed at the focal point of a collimator lens with a long focal distance. Its purpose is to make the divergent light rays parallel.

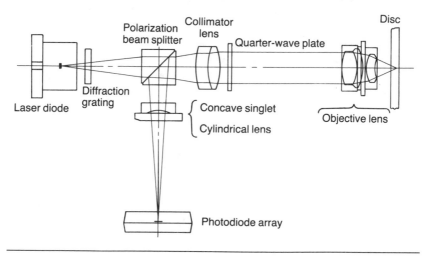

Figure 4.3  *Optical path of a three-beam pickup.*

A monitor diode is placed next to the laser diode to control power to the laser. It compensates for temperature changes and prevents thermal runaway. The monitor diode conducts current in proportion to the laser's light output. In other words, it stabilizes the semiconductor laser's output.

A three-beam pickup uses three beams for tracking and reading. To generate these beams, the light from the laser passes through a diffraction grating, a screem with slits spaced only a few laser wavelengths apart, as shown in figure 4.4. As the beam passes through the grating, the light diffracts; when the resulting collection is again focused, it will appear as a single, bright, centered beam with a series of successively less intense beams on either side. It is this diffraction pattern that actually strikes the disc. A three-beam pickup uses the center beam for reading data and focusing and two secondary beams for tracking only. A one-beam pickup accomplishes all of these tasks with one beam.

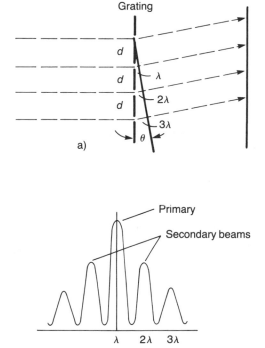

Figure 4.4 *In a three-beam pickup a diffraction grating (a) splits the beam into successively less intense secondary beams (b).*

The next part of the optical system, a polarization beam splitter (PBS), directs the laser light to the disc surface and angles the reflected light to the photo sensor. (In some designs, a half-silvered mirror is used.) The PBS consists of two prisms with a common 45 degree face acting as a polarizing prism. The collimator follows the PBS (in some designs, it precedes it). The light then passes through a quarter-wavelength plate (QWP), an anisotropic material that rotates the plane of polarization of the light beams (required to make the PBS work). Light which has passed through the QWP and been reflected from the disc back again through the QWP will be polarized in a plane at right angles to that of the incident light. Because the PBS will pass light in one plane, (e.g., horizontallly polarized) but reflect light in the other plane (e.g., vertically polarized), the PBS will properly deflect the reflected beam toward the photodiode sensor to read the digital data.

The final piece of optics in the path to the disc is the objective lens that is used to focus the beams on the disc data surface, taking into account the refractive index of the polycarbonate substrate (see figure 3.4). The objective lens focuses the laser light into a convergent cone of light. The convergence is a function of the numerical aperture (NA) of the lens. Most pickups use an objective lens with an NA of about 0.5 (this corresponds to f/1.0 in a photographic lens). The main spot is about 800 micrometers in diameter on the outer surface of the disc's transparent polycarbonate substrate. The refractive index of the polycarbonate substrate is 1.55 and its thickness about 1.2 millimeters, so the spot is narrowed to 1.7 micrometers at the reflective surface (see figure 3.4), slightly wider than the pit width of 0.5 micrometer and comparable in width to the wavelength of the light itself.

The data encoded on the disc now determines the fate of the laser light. When the spot strikes land, the smooth interval between two pits, the light is almost totally reflected. When it strikes a pit (seen as a bump by the laser) with a depth in the transparent layer of about a quarter wavelength of the laser light, destructive interference and diffraction cause less light to be reflected (see figure 3.5). All three intensity-modulated light beams return through the objective lens, the QWP, the collimator lens, and the PBS. Finally, they pass through a singlet lens and a cylindrical lens en route to the photodiode.

### *Three-Beam Auto-Focus*

Auto-focus is an absolute prerequisite in an optical pickup system. Disc warpage and other irregularities can cause vertical deviations in the disc data surface. This movement would place the data out of the pickup's depth of focus, making it impossible to distinguish the phase difference between pit height and land.

In a three-beam player, the unique properties of astigmatism are used to achieve automatic focusing. The cylindrical lens just prefacing the photodiode (see figure 4.3) is used to detect an out-of-focus condition. As the distance between the objective lens and disc reflective surface varies, the focal point of the optical system also changes, and the image projected by the cylindrical lens changes its shape. This is illustrated in figure 4.5. The change in the image on the photodiode generates the focus correction signal. When the disc surface lies precisely at the focal point of the objective lens, the image reflected through the intermediate convex lens and the cylindrical lens is unaffected by the astigmatism of the cylindrical lens, and a circular spot strikes the center of the photodiode. When the distance between the disc and the objective lens decreases, the image projected by the objective lens, the convex lens, and the cylindrical lens moves further from the cylindrical lens, and the pattern becomes elliptical. Similarly, when the distance between the disc and the objective lens increases, the image moves closer to the lens, and an elliptical pattern again results, but it is rotated 90 degrees from the first elliptical pattern.

The four-quadrant photodiode uses the light's intensity level from each of the quadrants to generate focus correction voltages. An elliptical pattern mainly striking quadrants A and C, as shown in figure 4.5b, indicates the disc is too near, and a positive voltage is created. When the disc is in focus, no net voltage is created from the round pattern. An elliptical pattern striking quadrants B and D indicates the disc is too far, which creates a negative voltage. This varying voltage, as shown in figure 4.5d, is used to correct the focusing mechanism continually towards a zero voltage, thus maintaining a focused laser beam. The center beam is used to convey data from the disc, using a signal summed from the four-quadrant photodiode $(A + B + C + D)$.

The correction voltage also generates a control signal in the form of $(A + C) - (B + D)$. This electrical input controls the mechanical motion of a servo motor. In this case the servo's job is to move the objective lens along the optical axis in response to vertical disc motion, and thus maintain focus. This servo motor consists of a coil and permanent magnet structure similar to that used in a loudspeaker, with the objective lens taking the place of the speaker cone, as shown in figure 4.6.

When a disc is first loaded, initial focus is achieved by injecting a signal into the system which causes the laser to turn on and the objective lens to move up and down several times until a focus condition is found. Then, the automatic focusing system takes over. If no disc is detected, the system typically tries again, shutting off if it fails again. When the auto-focus is not operative (e.g., disc tray is open) the system pulls the objective lens back to prevent damage to the lens or disc. The auto-focus system is slightly complicated, but its task is complex, and it performs well at keeping the

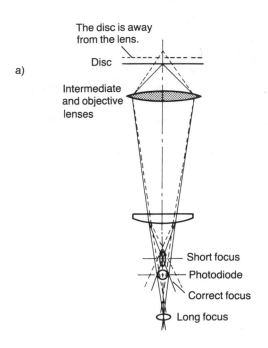

The disc is away
from the lens.

a)

Disc

Intermediate
and objective
lenses

Short focus
Photodiode
Correct focus
Long focus

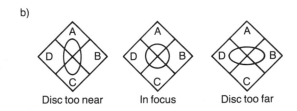

b)

| A | A | A |
| D B | D B | D B |
| C | C | C |

Disc too near      In focus      Disc too far

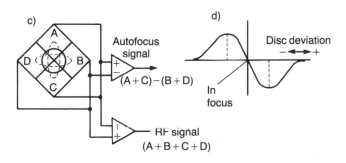

c)

Autofocus
signal

$(A+C)-(B+D)$

d)

Disc deviation

In
focus

RF signal
$(A+B+C+D)$

Figure 4.5    *A three-beam pickup uses the properties of astigmatism to generate
an auto-focus correction signal.*

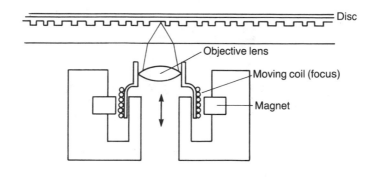

Figure 4.6 *A coil and magnetic structure are used to move the objective lens in the optical path.*

pickup floating underneath the spinning disc, maintaining focus to within a tolerance of approximately ±0.5 micrometers.

### Three-Beam Auto-Tracking

The track pitch, the distance between adjacent laps of the pit spiral, is 1.6 micrometers on a CD, which is too fine a tolerance for any mechanical tracking system to be cost-effective. An auto-tracking system is required. In three-beam pickups, the two secondary beams are used for auto-tracking. The center beam, which carries the information from the disc, is accompanied by the two secondary beams from the point of generation at the diffraction grating. The tracking beams also strike the data surface and are reflected. Their varying intensities are used at two separate photo-diodes mounted alongside the four-quadrant photodiode.

The central beam spot covers the pit track while the two tracking beams are aligned above, below, and to either side of the center beam. Their relative position is firmly fixed. When the beam is tracking the disc properly, part of each tracking beam is aligned on the pit edge; the other part covers the mirrored land between pit tracks. The three beams are reflected through the quarter-wave plate and polarizing beam splitter; the main beam strikes the four-quadrant photodiode, and the two tracking beams strike two separate photodiodes (E and F) mounted to either side of the main photodiode, as illustrated in figure 4.7.

As the three spots drift to either side of the pit track, the amount of light reflected from the tracking beams varies. There is less average light intensity reflected by the beam which encounters more pit area, and greater reflected light intensity from the beam which encounters less pit area. The

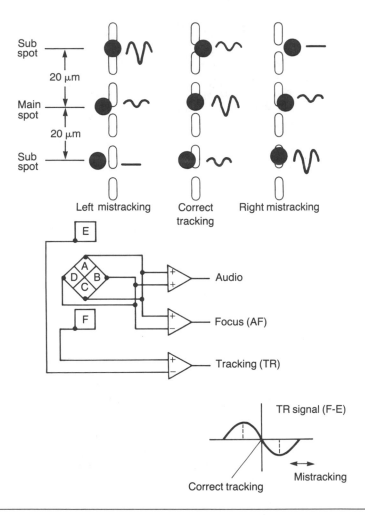

Figure 4.7  *In a three-beam pickup, two tracking beams are precisely aligned to either side of the center of the pit track. When reflected, they strike outrigger photodiodes, to generate an auto-tracking correction signal.*

relative output voltages from the two tracking photodiodes thus form a tracking correction signal (F–E).

The varying output from the tracking photodiodes is converted into a useful correction signal. Because the tracking beams are aligned to different areas of the disc, the signal from the leading beam is delayed 30 microseconds to permit comparison on the basis of the same pit, as if they were reading the same pit simultaneously. The outputs are constantly compared and used to control a servo system. If the tracking is precisely aligned, the difference is zero. If the beams drift, a difference signal is generated, varying positively for a left drift, for example, and negatively for a right drift.

### Three-Beam Pickup Mechanism

In many designs, both the tracking and focus difference signals are applied to a two-axis actuator, with a focus/tracking coil and a permanent magnet. The top assembly of the pickup is mounted on a base with a circular magnet ringing it. A circular yoke supports a bobbin containing both the focus and tracking coils. Control voltages from the focus circuit are applied to the bobbin focus coil, and it moves up and down with respect to the fixed magnet. The objective lens thus maintains its proper depth of focus. The other axis of movement, from side to side, is used to achieve tracking accuracy. When the tracking difference signal is applied to the coil, the bobbin swings around a shaft to move the objective lens laterally, in the direction dictated by the polarity of the signal, so the main laser beam is again centered, and the tracking signal is again zeroed.

A three-beam pickup requires a linear movement because the three beams must stay in a fixed position relative to the pit track. The three-beam pickup is thus mounted in a sled that moves radially across the disc. The sled can be driven by a lead screw; the pitch of the screw's thread is a compromise between the fine thread required for normal tracking (35 millimeters per hour) and the coarse thread needed for fast forward and reverse (perhaps 35 millimeters per second). In some designs, a moderate thread is used to achieve disc access, and a movable mirror is inserted into the laser's path to deflect the beam quickly to handle small differences, such as track eccentricity. Alternatively, many designs use linear motors to provide smooth and rapid movement of the pickup across the disc surface.

### One-Beam Optical Design

The optical components of a one-beam design are shown in figure 4.8, along with the photodiode array used to generate tracking and focusing signals, as well as the data signal. A laser diode generates the laser beam which strikes a semitransparent mirror (used in place of a PBS and QWP). A collimator and objective lens focus the beam on the disc's reflective pit track surface. As the pits fly by, the data encoded as pits and land results in a reflected laser beam with varying intensity.

On its return path, some of the reflected laser light passes through the semitransparent mirror and strikes a wedge lens. It is then split into two beams, adjusted to strike an array of four horizontally arranged photodiodes. The outputs of all the photodiodes are summed to provide the data signal $(A + B + C + D)$, which is demodulated to yield audio data and speed control signals.

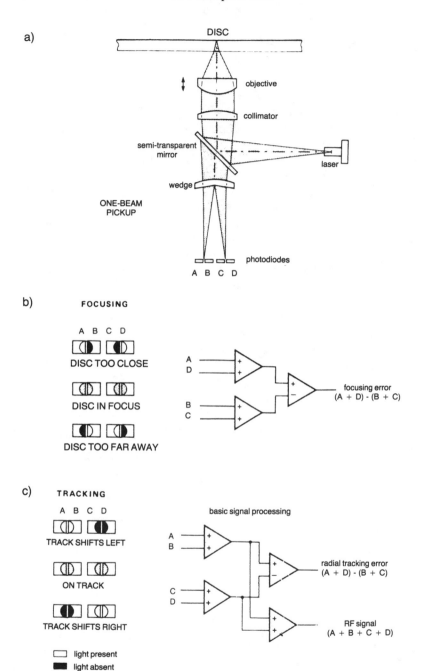

Figure 4.8    *A one-beam pickup (a) derives data, focus, and tracking signals
from one beam. Auto-focusing (b) utilizes the shift in split beams. Auto-tracking
(c) utilizes asymmetry in the beam, caused by beam interference. (Courtesy Philips)*

### One-Beam Auto-Focus

Auto-focus is accomplished by the four photodiodes. As noted, Foucault focusing is often used. When correct focus is achieved, two sharp images are located between photodiode pairs. When focus varies, the focal point of the system is shifted, and the split beams draw closer together (when the disc is too far) or further apart (when the disc is too near), as shown in figure 4.8b. The difference between diode pairs A/D and B/C forms a focus error signal $(A + D) - (B + C)$, used to maintain the focus of the servo-driven objective lens. The capture range of the one-beam focus system is sufficient to accommodate normal tolerance without special start-up focusing procedures, as in three-beam designs.

### One-Beam Auto-Tracking

The diodes also generate error signals for auto-tracking. When the laser spot strikes the center of the pit track, a symmetrical beam is reflected. As the laser beam wanders from the pit track, interference creates asymmetry in the beam, resulting in an intensity difference between the two split beams, as shown in figure 4.8c. For example, as the beam moves off track, one side of the beam encounters more reflective land; consequently, less interference occurs on that side of the beam. Thus reflected light is more intense there. As a result, the split beam derived from that side of the beam will be more intense, and the photodiode's output will be greater. Either photodiode pair A/B or C/D generates a greater signal from the increased laser light. The difference between the pairs $(A + B) - (C + D)$ produces an error signal used to maintain the pickup on track.

Aging or soiling of the one-beam pickup could cause the reflected beam to become increasingly asymmetrical. This asymmetry would generate a constant offset in the tracking correction signal, causing the pickup to remain slightly off track, requiring readjustment. To prevent this, a second tracking error signal is generated. A low-frequency (e.g., 600 Hz) alternating voltage is applied to the coil that controls the tracking. The output signal from the four photodiodes is thus modulated by the alternating tracking signal. As the pickup wanders off track, a deviation in the tracking signal occurs in the modulated signal, as shown in figure 4.9. When the modulation signal is rectified, a drift-free tracking error signal is produced. This tracking signal is used to correct the primary tracking signal with a direct voltage. The data signal from the four photodiodes is thus always returned to its maximum value. In practice, of course, the four photodiodes must simultaneously perform all three tasks of data reading, tracking, and focusing.

Although most one-beam pickups are mounted on a pivoting arm, a linear sled may be used as well. In the former, the pivoting arm describes a radial arc across the data surface. A coil and permanent magnet are

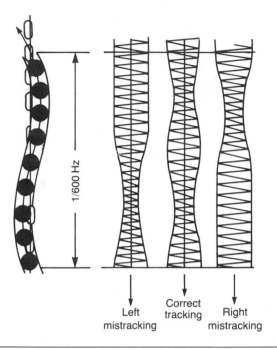

Figure 4.9    *In a one-beam pickup, a modulation signal is sometimes injected into the servo system to compensate for any tracking offset.*

mounted around the pivotal point of the arm. When the coil is energized, the pickup may be positioned anywhere on the pit track, and its position corrected by the auto-tracking system. The objective lens is provided with a coil and a permanent magnet for displacement in the direction of the optical axis to achieve auto-focusing.

### One-Beam Versus Three-Beam

Which is better, three-beam or one-beam? In the final analysis, both designs perform the same function, but the engineering advantages may favor the one-beam design. The optics in a three-beam design are inherently more complicated; there are at least five components (objective, collimator, grating, cylindrical, and beam splitter) compared to the four components in a one-beam design (objective, collimator, wedge, and semitransparent mirror). In addition, the three-beam design requires several critical adjustments, including secondary beam and diffraction grating alignment, as opposed to the single adjustment of the horizontal position of the photodiode assembly in a one-beam design. Both designs require adjustment of drive current for the laser diode.

A three-beam design is also more complex from a mechanical viewpoint. A one-beam design can be mounted on a single pivoted arm which describes an arc across the disc surface; since there is only one moving part, wear is minimal and reliability is high. A three-beam design requires a linear sled mechanism because the tracking beams must stay in a fixed position relative to the pit track. In terms of traditional specifications, such as frequency response and channel separation, there is no sonic difference between one-beam and three-beam designs. Ultimately, pickup performance must be evaluated on the basis of individual players.

### Pickup Control

Aside from the tracking accuracy needed to keep the laser beam on track, the pickup must properly move across the disc surface to track the entire pit spiral. The pickup must also be able to jump from one place on the disc to another.

In the search mode, the player's microprocessor takes command to provide faster motion than is possible during normal tracking. Control signals are directed to the pickup for accelerated movement in the forward or reverse direction. Subcode data added to each CD frame is used to determine the pickup's location on the pit spiral.

For forward or reverse jumps to programmed locations on the disc, the tracking signal is disabled, and the microprocessor controls the pickup. Just prior to alignment, a brake pulse is generated to compensate for the pickup's inertia. When the correct location is reached, the microprocessor informs the system that proper alignment is imminent, the tracking signal is again activated, the pickup comes to rest on the correct track, and the system resumes auto-tracking.

It is interesting to note that the movement of a CD player's pickup is similar to that of a stylus in an LP groove. With the aid of the auto-tracking system, the pit signal "pulls" the pickup across the disc in the same way that the phono cartridge is pulled across an LP by the groove. Of course, a CD pickup uses a lot more technology than a phonograph cartridge to achieve tracking, but most would agree that the outcome is much more satisfactory, especially in terms of the longevity of CDs compared to LPs.

## DIGITAL-TO-ANALOG CONVERTER

All compact disc players have digital-to-analog converters, otherwise known as D/As or DACs. Increasingly, however, CD players optionally output their digital information directly to preamplifiers and power amplifiers with their own D/A converters. Ultimately, all-digital stereo systems will appear. The analog signal that our ears require will not appear until the last possible moment, at the loudspeaker. Until then, players contain D/As to convert the digital bit stream to an analog signal, so that analog preamplifers and power amplifiers can process it.

A D/A must produce an analog voltage corresponding to each digital audio sample. The sum total of these sample voltages creates an analog waveform—actually, one waveform for each stereo channel. The signal output from the D/A (following the output sample-and-hold) is thus equivalent to the signal appearing after the sample-and-hold circuit in the recording side of the chain. There are several excellent ways to accomplish this task.

### Ladder Network D/A Converter

D/As have traditionally used resistor ladder networks, such as the one in figure 4.10. The reference voltage source $V_{ref}$ produces a voltage along the ladder, which is converted to a current by the resistors. Each successive rung of the ladder taps off part of the current: that is, each current is a binary power of two less than the preceding current. This corresponds to the values of the bits of the digital word. The bits of the word are used to open and close switches, turning their appropriate currents on and off. For example, a word with all 0s would keep the switches open, and no current would flow. A word with all 1s would close all the switches, and maximum currrent would flow. When the output current is converted to a voltage, the result is a voltage from the circuit which corresponds to the input binary word. Our conversion is thereby accomplished.

### Integrating D/A Converter

Other circuit designers have devised D/As that differ significantly in design but accomplish the same purpose. For instance, an integrating D/A uses a

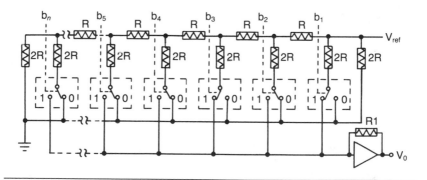

Figure 4.10  *Circuit diagram of a R-2R ladder network D/A converter.*

constant current that flows for a period of time controlled by the digital
input. Figure 4.11a illustrates the concept behind this design: a current
source produces a changing voltage by means of an integrator. The input
word determines how long the current is applied to the integrator, thus
establishing the value of the output voltage. A small digital value allows a
small amount of time for current flow, whereas a large value would allow a
long time for current flow. By measuring the amount of current that has
flowed and converting that current to a voltage, we receive a voltage that
corresponds to the input word.

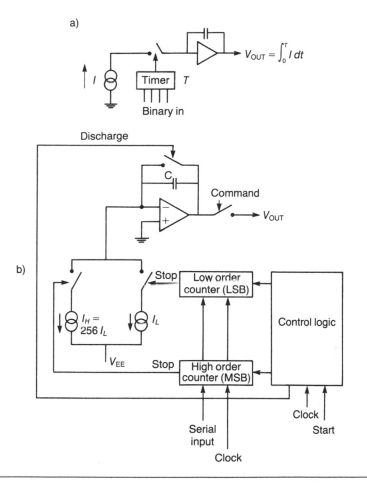

Figure 4.11 *An integrating D/A converter (a) uses a current source, integrator
and timer to produce an output voltage. A dual slope integrator (b) separates low
and high order bits, and uses two current sources to produce a segmented output
voltage.*

In practice, a single current source and timer are not used, because the timer cannot operate quickly enough to achieve high resolution. To achieve conversion speed without sacrificing accuracy, two current sources are used, as shown in figure 4.11b. This design is called a dual slope integrating D/A converter. The two current sources have a precise ratio of 256:1; the larger current, for every time period it flows, is equivalent to the smaller source operating over 256 periods. The two current sources are thus assigned to the eight least significant bits and the eight most significant bits of the input word respectively. The high-order bits first generate a coarse ramp output. Then the low-order bits take over to generate an accurate ramp output. The result is a highly accurate output voltage, quickly achieved.

### Dynamic Element Matching D/A Converter

Another D/A design, called dynamic element matching (DEM), uses the principle of current adding. This is illustrated in figure 4.12a. In practice, as shown in figure 4.12b, an accurate current source is obtained by dividing a reference current source with a pair of resistors, then by averaging their outputs with a pair of switches and capacitors. By cascading these or other types of current-dividing stages, a binary weighted series of currents can be obtained. Their selected summation accomplishes the task of conversion. Although a DEM converter may require more external parts than other designs, it is cost efficient because it requires no calibration.

Whichever method is employed, the D/A converters used in most CD players do not pose major design problems. Contemporary players utilize one or two converters, typically converting a 16-bit word. In some designs, 18-bit D/A converters are employed; the longer word lengths present following oversampling permits this technique, which yields an increase in the system's S/E ratio.

### Output Sample-and-Hold

The sample-and-hold (S/H) circuit following the D/A, which is sometimes contained on the D/A chip, performs a hold function to create a pulse amplitude staircase. The impulses in the output staircase waveform are the width of a sampling period, but reconstruction theoretically requires impulses of infinitely short duration. This is impossible to achieve because it would require, among other things, infinitely large current flow. Because of the finite duration of the output samples, a filtering effect occurs in which the amplitude response (a $\sin(x)/x$ curve) gradually falls to zero at the sampling frequency, which can be seen in figure 4.13. Supersonic frequencies are partly attenuated. However, the filtering results in a loss of about 4 dB at the Nyquist frequency. This is sometimes called aperture

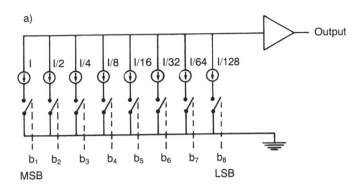

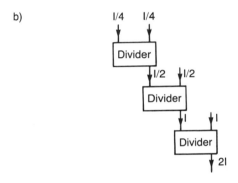

Figure 4.12  *A dynamic element matching D/A converter uses current adding (a). The current sources are obtained from a current source and current dividers (b).*

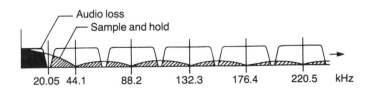

Figure 4.13  *Aperture error results in a slight attenuation of high audio frequencies.*

error. To minimize this loss, the impulses can be narrowed closer to their original width. Such shorter duration impulses result in a frequency characteristic closer to the originally flat response for the pulse amplitude signal. Figure 4.14a shows the sample pulses narrowed by four amounts. The aperture time $A$ is defined by

$$A = t_o/t_s$$

where $t_s$ is the sample time and $t_o$ is the duration of the pulse. Figure 4.14b shows the resulting frequency roll-off due to aperture effects. The filter design can compensate for any slight remaining high-frequency attenuation with an inverse, or $x/\sin(x)$ characteristic.

In addition to its role in correcting aperture error, the sample-and-hold circuit is also useful in removing glitches from the staircase waveform. The D/A converter output is not a smooth transition from one analog level to the next. Instead, inaccurate transition voltages known as glitches are often generated. Although they are momentary and disappear when the D/A's output value settles to its correct voltage, these glitches would increase distortion in the output signal. A sample-and-hold circuit can be

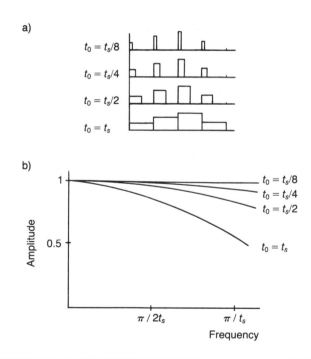

Figure 4.14 *Shorter duration output samples minimize aperture error, resulting in a flat frequency response.*

used to gate them out. This circuit is timed to wait for them to settle before it samples the D/A output. In this way, only accurate values are propagated. Other types of de-glitcher circuits have also been devised to solve this problem. For example, a shunting circuit could switch the output to ground during glitching transitions.

### One Versus Two Converters

A question over which circuit designers (or at least their company's accountants) disagree is the number of D/As to use in a player. Until the all-digital system becomes commonplace, and CD players omit D/As altogether, we have the option of using either one or two D/As in a player.

At first glance, two D/As seem necessary. Since the compact disc is a stereo playback medium, two audio channels are reproduced. As figure 4.15a shows, the digital data stream can be demultiplexed to left and right channels and fed to two D/As, resulting in two audio outputs. For strictly budgetary reasons, however, many players employ only one D/A, as in figure 4.15b. The multiplexed data of the two audio channels is handled by one D/A (operating twice as fast as the dual D/As). Only after the D/A has performed its conversion are the two analog channels separated into left and right channels.

Although the results of each method are apparently identical, small differences are introduced. The single D/A design creates several anomalies

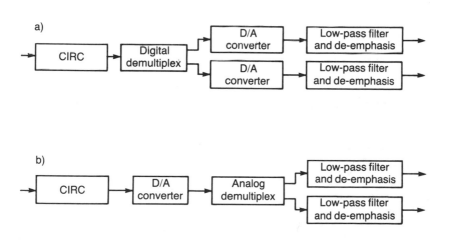

Figure 4.15 *A CD player may employ two D/A converters (a) or only one multiplexed converter (b).*

in the signal. First, while the data bits from different channels are easily split apart in the dual D/A design, the interleaved segments of analog voltages produced from single D/A design are not so easily separated. A switch must be used to route these pieces of waveform (88,200 per second) to the correct output channel. The switch might cause distortion as it flips back and forth.

Second, the single D/A design introduces a slight time difference (11.34 microseconds) between the two audio channels. In a dual D/A design, the demultiplexed data appears at the two converters simultaneously, exactly as it appeared at the A/D converters of the digital recorder. The output analog channels are thus exactly in phase—that is, exactly matched in time. It is possible to compensate for the offset introduced by a single D/A. However this is difficult to achieve uniformly over the entire frequency range.

Acoustically, the use of a single D/A converter and the resulting 11.34 microsecond interchannel difference can affect stereo imaging. In addition, the offset could affect downstream equipment. In stereo broadcasting, for example, cancellation could result in high-frequency roll-off of the L + R component and reinforcement of the L − R component. Dual D/As avoid these liabilities.

Unfortunately, not everything is sunny in dual D/A land; a pair of converter chips might mistrack because of fluctuations in their reference voltages or anomalies in the chips themselves. The result could again be phase error. Some manufacturers have solved both problems by offering dual D/A converters on a single chip, which is nearly an ideal solution. Nevertheless, the evidence weighs in favor of dual D/A converters, even with dual-chip designs.


## ANALOG FILTERING

Although analog filters seem innocuous enough, the particularly steep kinds required for digital audio applications cause some unexpected problems. In fact, the more we look at analog filters, the more suspicious we become that they potentially contaminate digitized audio. It would be ironic if the worst sonic offenders in digital audio recording systems were filters that were *analog* in nature, and this may be likely.

Filtering is an unfortunate fact of life for digital audio systems. An input anti-aliasing filter must precede the sampler to uphold the Nyquist theorem's criteria for bandlimited, and thus lossless, sampling. Similarly, the output anti-imaging filter must filter out all frequencies above the half-sampling frequency. The analog signal at the output of the digital-to-analog converter is a pulse amplitude modulation waveform whose staircase appearance is easily spotted by waveform watchers. These sudden shifts in amplitude represent high-frequency components not present in the original analog waveform; such artifacts of sampling must be removed to create a smooth waveform that eliminates high-frequency components. In fact, the output filter is sometimes referred to as a smoothing filter.

Mathematically, a low-pass filter has a $\sin(x)/x$ impulse response. It is the filter's impulse response to the individual samples, when added together, that reconstruct the original waveform. This superposition of individual impulse responses results in a smooth curve passing exactly through the input sample points being filtered.

Sharp-eyed readers might question the need to worry about frequencies such as 88.2 or 176.4 kHz, since they lie so far above the limits of audibility. Why waste money on a filter, when the ear itself is rather effective at filtering everything beyond 20 or 25 kHz? The original waveform is reproduced without filtering, but the accompanying image bands could stress the player's output amplifier or cause intermodulation in downstream analog equipment through which the signal passes. For example, the high frequency components might create intermodulation components with baseband frequencies or with the high-frequency bias current of an analog tape recorder. That, in turn, could add audible distortion to the signal. Filtering is therefore mandated. A filter must precede and follow every audio digitization system. As we shall see, either analog or digital varities can be employed.

### Ideal Filters

Because engineers have been designing analog filters for a long time, we would expect little trouble with this particular assignment. Both the input and output filters can share similar designs, and the design criteria can be easily summarized. Ideally, we would like to attenuate all audio frequencies above the half-sampling frequency without affecting the lower audioband frequencies. Moreover, we would like the transition to occur instantaneously so that the useable bandspace is extended as far as possible in order to yield an extended and flat frequency response. Thus, an ideal filter, such as the one in figure 4.16, would have a flat pass-band (the audio range the filter passes), an immediate, or brickwall filtering characteristic, and a stop-band (the frequencies the filter eliminates) attenuated to below the system's quantization resolution. In addition to these frequency response criteria, an ideal filter would not affect the phase or any other time-domain characteristic of the signal.

### Actual Filters

Although an ideal filter may be approximated, in practice its implementation presents a number of engineering challenges. A brickwall design re-

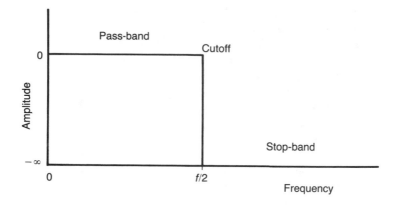

Figure 4.16   *An ideal low-pass filter has a flat pass-band, instantaneously sharp cutoff, and infinitely attenuated stop-band.*

quires compromise in other specifications, such as flat pass-band and low phase distortion. To alleviate these problems inherent in a brickwall response, we could design filters with more gradual cutoff which would not exhibit phase nonlinearities. However, the frequency of the half-sampling point would have to be increased to make sure that it was placed in a sufficiently attenuated part of the filter characteristic. This is the case shown in figure 4.17. Consequently, a higher sampling frequency, much higher than that required for a sharp cutoff filter, would be needed to achieve the same flat audio frequency response. To limit the sampling rate and make

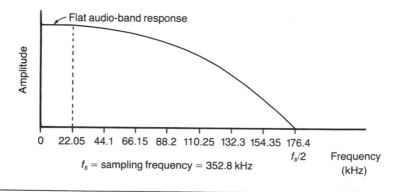

Figure 4.17   *Problems associated with brickwall filters can be overcome with more gentle filter characteristics. However, a higher sampling rate would be required to ensure a flat audio band.*

full use of the bandspace below the half-sampling point, a brickwall filter, at both input and output of the system, is the only alternative. Our problem is thus stubbornly defined.

Let's consider an analog output filter design, such as those found in some compact disc players. With a sampling rate of 44.1 kHz, the output filters (one for each channel) are usually designed for flat response from DC to 20 kHz. This provides a guard-band of about 2 kHz to ensure that attenuation is sufficient at the half-sampling point. The pass-band undoubtedly exhibits some frequency response irregularity, called ripple, which is typically specified to be less than ±0.1 dB, as represented in figure 4.18. The stop-band's attenuation is designed to be equal to or greater than the system's dynamic range, as determined by word length. Ideally, a 16-bit system would require a stop-band attenuation of greater than 95 dB. The stop-band also typically exhibits ripple.

### Cascade Filter Design

Although there are many types of filter design, only a few are able to achieve the performance criteria required of a high fidelity digital audio system. One filter type often employed is an elliptical filter, sometimes called a Cauer filter. The design generally uses a low-pass filter combined with a band-reject notch filter to sharpen the cutoff. The elements of an elliptical filter interact with each other, making them challenging to design. High precision parts are also required.

Basic filter elements of various types can be cascaded (repeated in series) to sharpen the cutoff. As the number of cascaded stages is increased, the filter characteristic steepens until the ideal filter frequency response is approximated. Unfortunately, as the cutoff steepens, the phase shift increases as well. Compact disc players might require ninth-order filters with

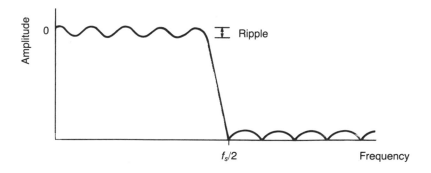

Figure 4.18    *Actual low-pass filters exhibit ripple in both the pass- and stop-bands. In addition, cutoff is not instantaneous.*

characteristics such as those indicated in figure 4.19. The cutoff shown in figure 4.19a looks like the north rim of the Grand Canyon, but the phase shift shown in figure 4.19b might exceed 360 degrees at 20 kHz. This phase shift introduces nonlinear time delay across the audio band.

The resulting group delay shown in figure 4.19c, which measures the change of phase shift with respect to frequency, causes high frequencies to be shifted in time (delayed) relative to lower frequencies. The delay increases toward the cutoff frequency of an analog filter in a CD player. This creates a kind of time smear in the signal. (Ultrasonic frequencies are theoretically delayed "forever," which is how they are filtered out.)

Absolute, non-frequency-dependent phase shift is inaudible. Recordings of Enrico Caruso may be 85 years old, which is a lot of time delay, but the CD suffers no distortion on that account, because all of the frequencies of the recording have been delayed by the same amount. But frequency-dependent group delay is different. Conceptually, we might compare such delay to the worst case example of an extremely strange loudspeaker in which the tweeter is located a mile behind the woofer. If properly equalized, steady-state tones would sound fine. But when the tone ended, we would hear sound emanating from the tweeter a full 5 seconds after the sound from the woofer had ended. Conversely, at the onset of a tone, the tweeter's attack would arrive 5 seconds late. Such long frequency-dependent delays would obviously be audible. What about a real brickwall filter, in which delay at 20 kHz might be 100 microseconds relative to 0 Hz? Is that audible? The answer has yet to be fully determined, but manufacturers have certainly hesitated to feature the relevant specification in full color advertisements. Obviously, we would prefer to avoid any such group delays in frequency response. The point is that the filters necessary in CD players are by no means trivial design exercises. It is becoming increasingly clear that these analog circuits demand careful design specifications to avoid contamination of the audio signal.

## DIGITAL FILTERING

The digital filter used in CD players is a circuit which accepts audio samples and outputs audio samples. Filtering takes place precisely because the values of the output samples have been altered to produce filtering. Moreover, a technique called oversampling is utilized in which additional sample values are computed by interpolating between original samples. Because additional samples have been generated (perhaps two, four, or eight times as many), the sampling rate of the output signal is greater than the input signal.

Each intermediate sample is multiplied by the appropriate $\sin(x)/x$ coefficient corresponding to its contribution to the overall impulse response of

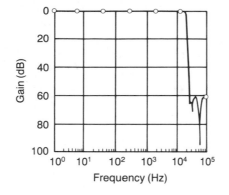

a)

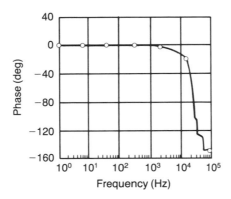

b)

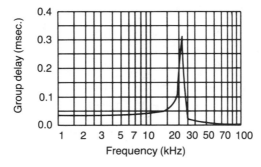

c)

Figure 4.19    *A brickwall filter will have a sharp cutoff (a), high-frequency phase shift (b), and high frequency group delay (c). (Courtesy Sony)*

the filter. The multiplication products are summed together to produce the output filtered sample. It thus digitally simulates the impulse response of an analog filter. The spectrum of the signal is changed, with the images appearing at multiples of the new (oversampled) sampling rate. Because the distance between the baseband and sidebands is larger, a gentle analog filter can be used to remove the images without causing phase shift or other artifacts.

### Time Delay

Rather than using an analog brickwall filter to suppress the high-frequency image components after the signal has been converted to analog form, it is possible to process the digitized signal before D/A conversion using a digital filter. The basic mechanism used in the digital filters found in CD players is time delay. A delayed signal added back to itself results in a wholly new frequency response. In this case, the effect is called a comb filter response. If a signal is delayed by time $T$, as shown in figure 4.20, and mixed with the original undelayed signal, the two will be out of phase, and cancellations will occur at odd multiples of the frequency $= 1/(2T)$. For example, a 1 millisecond delay will produce notches at 500 Hz, 1500 Hz, 2500 Hz, etc. In the same way, digital filters use summed delays to produce phase cancellation in the signal, and consequently a filtered frequency response.

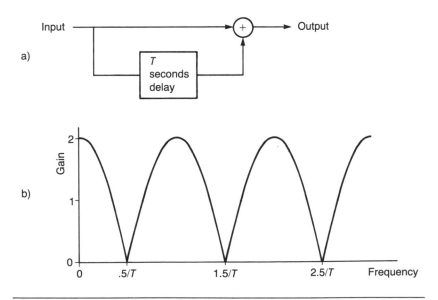

Figure 4.20    *A delayed signal added to itself (a) results in a filtered frequency response (b).*

Although the notion of filtering a signal with a delay line might seem unusual, the phenomenon is common in the acoustical world. For example, a sound travelling to a microphone can take a direct path or a reflected (delayed) path (such as a bounce off the floor). The summed difference in path lengths creates a comb filter.

In a digital filter, delay lines comprised of shift registers are used to create time differences in the signal. Furthermore, multiple delays are taken from the line. For example, delays of 3, 4, and 5 microseconds will yield notches at odd multiples of 166, 125, and 100 kHz. In addition, the notches will overlap, attenuating all frequencies in that band. In the case of a CD player's digital filter, the delays are greater in number and specifically calculated to attenuate image spectra above the audio band.

### Transversal Filters

Remembering that each sample point of filtered output signal is the sum of many filtered samples, we can demonstrate how a digital filter works. We may employ a shift register with output taps after each delay element, as shown in figure 4.21. Input samples enter the shift register. The output of each tap is multiplied by a coefficient associated with the impulse response, and the product is summed with other products to yield the new output sample. The coefficients are taken from the $\sin(x)/x$ curve and thus impose that characteristic on the audio data when it is multiplied by the coef-

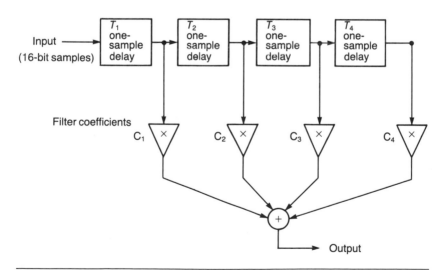

**Figure 4.21** *A transversal filter uses a shift register, coefficient multipliers, and an adder to produce a filtered output.*

ficients. The sum of many such multiplied samples results in low-pass filtered data. To access many such samples, each time a new sample is input, the samples in the shift register are shifted one delay to the right, and the new sum of products is recalculated. Because of the movement of the samples across the shift register, this design is often called a transversal filter.

A step by step example may illustrate the filter's operation. First (referring again to figure 4.21), assume that data has already shifted through the filter. We observe that the output sample is equal to the $T_1$ input sample times the $C_1$ coefficient, plus the $T_2$ input sample times the $C_2$ coefficient, plus the $T_3$ input sample times the $C_3$ coefficient, plus the $T_4$ input sample times the $C_4$ coefficient. When the next new sample is entered, the previous samples are shifted one delay to the right to make room for it, and the calculation is repeated. Thus, in this example, each sample shifted through the filter requires four multiplications and four additions.

In practice, a number of considerations determine the design of implemented filters. The analog signal is the sum of the $\sin(x)/x$ waveforms resulting from each sample. The $\sin(x)/x$ waveform extends to infinity in both the positive and negative directions, so theoretically all of the values of that infinite waveform would be required to reconstruct the analog signal. (In our example above, only four coefficients were used.) Fortunately, we can find a point on the waveform where neglecting any further response results in an error less than the system error; such a design is called a finite impulse response (FIR) filter. We can disregard the rest of the response values. In some implemented designs, perhaps 24 or 30 samples are summed.

Moreover, as noted, the number of samples must be increased through oversampling. To achieve oversampling, a transversal filter could, for example, be constructed so that each delay is now 1/4 sample period. This would result in 4 times the number of output samples, with the filter calculating three new sample values for each input sample. To provide enough impulse response values to permit a good response after summation, perhaps 96 delay elements would be required. It would input new data four times each sample period. Every fourth sample would be an audio sample from the disc, and the other three would be zero intermediate samples. Thus only 24 of the 96 elements would be filled with non-zero samples at any time. The filter would output data at a rate of 176.4 kHz, each new sample the sum of 24 non-zero multiplications. The filter thus calculates three new sample values at the location of the zero input samples. However, this oversampling design is inefficient; the same result can be obtained with fewer delay elements.

A more cost-effective approach is shown in figure 4.22. It shows the architecture of a practical four-times oversampling digital filter, generating three intermediate samples between each input sample. The filter consists

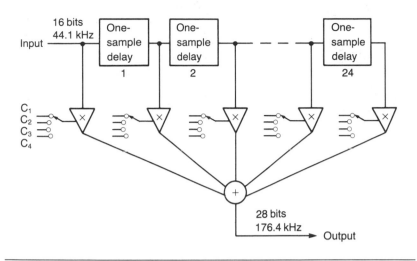

Figure 4.22    *A practical four-times oversampling transversal filter may use 24 delay elements and four sets of coefficients.*

of a shift register of 24 delay elements, each delaying a 16-bit sample for one sampling period. Thus each sample remains in each element for a sample period. During this time each 16-bit sample is multiplied four times by a 12-bit coefficient stored in ROM, a different coefficient for each multiplication. In total, the four sets of coefficients are applied to the samples in turn, thus producing four output values. The 24 multiplication products are summed four times during each period, and output from the filter. The data is shifted one place, and the process is repeated. After multiplication and summation, the weighted average of a large number of samples is generated. Four times as many samples are present after oversampling, with new intermediate values calculated by the filter. The sampling frequency is increased four times, to 176.4 kHz. The filter's coefficients produce a transition region between 20 and 24.3 kHz, and again around 154 kHz. Figure 4.23 shows the effect of the filtering. The values of the intermediate samples, obtained by the calculation process, determine the filter characteristic; the bands centered at 44.1, 88.2, and 132.3 kHz have been largely suppressed.

### Noise Shaping

Following the multiplications occurring during oversampling, the word length is much longer than the original 16 bits. Oversampling reduces the audio band quantization noise by distributing it over a wider bandwidth, four times the bandwidth in the case of four-times oversampling. How-

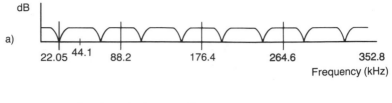

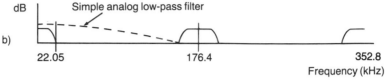

---

Figure 4.23 *After four-times oversampling, the image spectrum is moved to 176.4 kHz.*

ever, the output word cannot simply be truncated to 16 bits; this could increase distortion. Sometimes employed is a special rounding-off mechanism known as noise shaping. Quantization noise and the distortion from truncating are distributed over the entire oversampling spectrum. Thus the distortion in the audio band is a fraction of the total. With noise shaping, the dynamic range of the system can be extended.

### Output

Following digital filtering, the data is converted back to analog with a digital-to-analog converter. An output sample-and-hold circuit, implemented, for example, by a DC hold function of the D/A converter, creates a staircase waveform of samples. The $\sin(x)/x$ aperture effect causes greater suppression of the remaining spectra centered on 44.1 kHz, 88.2 kHz, 132.3 kHz and especially 176.4 kHz, present in a four-times oversampling design. Designing a slight high-frequency boost in the digital filter can compensate for the slight attenuation of high audio frequencies.

Finally, the remaining band around 176.4 kHz must be completely suppressed by an analog filter. This anti-imaging filter follows the converter, just as in players without digital filtering, but it is tame compared to brick-wall filters. Since the remaining band is so high in frequency, we can use a filter with a gentle, 12 dB/octave response and a −3 dB point between 30 and 40 kHz. It is a noncritical design, and its low order guarantees good phase linearity; phase distortion can be reduced to ±0.5 degrees across the audio band.

## Relative Performance

In this example, we have focused on a four-times oversampling circuit. However, CD players may use two-times, four-times, eight-times, or even sixteen-times digital filters, in which the 44.1 kHz sampling rate is oversampled to 88.1 kHz, 176.4 kHz, 352.8 kHz, or 705.6 kHz, respectively. At any rate, such digital filters are similar in operation to the four-times scheme. However, the characteristic of the analog low-pass filter must vary. The lower the oversampling frequency, the closer to the audio band the image spectrum will be, and hence the sharper the analog filter required. Some designers feel that in oversampling designs of eight-times or more, the remaining image spectrum is at such a high frequency that no analog filtering is needed.

A digital filter design is thus an efficient method of accomplishing the task of anti-imaging without resorting to analog brickwall filters. This alleviates the problem of phase distortion introduced by analog filters. A digital filter can have almost perfect linear phase response.

In terms of overall performance, digital filters represent a great improvement over analog filters because a digital filter can be designed with considerable, stable precision, whereas an analog filter design is inherently limited. Other specific advantages of digital filtering are more subtle: the filter characteristic varies with the clock rate. Thus its parameters may be altered. For example, variable speed CD players could be easily designed for special applications where the data rate and the pitch of the music are varied.

In addition, the output circuits have an easier time dealing with the waveform because the successive changes in amplitude are smaller in an oversampled signal. More precisely, the slew rate, the rate of variation in the output waveform, is lower. This, along with less ringing and less overshoot, reduces intermodulation distortion. Finally, because digital filtering is a purely numerical process, the characteristics of the digital filtering, as opposed to analog filtering, cannot change with temperature, age, and so on.

On the other hand, a digital filter performs its calculations at high speed, which is a power-hungry operation that tends to make portable applications more difficult. In addition, the software design of the filter's numerical circuits is a somewhat esoteric task, so great care must be taken to provide for correct computation. Furthermore, because the number of samples has been increased by several times, the D/A converters must do their job two or four times faster. Thus higher quality, more expensive D/As are required. This cost may be offset by the lower cost of the digital filter chip relative to an analog filter. While many CD player manufacturers still employ analog filters, oversampling appears to be winning out.

In terms of sonic performance, does digital filtering do a better job than analog filtering? Do CD players with digital filters sound better than those with analog filters? After careful listening, many critics tend to favor digital filter designs. There are exceptions, however, and complete generalization would be a mistake.

So much for filtering problems in CD players. But what about digital audio recorders? What good is perfect phase linearity at playback when every disc contains phase nonlinearity introduced by the anti-alias brickwall filters of the digital recorder? At first glance, the problem is insurmountable. The Nyquist theorem dictates that the input anti-aliasing filter be present before sampling occurs. In other words, because filtering must take place on the analog signal before digitization, the filter must be an analog design.

There is, however, a way to put the cart before the horse using oversampling techniques. In short, an oversampling digital input filter can be designed. In essence, such a filter samples at a very fast rate (following a very gentle analog low-pass filter) to greatly extend the Nyquist frequency. A computational process called decimation is used to lower the initial high sampling rate to the 44.1 kHz. Digital filtering provides the anti-aliasing function to prevent aliasing between audio signals and the 44.1 kHz sampling rate. With this technique, at least in theory, perfect phase linearity throughout the digital audio chain is possible.

## A CHIP SET

When circuitry is reduced to an integrated circuit, several interesting things happen. First, everything's a lot smaller. Instead of a king-size circuit board populated with several thousand transistors and other discrete components, we have something considerably more compact. Furthermore, power consumption is dramatically reduced, decreasing the size of the needed power supplies or batteries.

Cost is the bottom line and the most interesting asset of integration. While the development cost of a new chip can be very expensive, the manufacturing costs are quite low. If these costs are amortized over the market life of the chip and divided over the number of chips sold, the cost per chip can be about as small as the microcircuitry itself. In addition, labor costs, packaging costs, and shipping costs of the finished product are all lower. The result is a product that is smaller, lighter, less sensitive to environmental changes, less power hungry, more reliable, and cheaper—all thanks to chips.

Most of the signal processing in a compact disc player is handled by chips. In fact, CD players are prime examples of the benefits of digital microelectronics. A CD player without chips would be enormously large, power-hungry, costly, and wouldn't sound very good. Its hundreds of circuit boards would be extremely unstable, particularly with respect to temperature changes. Even with a full-time engineer crawling around inside to adjust potentiometers, fluctuations would make a joke of operating tolerances.

### A Philips Chip Set

For these and other reasons, manufacturers are anxious to reduce CD player circuitry to the fewest possible number of chips. The decrease in the number of parts marks the evolution of player design. For example, Philips, coinventor of the CD system, has achieved a high degree of integration. Its second-generation chip set is shown in figure 4.24. The SAA7210 handles demodulation, error correction, and basic interpolation. The SAA7220 contains circuitry for enhanced interpolation and a phase-linear digital FIR (finite impulse response) filter. The TDA1541 is a dual 16-bit D/A converter chip.

For design flexibility, the I²S (inter-IC signal) format is used between the SAA7210, SAA7220, and TDA1541 chips. It provides a three-line bus comprising serial data line, clock, and left/right channel select line. Using this bus, the SAA7210 and TDA1541 could be connected directly, omitting the SAA7220. For example, a low cost player design could omit digital filtering and use a downstream brickwall analog filter instead.

### Features of SAA7210 Decoder

Of course, the time and trouble required to compress circuitry into a few chips provides the opportunity for greater performance. In this case, these three decoding chips offer significant improvements over first-generation chips. The SAA7210 contains a demodulator with adaptive data slicer, a fully integrated phase-locked loop demodulator for bit-clock generation, and a motor speed control to stabilize the input data rate.

Part of the SAA7210's job is to process subcode information from the disc—the non-audio data representing track numbers, playing times, titles, and so forth. In some designs the control processor wastes a lot of time working with the subcode. The SAA7210 continually collects the subcode, sending a full frame of subcode only when the processor requests it. If the processor requires only a portion of the subcode—for instance, only a track number (contained in the first sixteen bits of the subcode block)—it can prematurely reset the SAA7210, returning it to subcode collecting.

The SAA7210 decoder also handles error correction chores, using CIRC. The CIRC is standard for all compact discs, but decoding strategies vary considerably. Prior to the SAA7210, no error correction chip made full use of the CIRC's correcting capabilities. The SAA7210 can make four

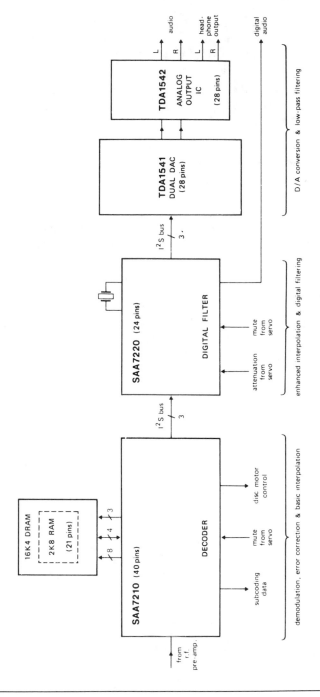

Figure 4.24   *Second generation Philips chip set. (Courtesy Philips)*

erasure corrections (the position of the error is known) per 32-symbol block and up to four corrections when the position of the errors is not known. In some other chip sets, only two erasure corrections are possible.

Furthermore, unlike other decoders, the SAA7210 uses adaptive error correction to discriminate between the types of errors found on a disc. This makes better use of the CIRC correction capability, permitting correction of longer burst errors and more reliable corrections. All decoders use error flags to pinpoint troubled data, but the SAA7210 uses extra flags. They are generated by the EFM decoder to mark symbols that violate the $3T$–$11T$ criterion.

In designing the chip, laboratory testing of defective discs resulted in the identification of types of defects and the development of three 2-bit error flags: a hard error flag (the most reliable flag), a medium error flag, and a soft error flag (the least reliable flag). A no-error flag identifies valid data. The optimum error-correction strategy is selected from one of 60 possibilities by a flag processor, as shown in figure 4.25, depending on the type (soft, medium, or hard) and number of flags caused by disc defects.

After correction, more flags are generated and compared to incoming flags to fine-tune the strategy by updating and hardening the flags. Progressive flag-hardening improves the reliability of the error correction, so that very reliable corrections can be made. The various strategies are programmed in the SAA7210's ROM and can be altered for non-audio CD applications which might call for different strategies.

The SAA7210 must also communicate with RAM; a FIFO (first in, first out) memory is needed to de-interleave data and to buffer data rate irregularities. The SAA7210 is designed to operate with a 4 × 16K RAM which accomodates 64 frames of data. Among other benefits, the large FIFO helps smooth data disruptions occurring in car and portable players. The

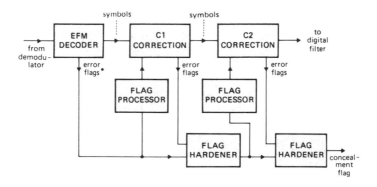

Figure 4.25  *Philips flag processor for selecting error correction algorithms. (Courtesy Philips)*

SAA7210 can be connected directly to an output analog low-pass filter or can deliver its data to the SAA7220 digital filter.

### Features of the SAA7220 Filter

The SAA7220 is a dual-channel linear-phase FIR digital filter chip. The SAA7220 chip employs a four-times oversampling design. The number of filter coefficients has been increased over the first-generation filter by 24 per channel to a total of 120. Passband ripple has been reduced to 0.02 dB to reduce the possibility of that artifact's audibility. (Experiments have shown that passband ripple of ±0.2 dB can be heard.) In addition, the SAA7220 mutes the signal smoothly so that no clicks or pops occur when the player starts, stops, or pauses. Uncorrected data errors stemming from burst errors are masked with an 8-sample interpolator on-board the SAA7220 to create a smooth bridging waveform over the bad samples, as shown in figure 4.26. Improved interpolation and error correction result in significantly better tolerance to burst errors compared to earlier chip sets. The SAA7220 can deliver a digital-format audio output for interfacing to outboard digital signal processors.

### Features of the TDA1541 D/A Converter

The TDA1541 employs a dynamic element matching design technique. Moreover the TDA1541 is a dual 16-bit D/A chip. Since the TDA1541 offers two D/As on one chip, there is no chance of mismatched performance or thermal drift between single D/A chips. Internal bit switching is performed with a diode transistor configuration for fast and accurate switch-

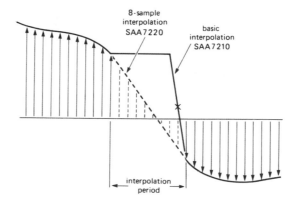

Figure 4.26    *An 8-sample interpolation on the SAA7220 is used for error concealment. (Courtesy Philips)*

ing. When the filter's coefficients were selected, the designers compensated for both the sin($x$)/$x$ response of the hold function on the D/A converter and the analog output Bessel filter's response. The combined conversion function is thus flat in the audio band.

The TDA1541 also looks ahead to the possibility of digital signal processing, such as digital tone controls. Such processing requires increasing the dynamic range of the output signal when select frequencies are boosted. When the 16-bit TDA1541 is coupled to noise shaping circuits to shift quantization noise out of the audio band, resolution equivalent to eighteen bits can be achieved. For example, a digital tone control using the TDA1541 could boost a frequency band by 12 dB while maintaining a 16-bit dynamic range over the audio band.

### Output Stage

To wrap things up, the audio output is handled by the TDA1542 dual channel analog filter chip. As we have seen, digital filtering cleverly shifts frequency components away from the audio band, but they reappear again at higher frequencies. The TDA1542 removes those artifacts with an active third-order filter. Choice of external components determines the filter type (Bessel, Cauer, and so forth). In Philips players, a Bessel filter is used.

These new chips offer significant improvements over first-generation chip sets. These improvements result in improvements in player cost, size, and power consumption, while improving reliability and audio performance.

### SUBCODE

A compact disc player does some amazing things, but some of the credit should rightfully go to the disc itself. Many of the player's operational features derive their ability from special subcode control information encoded on every music disc. Although the user cannot access the subcode directly, it provides much of the information for the front panel controls and display. All players contain the circuitry required to interpret and utilize this information.

### Subcode Blocks

All the data on a CD is arranged into a frame format, which is identified in figure 4.27. By definition, a frame is the smallest recognizable section of data on a disc. Each frame contains audio data, parity, the synchronization word, and an 8-bit field called the subcode. Following modulation, each subcode field is conveyed by one 14-bit EFM symbol. Upon playback the

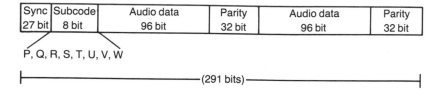

| Sync<br>27 bit | Subcode<br>8 bit | Audio data<br>96 bit | Parity<br>32 bit | Audio data<br>96 bit | Parity<br>32 bit |
|---|---|---|---|---|---|

P, Q, R, S, T, U, V, W

⊢————————————————————(291 bits)————————————————————⊣

**Figure 4.27**  *A CD frame is comprised of 291 bits before EFM modulation, including 8 subcode bits per frame.*

subcode data is demodulated and separated from the audio data to be decoded independently.

The eight subcode bits are contained in every frame and are designated as P,Q,R,S,T,U,V, and W. Only the P and Q subcode bits are used in the audio format. (There is no relation to the P and Q codes in CIRC.) Since the number of bits available in each frame is small, the entire number of subcode bits available from 98 frames is collected to form a subcode block. In other words, the subcode is constructed a byte at a time from 98 successive frames. Thus the 8 subcode bits (P through W) are used as 8 different channels, with each frame containing 1 P bit, 1 Q bit, 1 R bit, and so forth. This interleaving helps minimize the effect of disc errors on subcode data.

A little mathematics determines just how fast subcode blocks accumulate. A CD contains 44,100 left and right 16-bit audio samples every second, so the byte (8-bit) rate is 44,100 × 4, or 176.4 kbytes/second. There are 24 audio symbols in every frame, so the frame rate is 176.4/24 or 7350 Hz. Because it takes 98 frames to make one complete subcode block, the subcode block rate is 7350/98 or 75 Hz; that is, 75 subcode blocks appear every second. Incidentally, if you take 7350 frames per second and multiply it by the number of channel bits, 588, you wind up with 4.3218 MHz, the overall bit rate.

A subcode block is complete with its own synchronization word, instruction, data, commands, and parity. The start of each subcode block is denoted by the presence of $S_0$ and $S_1$ sync patterns in the first symbol positions of two successive blocks. Because $S_0$ and $S_1$ are two patterns (00100000000001 and 00000000010010, respectively) not used in the EFM code, they can be uniquely identified. (You might recall that there are 267 legal EFM patterns, but only 256 of them are used to encode regular data on a disc.)

### The P Channel

The P channel contains a flag bit. It designates the start of a track, as well as the lead-in and lead-out areas on a disc, as shown in figure 4.28. The music

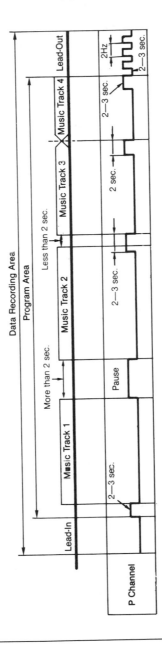

Figure 4.28 *The P channel contains a flag bit designating lead-in, program, and lead-out areas on the disc. (Courtesy Sony)*

data is denoted by 0, and the start flag as 1. The length of a start flag is a minimum of two seconds, but equals the pause length between two tracks if this length exceeds two seconds. Lead-in and lead-out signals tell the player where the music program on the disc begins and ends. A lead-in signal is encoded in the P channel; it consists of all 0s appearing just prior to the beginning of the music data. At the end of the lead-in, a start flag two to three seconds long appears just prior to the start of music. During the last music track, preceding the lead-out, a start flag of two to three seconds appears. The end of that flag gives the start of lead-out and the P channel remains at 0 for two to three seconds. Following that time, a P signal consisting of alternating 1s and 0s (at a 2 Hz rate) appears. These various sets of identity signals can be used by players of basic design to control the optical pickup. For example, a player could count start flags placed in the blank interval between tracks to locate any particular track on a disc. In practice, virtually all players use only the more sophisticated Q code. During master disc encoding, the P code is generated automatically from the Q code.

### The Q Channel

The Q channel contains four basic kinds of information: control, address, Q data, and an error detection code. Figure 4.29 illustrates the Q channel data format. The control information (four bits) handles several player functions. The number of audio channels (two or four) is indicated; this distinguishes between two- and four-channel CD recordings. Although

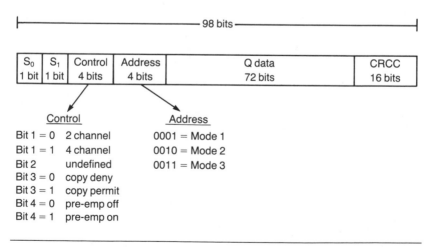

Figure 4.29 *The Q channel contains control, address, data (for three data modes), and CRCC.*

not widely used, a properly equipped player would thus automatically switch its outputs to provide a quadraphonic output. The digital copy (permit/deny) bit regulates the ability of other digital recorders to record the CD's data digitally. Pre-emphasis (on/off) is also indicated. The player reads the code and automatically switches to the appropriate de-emphasis circuit.

The address information consists of four bits designating the three modes for the Q data bits. Primarily, Mode 1 contains number and start times of tracks, Mode 2 contains a catalog number, and Mode 3 contains the International Standard Recording Code (ISRC) code. Each subcode block contains 72 bits of Q data, as described below, and 16 bits for cyclic redundancy check code (CRCC), a code used for error detection on the control, address and Q data information.

As noted, there are three modes of Q data. Mode 1 stores information in the disc lead-in area, program area, and lead out area. The data content in the lead-in area differs from that in the other areas, as illustrated in figure 4.30a. Mode 1 lead-in information is contained in the table of contents (TOC). The TOC stores data indicating the number of music selections (up to 99) as a track number (TNO) and the starting times (P times) of the tracks. The TOC is read during disc initialization, before the disc begins playing, so that the player can respond to any programming or program searching that is requested by the user. In addition, most players can display this information.

In the lead-in area, the TNO is set to 00, indicating that the data is part of a TOC. The TOC is assembled from the point field; it designates a track number and the absolute starting time of that point in minutes, seconds, and frames (75 frames per second). The times of a multiple disc set can also be designated in the point field.

When the point field is set to A0 (instead of a track number) the minute field shows the number of the first track on the disc. When the point field is set to A1, the minute field shows the number of the last track on the disc. When set to A2, the absolute running time of the start of the lead-out track is designated. During lead-in, running time is counted in minutes, seconds, and frames. The TOC is repeated continuously in the lead-in area, and the point data is repeated in three successive subcode blocks.

In the program and lead-out area, shown in figure 4.30b, Mode 1 contains track numbers, index numbers (X) within a track, time within a track, and absolute time (A-time). TNO designates individual tracks and is set to AA during lead-out. Running time is set to zero at the beginning of each track (including lead-in and lead-out areas) and increases to the end of the track. At the beginning of a pause, time decreases ending with zero at the end of the pause. The absolute time is set to zero at the beginning of the program area (the start of the first music track) and increases to the start of the lead-out area. Program time and absolute time are expressed in min-

a)

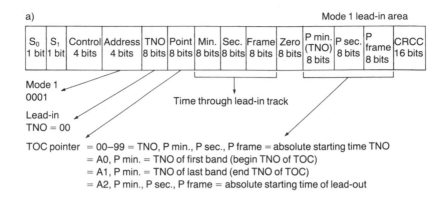

Mode 1 lead-in area

| S₀ 1 bit | S₁ 1 bit | Control 4 bits | Address 4 bits | TNO 8 bits | Point 8 bits | Min. 8 bits | Sec. 8 bits | Frame 8 bits | Zero 8 bits | P min. (TNO) 8 bits | P sec. 8 bits | P frame 8 bits | CRCC 16 bits |

Mode 1
0001

Lead-in
TNO = 00

Time through lead-in track

TOC pointer = 00–99 = TNO, P min., P sec., P frame = absolute starting time TNO
= A0, P min. = TNO of first band (begin TNO of TOC)
= A1, P min. = TNO of last band (end TNO of TOC)
= A2, P min., P sec., P frame = absolute starting time of lead-out

b)

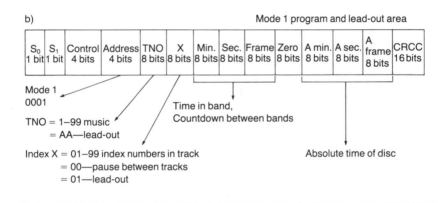

Mode 1 program and lead-out area

| S₀ 1 bit | S₁ 1 bit | Control 4 bits | Address 4 bits | TNO 8 bits | X 8 bits | Min. 8 bits | Sec. 8 bits | Frame 8 bits | Zero 8 bits | A min. 8 bits | A sec. 8 bits | A frame 8 bits | CRCC 16 bits |

Mode 1
0001

TNO = 1–99 music
= AA—lead-out

Index X = 01–99 index numbers in track
= 00—pause between tracks
= 01—lead-out

Time in band,
Countdown between bands

Absolute time of disc

Figure 4.30  *The information in the Q channel, Mode 1 varies between lead-in area where TOC contents such as track numbers and times are stored (a), and program and lead-out areas where track number, running and absolute time, and index information are stored (b).*

utes, seconds, and frames. Index numbers both separate and subdivide tracks. When set to 00, X designates a pause between tracks, and count-down occurs. Non-zero X values set index points inside tracks. A 01 value designates a lead-out area. Using indexing, up to 99 locations within tracks can be indexed. Mode 1 information occupies at least 9 out of 10 successive subcode blocks. Figure 4.31 summarizes the timing relationships con-tained in Mode 1 Q channel information.

In Modes 2 and 3, the program and time information is replaced by other kinds of data. These are displayed in figure 4.32. Mode 2 contains a catalog number of the disc, such as the bar-code of UPC (Universal Prod-uct Code). Mode 2 also continues absolute time count from adjacent

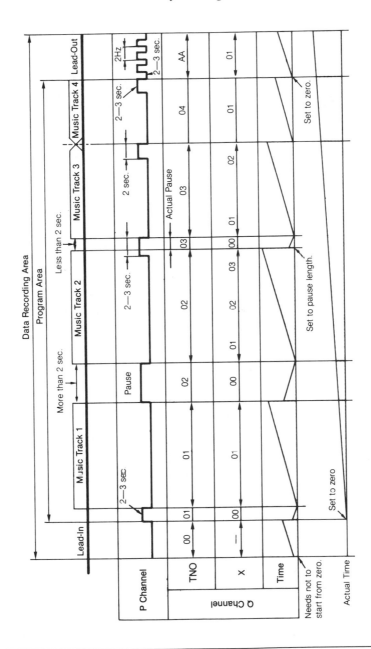

Figure 4.31 *The Q channel stores track numbers, index points, and program and absolute times, in order to form an information map across the disc. (Courtesy Sony)*

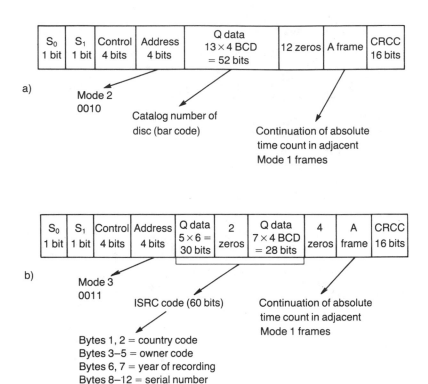

Figure 4.32    *The Q channel Mode 2 contains the disc catalog number (a), and Mode 3 contains an ISRC code (b).*

blocks. Mode 3 is used to give ISRC for identifying each music track. The ISRC number gives the country code, the owner code, the year of recording, and a serial number. Mode 3 also continues absolute time.

Modes 2 and 3 can be deleted from the subcode if they are not required. If they are used, Mode 2 and Mode 3 must occupy at least 1 out of 100 successive subcode blocks, with identical contents in each block. In addition, Mode 2 and 3 data can be present only in the program area.

Every audio compact disc contains additional data capacity in the subcode bits. The other six bits (R,S,T,U,V, and W), which account for about 20 megabytes of 8-bit storage per disc, are available for other data, such as video information. The R-W subcode area was reserved as contingency storage by the original disc designers. Manufacturers promote this feature of the CD standard through the CD + G (Compact Disc + Graphics) format, which will be discussed in Chapter Six.

## SERIAL TRANSMISSION FORMAT

Analog audio signals can be conveyed from one device to another with a minimum amount of confusion. However, the transmission of digital data is a great deal more complicated on account of the potential disagreements on the sampling rate, the synchronization method used, the block length, and many other factors. To permit an orderly exchange of data between professional digital audio devices, the Audio Engineering Society (AES) and European Broadcasting Union (EBU) jointly established a standard transmission format for linearly represented digital audio data. A number of digital audio devices with digital output use this format, which is known as the AES/EBU format; it has been codified as the ANSI S4.40-1985 standard. For compatibility, many manufacturers of consumer electronics have adopted a format derived from the AES/EBU format for transmission of digital audio data. It has been standardized by the International Electrotechnical Commission (IEC) in a draft document, 84/WG11.

The AES/EBU digital audio format transmits both left and right channel data using one digital cable. A time-sharing, multiplexing transmission transmits or receives frames, each containing left and right channel data alternatively. The transmission rate corresponds exactly to the source sampling frequency. When the sampling frequency is 44.1 kHz, 44,100 frames are transmitted per second. One frame consists of two subframes, labelled A (left channel) and B (right channel), each with 32 bits.

Each subframe carries data for one audio channel, as shown in figure 4.33. The first four bits are used for synchronization and for identifying preambles, which will be described shortly. The next 24 bits carry audio data, with the MSB transmitted last. Since most digital audio devices use 16-bit words, the last 16 bits in the field are typically used. In addition, the first 4 bits in the field are set aside for auxiliary audio or other data.

The last four bits form a control field which carries special information. The validity bit indicates if the previous audio sample is error free. The user data bit can be used to form a block for data associated with the audio channel, such as labelling of program number and duration. The channel status bit is used to form a data block; for each channel, one block is formed from the channel status bit contained in 192 successive frames. The start of a block is identified with special forms of the subframe preamble. The parity bit is used to provide even parity for each subframe; this permits simple error detection.

Three preambles are used to designate three types of events. One preamble marks the start of subframe A and the start of a channel status data block. A second preamble marks the start of subframe A, otherwise. A third preamble marks the start of subframe B.

Each channel status data block consists of 192 bits (times 2) organized into two 24-byte sequences. Table 4.1 shows that these 8-bit bytes convey a

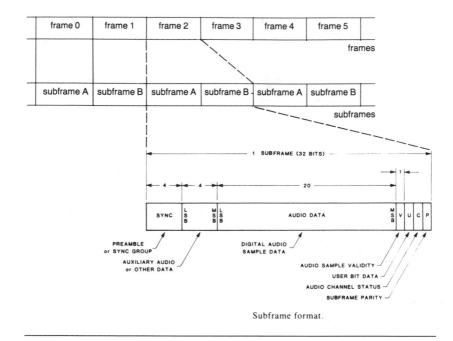

Subframe format.

Figure 4.33   *Subframe format for the AES/EBU serial transmission format.*
*(Courtesy JAES)*

considerable amount of information pertaining to the transmission. The first byte specifies a consumer or professional interface, use of pre-emphasis, and sampling frequency. The second byte specifies channel mode (e.g., stereo, or 2-channel mono). The third byte carries word length information. The remaining channel status bytes specify information on sample address, time-of-day timecode, channel status validity, and CRCC.

The data is modulated with biphase mark, in which a 0 corresponds to one inversion and a 1 corresponds to two inversions, as in the example in figure 4.34. However, the preambles ignore the inversion correspondences to provide unique identification, as shown in figure 4.35. The receiver input section uses this preamble portion for synchronization.

### Consumer Interface

The IEC serial format used in consumer digital audio equipment is derived from the AES/EBU standard (it is perhaps most appropriately known as the AES/EBU/IEC interface). It differs primarily in the definition of the channel status and user bits. The first bit of the channel status byte is set to

**Byte 0**

| Bits | Status | Defines: | As: |
|---|---|---|---|
| 0 | 0 | CSB usage | consumer |
|  | 1 |  | professional |
| 1 | 0 | mode | normal audio |
|  | 1 |  | non-audio |
| 2–4 | 000 | emphasis | undefined |
|  | 100 |  | defined as none |
|  | 110 |  | 50/15 µs |
|  | 111 |  | CCITT |
| 5 | 0 | sampling | unlocked |
|  | 1 | frequency | locked |
| 6–7 | 00 | sampling | undefined |
|  | 01 | frequency | 48 kHz |
|  | 10 |  | 44.1 kHz |
|  | 11 |  | 32 kHz |

**Byte 1**

| Bits | Status | Defines: | As: |
|---|---|---|---|
| 0–3 | 0000 | mode of | undefined |
|  | 0001 | channel | two-channel |
|  | 0010 |  | single-channel |
|  | 0011 |  | primary/sec-ondary ‡ |
|  | 0100 |  | stereophonic |
|  | 1111 |  | Byte-3 pointer |
| 4–7 | † | user bits | undefined |

**Byte 2**

| 0–2 | 000 | aux. bits not defined (20 bits) |
|---|---|---|
|  | 001 | aux. bits used with main audio (24 bits) |
| 3–7 | † | word length undefined |

**Bytes**

| 3 | Reserved for future channel modes. |
|---|---|
| 4, 5 | Reserved for future definition. |
| 6–9 | Channel origin data. (7 bits ASCII) |
| 10–13 | Channel destination data. (7 bits ASCII) |
| 14–17 | Recording index counter. |
| 18–21 | Time of day (sample address code). |
| 22 | Channel status validity flags. |

| Bits | Status | Defines: | As: |
|---|---|---|---|
| 0–3 | 0000 | reserved | undefined |
| 4 | 0 | bytes 0–5 | are OK |
|  | 1 |  | are unreliable |
| 5 | 0 | bytes 6 13 | are OK |
|  | 1 |  | are unreliable |
| 6 | 0 | bytes 14–17 | are OK |

**Byte 23** Channel status data CRCC (Cyclic Redundancy Check Character).

† Bit sequences not given above are reserved but not yet defined.
‡ (Byte 1) indicates A is main channel mono, B is a secondary channel.

Table 4.1 *Each channel status block consists of two 24-byte sequences. (Courtesy JAES)*

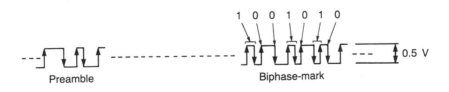

Figure 4.34 *Data is modulated with bi-phase mark. (Courtesy JAES)*

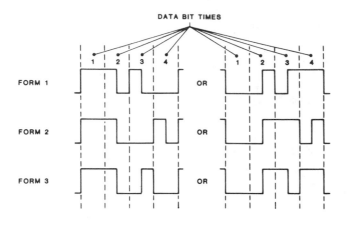

Figure 4.35    *Three preamble forms are used. Form 1 denotes channel A, sub-frame, and block synchronization, Form 2 denotes channel A, otherwise, and Form 3 denotes channel B. (Courtesy JAES)*

0, signifying a consumer interface. However, in the IEC version a different channel status specification is used, as shown in table 4.2. A general format defines a control code contained in the first six bits. A mode select is contained in the next two bits; presently only mode 00 is defined. The general format also defines bit 15; it is stipulated consumer/professional, or program transfer mode, in any selected mode. In mode 00, there is a control code (as above), category code, simplified source field, sampling rate field, and sampling rate tolerance field. A category code of 10000000 denotes a 2-channel CD player. This sets the subframe structure as 16-bit words sampled at 44.1 kHz, and other parameters.

In addition, when interfacing CD data, provision is made to transmit the subcode data in the user bit channel. Subcode data is transmitted as if it were output from the disc, one subcode channel bit at a time, over 98 frames. Each subcode field begins with a minimum of 16 zeros, followed by a high start bit. Seven subcode bits (Q-W) follow. The next start bit and subcode bits may follow, or up to 8 zeros may be inserted for timing purposes. The process repeats 98 times, until the subcode block has been transmitted. The interface provides a user bit for each data sample, but because there are fewer subcode bits than audio samples ($12 \times 98 = 1176$), the remaining bits are filled with zeros. The P subcode channel is not transmitted since it is merely a pickup location flag.

The AES/EBU standard specifies that the digital waveform is transmitted over twisted pair conductors, with 3-pin XLR connectors. In the IEC

**General Specification**

*Control Word* (bits 0–5)
bit 0  0 = consumer, 1 = professional
1  0 = normal, 1 = digital data
2  0 = copy prohibit, 1 = copy permit
3  0 = pre-off, 1 = pre-on
4  reserved
5  0 = 2-channel, 1 = 4-channel
*Mode* (bits 6, 7)
bit 67
00 = mode 00
01 ⎫
10 ⎬ reserved
11 ⎭
*Program* (bit 15)
bit 15  0 = consumer or professional use
1 = program transfer mode (if bit
0 = 0)

**Mode 00 Specification**

*Category Code* bits 8–15
00000000 = general format
10000000 = 2-channel CD player
01000000 = 2-channel PCM
11000000 = 2-channel DAT
*Source Number* (bits 16–19)
0000 = undefined
0001 = source 1
0010 = source 2
.
.
.
1111 = source 15
*Channel Number* bits (20–23)
0000 = undefined
1000 = A (left channel)
0100 = B (right channel)
1100 = C
.
.
1111 = 0
*Sampling Rate* (bits 24–27)
0000 = 44.1 kHz
0100 = 48 kHz
1100 = 32 kHz
. ⎫
. ⎬ reserved
. ⎭
1111
*Clock Accuracy* (bits 28–29)
00 = normal accuracy
10 = high accuracy
01 = variable speed

Table 4.2    *IEC channel status specification.*

version of the format used by consumer electronics manufacturers, video coaxial cable with phono plugs can be used to convey the data. Alternatively, many players feature fiber optic outputs with an optical connector to convey the digital data. Thanks to the transmission standard, digital audio devices from different manufacturers can connect for the transfer of digital audio information.

## FOR FURTHER READING

Adams, Robert. "Design and Implementation of an Audio 18-Bit Analog-to-Digital Converter Using Oversampling Techniques." *Journal of the Audio Engineering Society* 34(3):153–66, March, 1986.

Analog Devices. *Analog-Digital Conversion Handbook.* Englewood Cliffs, N. J.: Prentice-Hall, 1986.

Audio Engineering Society. "AES Recommended Practice for Digital Audio Engineering—Serial Transmission Format for Linearly Represented Digital Audio Data." *Journal of the Audio Engineering Society* 33(12):975–85.

Chamberlin, Hal. *Musical Applications of Microprocessors.* Rochelle Park, N. J.: Hayden, 1980.

Doi, Toshitada. "Recent Progress in Digital Audio Technology." In Blesser, B., B. Locanthi, and T. G. Stockham, Jr., eds. *Digital Audio.* New York: Audio Engineering Society, 1983.

EBU (European Broadcasting Union). "Specification of the Digital Audio Interface." *EBU Doc. Tech.,* 3250.

Fielder, Louis D. "Evaluation of the Audible Distortion and Noise Produced by Digital Audio Converters." *Journal of the Audio Engineering Society* 35(7/8):517–35, July/August, 1987.

Goedhart, D., R. J. Van de Plassche, and E. F. Stikvoort. "Digital-to-Analog Conversion in Playing a Compact Disc." *Philips Technical Review* 40(6):174–79, 1982.

IEC (International Electrotechnical Commission). "Draft Standard for a Digital Audio Interface." *IEC Report* TC 84/WG11, November 1, 1986.

Jung, W. G. "The Magnavox 16-Bit Series." *Audio Magazine* 71(6):74–80, June, 1987.

Lagadec, Roger, and Guy J. McNally. "Labels and Their Formatting in Digital Audio Recording and Transmission." *AES Preprint No. 2003,* 74th Convention, 1983.

Matull, J. "IC's for Compact Audio Disc Decoders." *Electronic Components and Applications* 4(3):131–41, May, 1982.

———. "IC's for Compact Audio Disc Decoders." *Signetics Linear Data and Applications Manual,* vol. 2, 1985.

Meyer, John. "Time Correction of Anti-Aliasing Filters Used in Digital Audio Systems." *Journal of the Audio Engineering Society* 32(3):132–37, March, 1984.

Naus, P. J. A., E. C. Dijkmans, E. F. Stikvoort, A. J. McKnight, D. J. Holland, and W. Bradinal. "A CMOS Stereo 16-Bit D/A Converter for Digital Audio." *IEEE Journal of Solid State Circuits* SC-22(3):390–95, June, 1987.

Nijhof, J. "An Integrated Approach to CD Players, Part 1: The Optical Pick-Up." *Electronic Components and Applications* 6(4):209–15, 1984 (Philips TP172).

———. "An Integrated Approach to CD Players, Part 2: The Decoding Electronics." *Electronic Components and Applications* 6(4):216–22, 1984 (Philips TP172).

Ranada, David. "CD Player Filters." *Stereo Review* 50(7):50–52, July, 1985.

Schott, W. "Philips Oversampling System for Compact Disc Decoding." *Audio Magazine* 68(4):32–35, April, 1984.

Schouwenaars, H. J., E. C. Dijkmans, B. M. J. Kup, and E. J. M. van Tuijl. "A Monolithic Dual 16-Bit D/A Converter." *IEEE Journal of Solid State Circuits* SC-21(3):424–29, June, 1986.

Talambiras, R. P. "Limitations on the Dynamic Range of Digitized Audio." In John Strawn, ed. *Digital Audio Engineering: An Anthology*. Los Altos, Calif.: Kaufmann, 1985.

Van de Plassche, R. J. "Dynamic Element Matching for High-Accuracy Monolithic D/A Converters." *IEEE Journal of Solid State Circuits* SC-11(6):795–800, December, 1976.

Van de Plassche, R. J., and E. C. Dijkmans. "A Monolithic 16-Bit D/A Conversion System for Digital Audio." In Blesser, B., B. Locanthi, and T. G. Stockham, Jr., eds. *Digital Audio*. New York: Audio Engineering Society, 1983.

Van der Kamm, J. J. "A Digital 'Decimating' Filter for Analog-to-Digital Conversion of Hi-Fi Audio Signals." *Philips Technical Review* 42(6/7): 230–38, April, 1986.

Watkinson, J. R. "Inside CD, Part 2." *Hi Fi News and Record Review* 31(12):46–47, December, 1986.

———. "Inside CD, Part 5." *Hi Fi News and Record Review* 32(3):41–43, March, 1987.

———. "Inside CD, Part 6." *Hi Fi News and Record Review* 32(4):45–47, April, 1987.

*Chapter Five*

# Practical Concerns

## INTRODUCTION

All CD discs and players offer considerable advantages over other audio media. The specifications are great: flat response, low noise, low distortion over the entire audio frequency band, and absolute speed stability and accuracy. The operational features are great: small size, long playing time, timing and contents information, indexing, and programmability. The longevity is great: discs are completely immune to damage from repeated playing and relatively impervious to handling damage. Still, as with any other product in the marketplace, there are good players and not-so-good players, good discs, and not-so-good discs. Remember—a smart consumer is a retailer's worst enemy.

## DESIGN CONSIDERATIONS

Evolution is the name of the technology game. While a company's marketing types are busy selling the public on the ultimate product, engineering has to be almost ready with its successor. When the compact disc was first introduced, a certain coinventor touted it as the "last word" and "pure and perfect." Perfection implies the impossibility of improvement, and everything, especially everything technological, can be improved. Sure enough, CD hardware has evolved quite nicely. Of course, take that with a grain of perspective. Once a system is standardized, improvements are usually orders of magnitude less impressive than the original achievement. But a few adjustments can often be quite significant, especially in something as subtle as audio.

Manufacturers are taking advantage of several opportunities to improve CD players, not radically, but nicely. Let's check out some of these improvements—some borrowed from audiophile lore, others stolen from customized players, and the rest inspired from good old common sense engineering.

## Power Supply

The power supply is probably the most unglamorous part of a CD player, mundanely contributing voltages, at prescribed current levels, to energize the system. Yet the power supply is a vital contributor to the player's audio performance. A player's servo control system, for instance, draws considerable current whenever the pickup moves around. This can occur normally—for example, in disc accessing—or under unusual circumstances—for example, when disc wobble (perhaps in the throes of acoustical vibration) stresses the servo. This power demand can translate into variations in the power delivered to other circuits and consequently affect their operating characteristics (rather like a brownout in a power grid). In short, fluctuations in the power supply modulate the rest of the player's circuitry. The distortion parameters of the output analog circuitry can change for the worse, or jitter might be introduced into the master clock, fouling up the digital circuitry. The solutions, increasingly endorsed by manufacturers, are high capacity power supplies which can meet demand under all conditions, or separate power supplies for each part of the system: pickup and servo, digital processing, analog output, and visual display. Separate supplies are particularly nice because they permit isolation of grounds, reducing electrical interference between circuits. Because of servo stress, and for all kinds of reasons, carefully designed power supplies make a lot of sense.

## Optical Pickups

Optical pickups have undergone extensive improvement. New types of lens assemblies have resulted in smaller and lighter pickups; this is important because a lower-mass pickup is better able to traverse the disc and respond to deviations in the pit track, such as the case of a disc with an eccentric center hole. Newer designs also require less calibration and are thus freer of misalignment, a problem with early-generation pickups.

Disc sleds have been greatly improved. They operate faster and smoother than their slow, bulky ancestors. Because they must carry the pickup across the disc surface, tracking and disc access is only as good as they are. Simple, linear motors are being used in many players, replacing rotary motors and their associated worm gears and reduction gear mechanisms. In a linear system, the motor's construction is flat underneath the disc surface, and the motor's torque is transferred directly to the pickup without any gears. The sled and its cargo, the pickup, may travel swiftly to access tracks quickly on a disc (some players can access any point on a disc in one second or less), yet provide precise tracking of the pit spiral. In addition, better sled suspension, ceramic material, and disc clamping help keep the pickup on track even when the room is rocking.

### Servo Systems

Servo systems must keep the laser pickup on track and in focus even under difficult conditions such as the presence of disc defects. When a disc defect passes by the laser, the RF (radio frequency) signal from the pickup momentarily drops in level. When this happens, the player loses its grasp on tracking and focusing information, as well as on audio data. The error correction code springs into action to correct or conceal audible errors, and the servo tries to keep the pickup on track.

In recent designs, the drop in the RF signal is detected more quickly, and the pickup's position is frozen to prevent it from wandering too far off track. In addition, the error correction circuits are alerted to the trouble. Figure 5.1 shows an RF signal interrupted by errors, and slow and fast detection circuits in action. Obviously, the faster circuit permits faster recovery from disc defects and more uniform tracking performance.

### Opto-electronics

Optical transfer devices have been introduced into CD technology. This solves a very basic problem for engineers: the incompatibility of analog and digital circuitry. The digital circuitry may cause interference in the analog signal: for example, digital circuitry often generates radio frequency

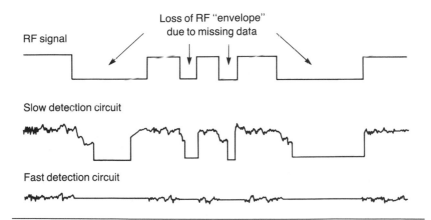

Figure 5.1   *With fast detection circuits, drop-outs in the RF signal may be sensed quickly, and the servo voltage held, until the RF signal is restored. (Courtesy Sony)*

interference, resulting in noise in analog sections. The conflict is especially worrisome in a device where digital and analog must coexist, as in a CD player.

Optical transfer devices help protect analog circuitry from digital interference. For example, some devices convert the electrical signals into light, which is focused and beamed through a short fiber optic cable to a receiver, and then converted back into an electrical signal. Thus data is transferred from the digital circuitry to the analog, but electrical isolation is preserved. When separate power supplies with separate groundings are provided, the two types of circuitry can easily coexist. Optical transfer also helps iron out fluctuations introduced into the signal by power supply modulation.

With optical transfer, much of the spurious noise present in the digital signal (to which digital circuitry is largely impervious) is isolated. Hence the analog section has a much cleaner signal to work with. Will optical transfer make the analog output signal cleaner? Yes. And will it *sound* cleaner? Well, maybe. Much of the spurious noise lies in the MHz region, along with television, radio, and other supersonics. However, the noise can create components in the audio band, and optical transfer can help eliminate them.

Another role for light in CD player design is the use of fiber optics. Increasingly, players feature fiber optic outputs that convey digital audio data via modulated light instead of electricity. In this way, noise and interference encountered en route is minimized. Moreover, grounding incompatibility between components is alleviated. Of course, your preamplifier must have both an optical input and D/A conversion circuitry.

### Electronics

Oversampling filters contain some extremely sophisticated bits of engineering, and the last word hasn't been said. One concern is passband ripple. Some studies indicate that even minute amplitude variations in frequency response cause other audible artifacts. High-resolution filters have been designed to hold ripple to less than $\pm 0.0001$ dB across the audio band; some digital filters achieve this. The oversampling rate employed in digital filters has increased from two- or four-times to eight-times and beyond. This increase moves image spectra to a higher frequency, thereby decreasing the required steepness of the analog filter needed to remove them. While this is an asset, the oversampling rate alone is not a measure of quality. More important is the accuracy of the numerical computation inside the filter. Roundoff errors and other considerations ultimately determine the quality of the digital filter.

Many players exhibit high-frequency components accompanying the audio signal at the player's output jacks. These components amount to spurious noise, ranging from 24 kHz on up, beyond the presumed range of hearing. In many cases, the components are actually beat frequency intermodulation products caused when various digital clocks react with each other. Some players create them and let them pass through, and other players create them and then filter them out. Recently, however, more emphasis has been placed on preventing them in the first place.

When the player is designed with a single master clock, rather than with several unsynchronized clocks, beat frequencies that result in spurious supersonic components are usually reduced. A single master clock is employed for all the processing circuits, including the oversampling filter and D/A converter. As a result, the data stream from the EFM demodulator to the D/A converter is synchronous, preventing any internal beating.

What difference would a beat frequency of perhaps 88.2 kHz make? Although inaudible in itself, the component could intermodulate with audio frequencies, creating distortion products in the audio band. In addition, in-band measurements are often improved as well. For example, figure 5.2 shows the frequency response of four players—one with a single master clock, and three without. The use of synchronous clocks clearly results in a flatter frequency response, because interaction between different clocks is reduced. In brands A and B, fluctuations occur at high frequencies. Even worse, brand C shows a high frequency roll-off. There is growing sentiment that a CD player should output the audio material present on the disc without any spurious supersonics.

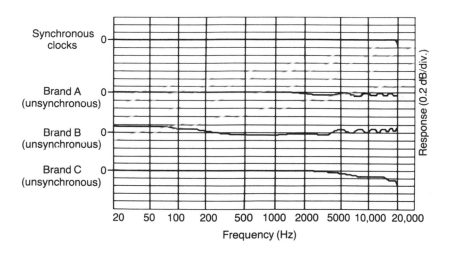

Figure 5.2  *Frequency response can be affected by design of the player's clocks. Frequency response of a player with synchronous clocks is compared to asynchronous clocks in players A, B, and C. (Courtesy Sony)*

While all CD discs use a standard 16-bit digital word, there is latitude in the number of bits actually converted into an analog signal. Some early players used 14-bit digital-to-analog converters and a noise shaping circuit to extend the otherwise limited S/N ratio (the more bits, the higher the S/N). Today, most players use 16-bit converters. However, manufacturers have introduced players with 18-bit conversion circuitry. Their intent is not to somehow improve the data from the disc, but to make better use of that data. Some players use a floating conversion design with 16-bit converters; however, two extra bits are tapped off the bit stream from the oversampling filter and shifted into the D/A converter. It works like this: Of the 18 bits from the filter, the lower 16 are normally fed to the D/A. When a loud passage occurs, the bits are shifted up to accommodate the top two bits. In this way, dynamic range is increased by 12 dB. To compensate for the bit-shifting, the output gain must be lowered by 1/4 when the lower bits are used. Figure 5.3 illustrates the pseudo-18 bit system. In other players, true 18-bit D/A converters are employed. Eighteen bits are taken from the oversampling filter and converted to an analog signal. The dynamic range of the conversion is increased by 12 dB. With either technique, 18-bit con-

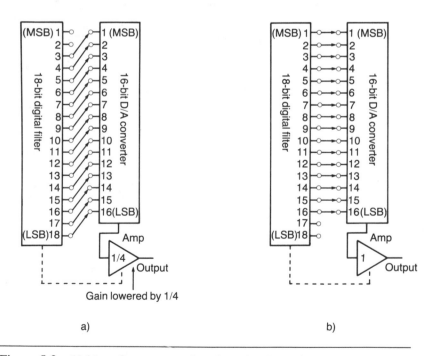

Figure 5.3    *18-bit performance can be achieved with a 16-bit D/A converter by using two lower bits from the oversampling filter during low audio levels (a). The bits are shifted when high levels occur (b). (Courtesy Yamaha)*

version provides an increase in conversion quality because, except in theory, 16-bit converters cannot fully decode a 16-bit signal without a degree of error. Eighteen-bit conversion circuitry provides a greater dynamic range than the recording and thus helps ensure a high quality conversion of the CD's data.

### Vibration

Vibration is bad. Transmitted to the analog circuitry, it can deteriorate sound quality; for example, mechanical vibration can be converted into electrical signals by capacitors. As we have seen, a vibrating disc can stress the servo system and the power supply.

Two sources of vibration common to every CD player are the disc and the sound output itself. Internal motor and disc-generated vibration can be damped by using ceramic or fiberglass material in the disc drive. These materials act as poor conductors of vibration, creating friction as vibration tries to pass through. It is quickly attenuated. Figure 5.4 shows the damping characteristics of a metal part as opposed to a ceramic part. In addition,

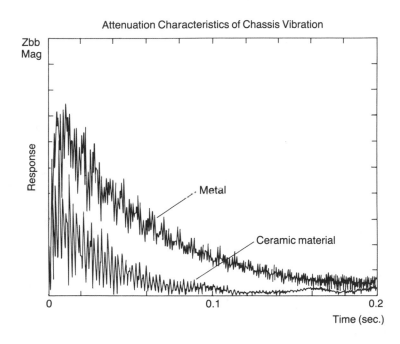

Figure 5.4 *Ceramic materials help damp vibration compared to metals. (Courtesy Sony)*

rubber bushings under the drive help isolate it from the chassis and the electrical components.

External vibration can be created acoustically from the pressure function of loudspeakers. The player's chassis forms the first line of defense. Player chassis are consequently becoming more massive, with thick plastic or metal panels, and are better braced in order to reduce resonance. Some players employ a dual-layer construction in which an impact-deadening material is sandwiched between two metal plates of different thicknesses. Alternatively, calcium carbonate material, reinforced with fiberglass, has been used. These chassis are remarkable; when you rap on them with your knuckles, the sound dies, along with any unwanted vibrations. In addition, the location and number of welds and screws and the placement of absorbing materials applied to inside areas all help damp vibration.

### Other Improvements

Capacitors used for the D/A chips can be susceptible to vibration. Capacitors with electrodes made of copper and dense film can be used for their antivibration characteristics. Heat sinks made of copper with a low $Q$ factor also help control resonance.

The search for good capacitors continues. Some manufacturers have added ceramic powder to their electrolytic capacitors for better impulse response and faster and more accurate rise-time characteristics. Of course, all other components must be audio-grade, including polystyrene capacitors with copper foil plate, one-percent tolerance metal film resistors, oxygen-free copper wire, and copper plated chassis.

Electrical interference must be controlled both internally and externally. Every circuit designer knows the importance of shielding and grounding. One might also contemplate the question of the effect of noise transmitted by a CD player on other audio components, such as amplifiers. The proliferation of digital audio gear increases the problem of radio frequency interference.

Operational amplifiers still aren't perfect, or even close to perfect. Manufacturers still struggle to find distortion, noise, slew rate, and heat dispersion specifications fully adequate for audio.

Manufacturers have taken a close look at early generation players and returned to the drawing board for some very worthwhile improvements. Are they drastic improvements? That depends on your perspective. If you liked CD playback from the beginning, you might hear a slight increase in the quality of the sound. If you had a problem with early generation players, these improvements might very well satisfy you, in which case the result would be considerable. In any case, they are worthwhile because

## SPECIFICATIONS

Perceiving nuances in the quality of different digital audio systems places great demands on even the best ears. Measured specifications are thus increasingly important in evaluating digital audio products. Most of us are lucky to hear 20 kHz, let alone a 0.1 dB deviation at that frequency. Specifications provide a standard of comparison. The CD player, the amplifier, the loudspeakers, the listening room acoustics, and personal subjectivity combine to produce an environment which is simply too unique to provide a meaningful reference. Thus specifications become an important part of any evaluation, for they permit us to probe both the limits of a player's sonics and the limits of our hearing in a standardized manner.

An understanding of specifications is crucial for the educated consumer. The numbers published by the manufacturer or quoted in a magazine test report are meaningful only if the basis for them is understood. Let's consider CD test procedures and some of the principal specifications for CD players. Specifications derived from analog technology are generally used; this is understandable because the analog output stages are often the limiting factor in many aspects of player performance.

### Test Discs

Any test needs a standard source. In the case of CD players, test discs are available from Philips (410 055-2/3, 410 055-2/5, and 410 055-2/5A), PolyGram (DHF19-410741-2), Sony (CD3-YED-S7), Denon (38C39-7147 and 33C39-7441), Technics (SH-CD001), Pierre Verany (PV788031/788032), CBS (CD-1), and other manufacturers, as well as organizations such as the Japan Audio Society (CD-1 YDDS-2), Hi-Fi News (HFN0-03), and the Electronic Industries Association of Japan (EIAJ CD-1 YGDS 13). They contain diverse test signals and musical selections.

The CBS test disc CD-1 deserves special mention. It includes all of the tests specified by both the Electronic Industries Association (EIA) and the EIAJ, along with several additional tests devised by CBS. It contains tracks of low-level amplitude-swept and amplitude-stepped signals (from about −70 dB to −100 dB) recorded with dither. These permit measurement of linearity and distortion without the effects of quantization noise. The use of dithered test signals is crucial at low amplitudes because it would be otherwise impossible to separate the player's distortion from those in the test signal itself. The −100 dB signal demonstrates the ability of the CD system to accurately reproduce signals below the least significant bit when proper dither has been added. The contents of the CBS CD-1 test disc are shown in table 5.1.

**CBS**
**CD-1 TEST DISC**

FOR MEASURING CD PLAYER
PERFORMANCE WITH E.I.A.
STANDARD SIGNALS

| | | |
|---|---|---|
| 1 Reference, L & R,<br>O dB, 1 kHz | 10 19 997 Hz<br>(Also used for Pitch<br>Error) | 16 Square Wave, L & R,<br>O dB, 1 002.27 Hz |
| 2 Left Separation, O dB,<br>1K, 125, 4K, 10K, 16K Hz | 11 Sweep Frequency<br>Response, | 17 Impulse & Polarity Test,<br>O dB, L & R |
| 3 Right Separation, O dB,<br>1K, 125, 4K, 10K, 16K Hz | O dB, 5Hz −22.05<br>kHz | 18 Linearity, 997 Hz,<br>L & R, |
| 4 Signal/Noise, L & R,<br>Infinity Zero w/o em-<br>phasis | 12 De-emphasis Error,<br>L & R, 1K, 125,<br>4K, 10K, | O dB, −1, −3, −6, −10,<br>−20, −30, −39.99,<br>−49.97, −59.94, −70.31, |
| 5 Dynamic Range, L & R,<br>1kHz, −60 dB w/o em-<br>phasis | 16K Hz<br>13 Intermodulation | −80.77, −90.31 dB<br>19 Linearity with Dither,<br>997 Hz, L & R |
| 6 Frequency Response,<br>L & R, O dB, 4, 8,<br>17, 31 Hz | Distortion<br>(SMPTE, Twin Tone),<br>L & R | *−70.31, −80.77,<br>−90.31, −100 dB<br>20 Fade to Noise with |
| 7 61, 127, 251, 499 Hz | 60 Hz + 7 kHz,<br>11 kHz + 12 kHz | Dither, L & R<br>*−60 dB, 500 Hz |
| 8 997, 1999, 4001,<br>7993 Hz | 14 Wow & Flutter, L & R,<br>O dB, 3150 Hz | 21 Monotonicity, L & R,<br>*1 102.5 Hz, 10 LSB |
| 9 10 007, 12 503, 16 001,<br>17 989 Hz | 15 Access Time, L & R,<br>O dB, 317 Hz | *Additional Test Tracks |

Table 5.1    *Contents of CBS CD-1 test disc. (Courtesy CBS)*

the following thirteen tests: frequency response, signal-to-noise ratio, dynamic range, total harmonic distortion, channel separation, de-emphasis error, wow and flutter, intermodulation distortion, phase difference between channels, level difference between channels, output voltage, pitch error, and access time. In addition, it specifies a standard method for performing and documenting the tests. "Test Disk for CD Players" describes a standard test disc to be used to perform such tests.

The signals on test discs are computer-generated to guarantee accuracy. Standard specifications can be measured with their menus of signals. Of course, test gear is needed to decipher the results; a good test bench has an oscilloscope, a distortion and level meter, and a harmonic analyzer. (Indeed, a good test bench should also have a CD player and test disc. They provide a highly accurate set of reference signals useful in testing other audio equipment, room acoustics, etc.) As an alternative to separate pieces of measuring equipment, integrated, computer-based test sets offer high accuracy and fast operation. Equipped with a test disc, measuring gear, and the player under test, we can run some numbers. Many of the following procedures are more fully described in an applications note by Audio Precision, as listed in the references at the end of this chapter. A word of warning: test discs contain maximum amplitude signals. Turn down your amplifier to avoid possible damage to the loudspeakers when playing them over a home system.

### Frequency Response

Frequency response measures a signal's amplitude deviation over the audio bandwidth of 0 to 20 kHz; any amplitude deviation, either positive or negative, is measured in decibels (dB) relative to a 0 dB (maximum) amplitude at 1 kHz. The test is easy to perform. By using either independent tones or a swept tone recorded at 0 dB, amplitude deviation is measured on a voltmeter. An actual measurement is shown in figure 5.5. The two channels are tested separately. By definition, the digital signal should have a perfectly flat response, but the output analog circuity usually interferes.

Frequency response measures one of the most audible aspects of any audio system. A slight difference in frequency response can account for diverse qualitative judgements, including image, depth, air, clarity, and warmth. Fortunately, the frequency response of digital audio equipment is one of its fortes. A good CD player will have an essentially flat response with a negative deviation of perhaps a few tenths of a decibel at the high frequencies.

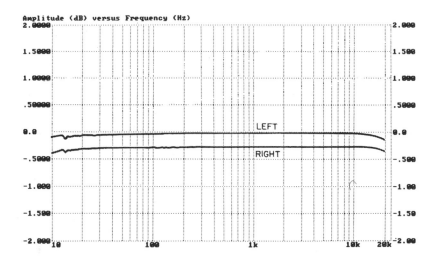

Figure 5.5 *Frequency response measurement. (Courtesy Audio Magazine)*

### Channel Separation

Channel separation measures the ability of the player to keep the stereo signals distinct from each other; again, the problem lies mainly in the analog output circuitry and usually grows more severe at high frequencies. For this test, 0 dB reference tones of various frequencies are played through one channel, and the crosstalk is measured on the otherwise quiet channel, as shown in figure 5.6. When a broadband measurement is taken, crosstalk of both the fundamental and its harmonic components are measured. Many manufacturers prefer to measure only crosstalk from the fundamental frequency under test. Thus a filter (a 22 kHz low-pass or a selected band-pass) is used to remove wideband signals which could decrease the measured value of separation.

Whatever method is employed, the crosstalk level is measured as an amplitude in dB. A figure of −90 dB at 1 kHz, for example, means that 1 kHz information on one channel will also appear on the other channel, but down 90 dB. A channel separation frequency response may thus be plotted. Curiously, channel separation is usually not reciprocal between two channels. A good player should have channel separation of more than 90 dB across the audio band.

### Total Harmonic Distortion Plus Noise

Total harmonic distortion plus noise (THD + N) measures a device's ability to reproduce a signal without adding components of its own. Speci-

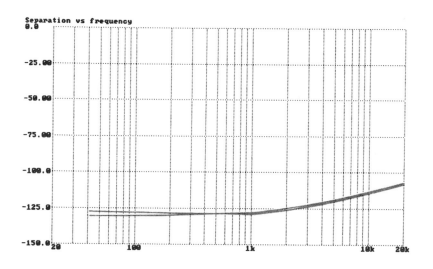

Figure 5.6    *Channel separation measurement. (Courtesy Audio Magazine)*

fically, distortion results if the device adds new harmonic information. For example, if a 50 Hz tone was applied, 50 Hz would be reproduced, as well as harmonics: 100 Hz second harmonic, 150 Hz third, 200 Hz fourth, etc. Devices such as D/A converters are often guilty of contributing harmonic distortion.

The THD + N of a device is measured by inputting a sine wave (a signal with no harmonics), then filtering out the sine wave at the output, and measuring the remaining harmonic signal as a percentage of the original signal. A THD + N analyzer accomplishes the process directly, as seen in figure 5.7. THD + N varies with respect to both amplitude and frequency. It must therefore be measured over a wide frequency range and at different levels. Unlike analog systems, in which THD + N increases with amplitude, a digital system's THD + N decreases with amplitude. CD player manufacturers wage war over THD + N measurements, often achieving levels below 0.002 percent.

The THD + N is typically measured at 14 frequencies recorded at 0 dB and lower amplitudes such as −24 or −30 dB. A dithered test signal should be used. Some players show a rise in distortion at high signal amplitudes, due to distortion in the analog output stages, as well as bit weighting errors in the D/A converter which increase quantization error. Steps in the measured distortion over amplitude indicate the latter. A rise in THD + N at high frequencies is often observed, particularly in players with poor low-pass filters. This is usually not due to harmonic distortion, but is caused by the beat frequency between the CD player's clock and the test signal. With

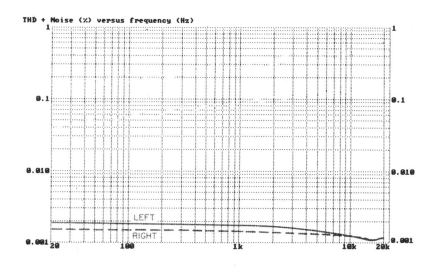

Figure 5.7  *Total harmonic distortion plus noise (THD + N) measurement.*
*(Courtesy Audio Magazine)*

a 44.1 kHz clock and 20 kHz test tone, for instance, the spurious signal will measure 24.1 kHz

The EIAJ and most manufacturers insert a 22 kHz low-pass filter between the player's output and the distortion meter. Otherwise, spurious beat frequency components related to the player's sampling frequency add to the distortion measurement, whereas in fact they are not harmonic distortion. While the use of a filter is thus justified in THD + N measurements, it limits the use of the measurement; for example, a 24 kHz low-pass filter removes all legitimate harmonic components for frequencies under test greater than 12 kHz (24 kHz is the first harmonic of 12 kHz). Thus THD + N cannot be accurately measured for frequencies greater than 12 kHz. Thorough reviewers are careful to examine the unfiltered output signal with a spectrum analyzer to detect any components, harmonic or otherwise, which might degrade performance. Because of the low distortion levels to be measured, care must be taken in grounding and interconnecting the player to the test equipment.

### Intermodulation Distortion

Intermodulation distortion (IM) measures the creation of new frequencies from a combination of any legitimate input frequencies. Some circuits generate a series of sum and difference frequencies related to two input frequencies. For example, if 50 Hz and 1,000 Hz are input, 950 Hz, 1,050 Hz, 1,100 Hz, and an entire series of frequences might be added in. Since these frequencies are not harmonically related to the originals, they tend to be audibly disagreeable and might contribute to listener fatigue. To measure IM, twin sine waves most often recorded at 0 dB are input to the device and then filtered at the output; any remaining intermodulation signals are measured and expressed as a percentage of the original signal. Several standard frequency pairs can be used. A SMPTE IM distortion standard specifies 60 Hz and 7 kHz signals in a 4:1 amplitude ratio. A CCIF IM distortion standard specifies 11 and 12 kHz in a 1:1 ratio. In either case, the percentage of the beat frequency at the player's output constitutes the measurement. A low-pass filter is usually inserted as part of the measurement. A good player's SMPTE IM distortion should be 0.004% or less. A spectral analysis of the IM products may yield insight into their cause.

Distortion measurements in CD players point up a unique problem: certain test frequencies must be avoided because they yield unrepresentative (and higher) distortion readings. Specifically, frequencies which are integral submultiples of the 44.1 kHz sampling frequency—they are thus synchronous with the clock frequency—will utilize a fewer number of quantization intervals than noninteger submultiples, resulting in higher distortion. The synchronous relationship does not test linearity of every state of the D/A converter because the points where the test waveform are sampled will repeat after a relatively small number of samples. A non-synchronous relationship is preferred because the waveform passes through many timing relationships, causing every converter state to be exercised. For example, a test frequency of 315 Hz (1/140 of 44.1 kHz) recorded at −20 dB would use 71 different quantization intervals in a period of 100 milliseconds, whereas a 317 Hz signal of the same amplitude and over the same time period uses 3,282 intervals.

Thus the EIAJ and manufacturers recommend avoiding test frequencies that are integer submultiples. Hence new test frequencies have been standardized by the EIAJ. These are presented in table 5.2. Measurements of criteria other than distortion, such as frequency response, are not affected by the anomaly.

| Normal Frequency (Hz) | Actual Frequency (Hz) | Difference (percent) |
|---|---|---|
| 4 | 4 | − |
| 8 | 8 | − |
| 16 | 17 | +6.250 |
| 32 | 31 | −3.125 |
| 63 | 61 | −3.175 |
| 125 | 127 | +1.600 |
| 250 | 251 | +0.400 |
| 500 | 499 | −0.200 |
| 1,000 | 997 | −0.300 |
| 2,000 | 1,999 | −0.050 |
| 4,000 | 4,001 | +0.025 |
| 8,000 | 7,993 | −0.088 |
| 10,000 | 10,007 | +0.070 |
| 12,500 | 12,503 | +0.024 |
| 16,000 | 16,001 | +0.006 |
| 18,000 | 17,989 | −0.061 |
| 20,000 | 19,997 | −0.015 |

Table 5.2   *Standardized non-integer submultiple test frequencies.*

### Signal-To-Noise Ratio

Ideally, an audio device should have no output signal when there is no input signal. In practice, the S/N (signal-to-noise) ratio measures the noise floor of the player's output relative to the player's rated maximum output level (0 dB). The number of bits in a digital audio system determines the maximum signal-to-error ratio possible, but the analog output circuitry is often the limiting factor. Any noise or hum in the output stages will determine the floor over which the signal may range. To make the test, a test disc track with 16 zeros per sample (digital silence) is played, and the noise which is measured is referenced to a maximum level of 0 dB. An S/N measurement with a digital silence track does not provide information on the player's digital circuitry since the D/A converter is not being exercised. The digital silence track is thus useful for separating analog noise from digital noise sources. Although the D/A converter is quiescent, and thus contributes no noise due to conversion, low frequency noise sources, such as the power supply, the analog circuitry, and poor grounding, as well as high frequency noise sources, such as clock leakage, will limit the noise floor of the player. A spectral analysis of the noise signal is often revealing.

Once again, there are different measuring methods. Some manufacturers measure a broadband S/N ratio, while others employ a low-pass filter to eliminate out-of-band components. (The EIAJ calls for a filter with cutoff at 4 Hz and 20 kHz, and with an attenuation of at least 60 dB at 24.1 kHz.) An "A" weighted filter may be used to attenuate low-frequency components of the noise signal. A good player should have an S/N of greater than 110 dB, unweighted, as shown in figure 5.8a. Careful attention to grounding and interconnections is required to measure such low levels.

### Quantization Noise

Quantization noise measurement differs from noise measurement with a digital silence track. To measure quantization noise, a test signal at various amplitudes is used. THD + N is measured, thus removing the fundamental component of the test signal. In addition, low and moderate order harmonics may be removed with a high-pass filter (400 Hz) to prevent distortion products from obscuring the quantization noise measurement across the audio spectrum above 400 Hz. Figure 5.8b shows quantization noise in dB (y axis) against signal amplitude from maximum down to −90dB (x axis).

### Dynamic Range

Dynamic range is often confused with signal-to-noise ratio, but there is a difference. The EIAJ defines dynamic range as the level of total harmonic

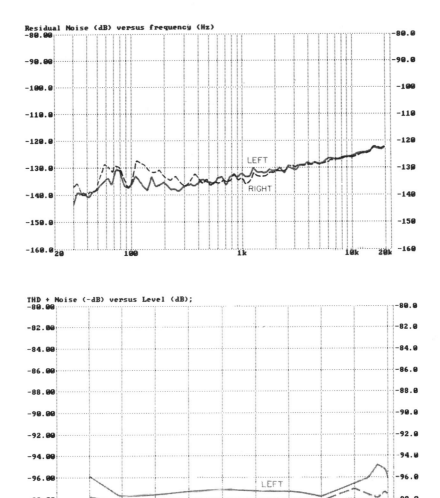

Figure 5.8 *Signal-to-noise ratio (S/N) unweighted (a), and A-weighted (b).*
*(Courtesy Audio Magazine)*

distortion plus 60 dB when a CD reproduces a 1 kHz signal recorded at
−60 dB below maximum level. For example, a THD + N reading of −25
dB plus 60 dB yields a dynamic range measurement of 85 dB. The measurement is thus not equivalent to S/N ratio. It is useful because it eliminates any distortion introduced at higher levels in the CD player. The
EIAJ specifies that an "A"-weighted filter and 22 kHz low-pass filter be
used to measure THD + N. This produces a noise measurement as op-

posed to a distortion measurement, and the results can be compared to "A"-weighted noise measurements. However, it may be misleading to measure only harmonic components; for example, D/A nonlinearities may produce alias frequencies. A more rigorous test is to measure the total power of all harmonic, nonharmonic, and noise components relative to the fundamental. The EIA has proposed means of measuring dynamic range using 500 Hz dithered test signals recorded at −60 and −120 dB. The player's output is passed through a ⅓ octave filter tuned to 500 Hz, and the output is measured in dB. The noise floor is determined by adding 3 dB to the output signal level from the −120 dB recorded level. This signal level is assumed to be the lowest signal that can be reliably distinguished from noise. Maximum signal level is thus 60 dB above the output signal level of −60 dB. Dynamic range is ascertained by subtracting the noise floor (−120 dB recorded + 3dB) from the signal level (−60 dB recorded + 60 dB).

### D/A Linearity

A D/A linearity test measures the D/A converter's ability to reproduce various signals, particularly low amplitude ones, at the proper recorded amplitude. The test is often performed with 1 kHz test tones, with descending test disc amplitudes of −1, −3, −6, −10, −20, −30, −40, −50, −60, −70, −80, −90 dB and −100 dB. A band-pass filter is inserted. It is important to note the difference between dithered and undithered test tones when making this test. For example, because of the distortion it creates, an undithered test tone of −90 dB will reproduce at −89 dB through a perfect D/A. When a dithered test tone is used, the fundamental level, as obtained from a spectrum analyzer, should fall precisely at −90 dB.

D/A converter nonlinearities can also be uncovered by ear. This is done by playing a dithered ramp signal, fading from approximately −40 dB to −120 dB where the signal disappears into system noise. Effects of nonlinearity are audible as harmonic distortion.

### Phase Measurements

Interchannel phase difference measures the shift between identical frequencies recorded on two channels. The stereo signal must be recovered from the single data stream and reconstructed with the original simultaneous phase between the two channels. Often a single D/A converter is used, and if compensation isn't applied, the channels will be out of phase with respect to each other as the converter delays one channel relative to the other. For example, a 44.1 kHz clocked player with a single D/A may show an 82 degree phase shift at 20 kHz (11.34 microseconds at the 44.1 kHz clock rate). Similarly, an 88.1 kHz clocked player may show a 41 degree shift, and a 176.4 kHz clocked player would show about a 20 degree phase shift. Time delay compensation used in single D/A players may improve this phase shift. Even dual D/As can contribute a slight error.

To measure any interchannel phase error, 20 kHz is output to each channel; any difference will be apparent from the misaligned waveforms, such as the ones in figure 5.9a. A good player should have negligible interchannel phase error. This is illustrated in figure 5.9b. Alternatively, time delay or phase error between channels can be measured through a Lissajous pattern. The output of one channel is connected to the horizontal (X) input of an oscilloscope, and the output of the other channel is connected to the vertical (Y) input. A trace angled at 45 degrees (from lower left to upper right) indicates the channels are in phase.

Phase linearity measures any phase shift between different frequencies. Digital filters and carefully compensated analog filters can reduce phase error to a few degrees or less. Although this is not a rigorous test, some test discs contain twin tones of 2 kHz and 20 kHz, each on a single channel output. The tones are encoded with simultaneous positive-going axis crossings. Any relative phase discrepancy can thus be observed on an oscilloscope. Simultaneous zero-crossing of the positive-going waveforms shows there is no phase discrepancy. An offset of the waveforms at that point would indicate a discrepancy. A CD player with digital filtering might show phase linearity of less than 0.5 degrees at 20 kHz.

### De-emphasis

To reduce noise, some compact discs are recorded with pre-emphasis, a boosting of high frequencies (50 microseconds at 3.18 kHz, 15 microseconds at 10.6 kHz). During playback, an automatic high frequency de-emphasis should restore a flat response. De-emphasis error measures any deviation occurring when the de-emphasis curve is not the correct reciprocal of the pre-emphasis curve. To accomplish the test, selected frequencies

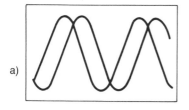
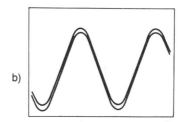

Figure 5.9    *Interchannel phase difference checked at 20 kHz: phase error (a), phase linearity (b).*

are output, and any de-emphasis deviation is measured in dB. The EIAJ proposes use of 125 Hz, 1 kHz, 4 kHz, 10 kHz, and 16 kHz.

### Other Evaluations

Any level imbalance between the two output channels is measured by comparing two 1 kHz signals recorded at 0 dB. The difference is expressed in dB. In addition, voltage readings of the maximum output values are often specified.

Although the wow and flutter in CD players should be unmeasurable, some test discs supply a 3.15 kHz tone, the frequency usually used to measure speed fluctuation in analog equipment, to accomplish the measurement for CD players. The EIAJ specifies that the test be made for at least 5, but no more than 30 seconds. Typically, the weighted peak value of CD wow and flutter is below the ±0.001 percent measurement threshold, and most manufacturers simply state, correctly, that it is below measurable limits.

Although an unlikely occurrence, any pitch error introduced by a CD player may be specified by measuring a 20 kHz output signal with a frequency counter and expressing the error as a percentage: $(F_1-F_0)/(F_0) \times 100$, where $F_0 = 20$ kHz.

The nature of the output filter can be examined through single pulses and square waves. A single pulse or a 1 kHz square wave will show the damped pattern of analog filtering or the symmetrical pattern of digital filtering as shown in figure 5.10. However, it is important not to misinterpret the ripple present on the waveform. A perfectly square square wave could only exist in the case of infinite bandwidth, that is, only if an infinite number of sine wave harmonics were present to completely comprise the square wave. In the case of a CD player, we know that our bandwidth is limited to about 20 kHz. Thus the square wave will show ripples and this is normal operation.

The single pulse response is also useful to uncover incorrect absolute polarity. A positive-going pulse is always recorded on the test disc; if the oscilloscope trace shows a negative signal, the player's absolute polarity is reversed.

The EIAJ also specifies a test to measure access time, the time it takes for a pickup to move to a location on the disc. Short and long access times are specified. Short access time measures the time for the pickup to move to the next adjacent track and begin playing. Long access time measures the time for the pickup to move from the innermost track to the outermost track and begin playing. Both measurements are specified in seconds.

Test discs can be used to exercise the error correction/tracking ability of the player. The Philips 5A test disc contains three types of intentional defects on specified tracks: simulated fingerprint, calibrated black dots on the

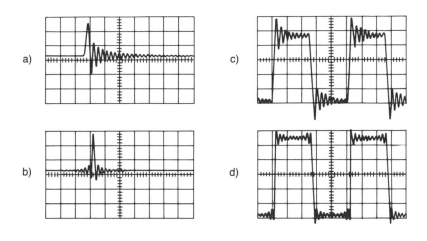

Figure 5.10    *Output filters can be examined through single pulse and square waves: analog filter impulse response (a), digital filter impulse response (b), analog filter 1 kHz square wave (c), digital filter 1 kHz square wave (d). (Courtesy Stereo Review)*

readout side, and calibrated interruptions on the information layer. The dimensions of the black dots are 300, 500, 600, and 800 micrometers, and the interruptions on the information layer are 400, 500, 600, 700, 800, and 900 micrometers. These obstacles help determine a player's limitations in error correction, concealment, and tracking.

All CD players should be able to play through the fingerprint and the smallest of the other defects. In theory a player with fully implemented error correction strategy (not all have this) should correct any defect up to 2400 micrometers. In practice most players handle all the defects on the Philips test disc. The more strenuous defects in the Verany 788032 disc may be used to determine the player's limits. Reviewers specify error correction/tracking performance by noting how many (if not all) of the defect sizes the player is able to negotiate.

### Caveats

The use of low-pass filters to limit measurements to in-band information has generated confusion. Some players output only in-band information with no spurious high-frequency components. Specifications such as THD + N can be measured directly. However, other players exhibit out-of-band frequency components. The rationale for bandlimited measurements is that supersonic components cannot be heard and should not therefore affect the measurement.

The difference between unfiltered and filtered measurements is illustrated in figure 5.11. The first oscilloscope trace of the unfiltered player under test shows a 20 kHz signal and an image frequency at 24.1 kHz (44.1 kHz−20 kHz), as well as images of those two frequencies at 64.1 kHz and 68.2 kHz. The second trace shows what happens when a 20 kHz seventh order low-pass filter is put on the player's output; the troublesome images are largely attenuated, leading to much better measurements.

We should note that some critics are not so sure of the validity of filtered measurements. Since many players measure satisfactorily without a special brickwall filter, is it fair to use special measuring conditions for the benefit of other players? Moreover, it is possible that some listeners can hear out-of-band components, or that the components might affect in-band signals. If a player has them, measurements should show that fact. Finally, unless the manufacturer wishes to supply the consumer with a special low pass filter, it doesn't seem right to measure the player *with* one.

The bottom line is that measurements are valid only if they accurately portray performance. If some players have higher THD + N, then that should be made clear. If THD + N measurements are made with a brickwall filter, then a spectrum analysis should also be supplied with the player to show the supersonic components. Honesty in specification is important, especially in a new technology such as digital audio. Only then can we expect evolution toward better performance.

A specification is meaningful only if we understand the conditions of measurement. Greater consumer awareness will lead the way to new specifications designed to clarify the performance of digital audio devices and to help supplement the pair of precision measuring devices you're naturally equipped with.

## BUYING A PLAYER

Are all CD players alike? The answer is definitely no. Some players are a lot more expensive than others, some players sound a lot better than others, and the correlation isn't always what you'd expect. Exactly how do you shop for the best buy? Let's consider a list of effective maneuvers for smart CD shopping—questions that will separate the great players from the merely good.

### Basic Questions

"Is this CD player free?" This question is often overlooked by many shoppers. I've found that it never hurts to ask. Moreover, if the answer is yes, you can skip the remaining questions.

a)

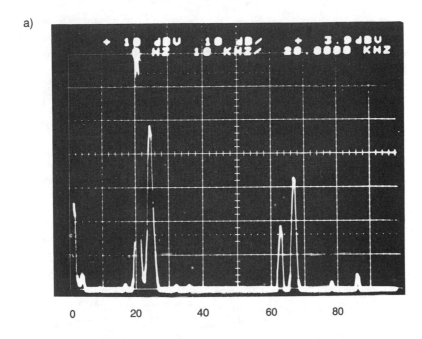

0    20    40    60    80

b)

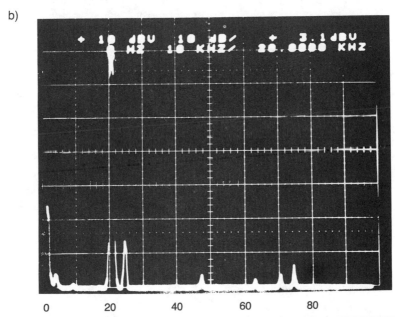

0    20    40    60    80

Figure 5.11    *Effects of output filters used in making measurements: Unfiltered spectra (a), and filtered spectra (b).*

Who is the manufacturer? This is a good overall measure of quality in CD players. After evaluating many players, one finds consistent quality among certain manufacturers, whereas other manufacturers may have hits and misses. Surprisingly, expense isn't always the reason. Do your homework and ascertain exactly which companies have the required expertise; read reviews in magazines and ask a lot of questions of knowledgeable people. It isn't always obvious.

Does the player have the features you want, or are you paying extra for gimmicks you'll never use? All players have the basic controls to start, stop, and move the optical pickup around, and many are programmable, but there are a lot of differences: remote control, multi-disc playback, headphone output, digital audio output, and so forth. Maybe a portable player better suits your needs. However at a given price, if the manufacturer added a feature, they probably sacrificed somewhere else. Some of the most important features include track number and index display, disc/track/elapsed/total time display, track and index programmability, disc and A-B repeat, multi-speed manual search, random track playback, headphone jack with volume control, digital output, remote control with volume control, multi-disc capability, and disc memory library.

Some players offer dynamic range compression. The high dynamic range of CDs presents a problem in environments with a low dynamic range. A compression circuit reduces the music's dynamic range to help compensate for high ambient noise conditions. This feature is particularly useful in a car player, or in a home player used to copy discs to tape for car listening.

Are the ergonomics well designed? Make sure the controls are easy to use and largely self-explanatory. Try out the controls and make sure the player does everything you expect it should. Similarly, verify that the display provides all the information you want. While you're at it, evaluate the player's responsiveness to your commands; some players have a considerable lag between your command and their response. In time, this might become very annoying.

Is the player's construction robust? Is the chassis made of metal or plastic? Do the disc drive and drawer operate smoothly and quickly, without a lot of racket? If you can manage a peek inside, are the circuit boards and components securely mounted? Does the disc drive appear to be solidly constructed?

### Performance Questions

Is the impact immunity good? When the sales people aren't looking, whomp the player a few times on the sides and top while it's playing. Good pickup servos are amazingly resistant to shock. Obviously, this test is even more crucial for a portable player.

How good is the error correction? Discs aren't indestructible, especially as they enter the harsh environments of car and portable players. Unfortunately, consistent specifications for error correction performance are not commonly available. Although error correction test discs are available, they are quite expensive and hard to find.

Even without a special test disc, it is possible to gauge a player's ability to play through errors without mistracking. You can make your own "torture disc" to test for tracking ability: take a strip of tape perhaps one millimeter wide and lay it radially across a disc data surface. A good player should play through it. Now try two strips and see if it plays. Keep loading them on until the player capitulates. While you're at it, try skipping around on the torture disc; some players are able to play straight through errrors but fail to locate damaged tracks.

Such a stripped disc simulates errors but cannot be used to fully determine a player's ability to track real-life defects. A player might perform poorly with the strips but do much better with scratches and dirt. Ideally, a badly damaged and soiled CD would make a better torture disc.

If you're caught without your torture disc, lay a few juicy fingerprints on any disc. This will stress a player with a real-life problem and may cause audible errors. Every player hiccups occasionally when it encounters a serious defect—evaluate its tenaciousness relative to other players. Repeat your impact immunity test with a torture disc; a pickup may have more trouble tracking a damaged disc.

Of course, even a normal disc contains errors, and the player's error correction and concealment circuitry must suppress their audibility. Correction strategies provide for absolutely correct data so that the error becomes nonexistent and inaudible. However, error concealment synthesizes data to the best of the circuit's ability. Because not all pickup/servo systems are equal, players' ability to read disc data varies; the poorer the data quality, the more concealment must be used. Concealment circuits aren't equal, either. The bottom line is audible errors—on some players you hear them once in a while. It isn't a mute or a click, just badly concealed data, and the distortion may be audible for an instant. On good players, you don't hear that very often.

Are there vibration problems? Airborne and structureborne vibrations from loudspeakers (CD listeners tend to play back at louder levels, which causes an augmented bass response) may cause vibration in discs that are not tightly clamped to the spindle motor shaft. As the disc vibrates, the pickup servos are worked harder, allowing greater chance for mistracking, and the result may be concealment distortion at loud listening levels. Even if the pickup tracks properly, its constant correction movements might draw excessive current from the power supply, leading to distortion in the analog output circuitry.

Checking for this problem in stereo showrooms is fun indeed. If you crank up the amplifier level, the problem may occur, but it might not audibly manifest itself because amplifier or loudspeaker overload will mask the problem. You have to crank up the level and then listen with closed-ear headphones. This is guaranteed to drive the sales staff crazy. Listen closely. On some players you may hear a deterioration of sound quality at high listening levels. It's difficult to describe the effect, but you'll know it when you hear it, if you keep an open mind. Remember that it's something you've never ever heard before in analog equipment.

### Design Questions

Does the player have separate power supplies for the servo, digital, and analog circuitry? This alleviates the problem caused by the fact that the servo system draws power intended for other circuitry and also helps isolate one circuit from another, reducing crosstalk, in the form of noise and interference, between different player circuits.

Does the player use a one- or three-beam pickup design? Don't overconcern yourself on this one. There is little difference between one-beam and three-beam designs, except on a one-to-one basis. The above tests determine the quality of the design. If it's a toss-up, opt for the one-beam type; it is inherently simpler, as we have seen in Chapter Four, and less prone to lose alignment.

Does the player have dual D/A converters? When the output data is multiplexed through a single D/A, its analog output signal must be alternately switched between the stereo channels. As discussed in Chapter Four, an 11.34 microsecond difference between left and right channels is created. The result is an interchannel phase difference. Dual D/As do not cause this phase error between channels.

On the other hand, a pair of converter chips might not be evenly matched. Some manufacturers have achieved the best of both worlds by placing both D/As on one chip, thereby ensuring good collaboration. Otherwise, dual D/A converter chips are still better than a single multiplexed chip.

Does the player have digital (oversampling) output filtering? In theory, there should be no audible difference between analog and digital output filters. In practice, the audible difference is sometimes significant. Primarily because it is much easier to design good digital filters, they tend to deliver consistently good sound. In addition, a digital filter is contained on a chip, whereas an analog filter is comprised of many discrete components. Thus the digital design yields greater reliability and long-term stability.

Furthermore, a digital filter is considerably cheaper for manufacturers to build. We hope this means they have reinvested some of that savings into the player by improving other subsystems, such as the audio output circuitry, including the gentle low-pass filter necessary to remove extreme high frequency components present at the output of a digital filter. Of course, they might have simply improved their profit margin.

In short, the question of filter design is a tough one. Many critics with golden ears are particularly impressed with the eight-times oversampling variety, but there are exceptions. Many four-times oversampling and analog-filtered players are very good. Take all advice (including this book's) with a pinch of salt, and let your own ears decide.

### Specification Questions

Do the specifications measure up? Although mid-priced players often have similar specifications, small differences begin showing up in high-priced players. In addition, independently measured specifications often reveal weaknesses. Look for a frequency response deviation of less than 0.3 dB, unfiltered total harmonic distortion plus noise (THD + N) of 0.0025% at 1 kHz and 0 dB, channel separation greater than 90 dB at 1 kHz, signal-to-noise ratio of 110 dB (A weighted), intermodulation (IM) distortion of 0.004% at 0 dB, and near-perfect phase linearity.

One specification problem to be aware of is supersonic artifacts (or at least those above 21 kHz). Beat frequency components caused by clock interactions and other high frequency signals can increase broadband distortion and decrease S/N values. When making measurements, most manufacturers insert brickwall filters to keep these spurious signals out of their published specifications, but they shouldn't be there in the first place. The answer, of course, is a player design using synchronous clocks so that beat frequencies are never generated.

### The Bottom Line

Does the player sound good? This question is tougher to answer than you might think. In general, most CD players sound okay. Most showrooms have always been a tough place to listen to anything other than the sales pitch. With digital audio, it's even rougher. The trick is to concentrate on one aspect of sound quality at a time. Play a familiar disc. Listen for badly corrected errors. Listen for stable localization. Listen for high-volume disc instability. Listen for full ambience with "air" around the music. Listen for naturally warm sound. Listen for tight bass response, smooth treble response, and low background noise. Relax. Take your time. Try several discs—one disc might bias your decision according to the type and quality of recording you're hearing. Some factors are difficult to evaluate with a music program. You might want to invest in a test disc for more critical evaluation. For example, deviations in frequency response are often exposed when one listens to noise. We discussed test discs earlier in this chapter.

When comparing players, compare only two at a time; otherwise it gets too confusing. Make sure they are playing at the same loudness level, or you'll tend to favor the louder player. Alternate between different loudspeakers, or else the loudspeaker's own coloration will bias your decision. Critical listening isn't easy, and it takes time. Sometimes it takes hours of comparison before a person can reliably choose the better player. Of course, you might have a better pair of ears. As we all become more familiar with what we're listening for in digital audio, we'll get better at it. (Manufacturers, are *you* listening?)

A shopper typically checks the player's features, construction, measured specifications, and, finally, sonic quality. In reality, though, the first thing you should do is to hook a player up and listen before your evaluation is influenced by knowledge of factors such as construction quality, the manufacturer's reputation, the price, and the specifications. While auditioning, you might even cover up the unit so that its front panel styling won't influence your decisions. Whenever possible, make double-blind listening comparisons in which the players' identities aren't revealed until you have recorded your results.

In summary, we can list the important evaluation criteria, roughly ranked in order of importance: sonic quality, robust construction, error correction and concealment performance, specifications, oversampling filter, dual D/A converters, separate power supplies, immunity to air and structureborne vibration, manufacturer, features, ergonomics, impact resistance, optical coupling, and vibration-damping chassis and parts.

## PLAYER NOTES

Unlike plants, animals, lawns and fine woolens, CD players require little care. Nevertheless, it is important to treat your player with at least a little respect. It is, after all, the most sophisticated piece of audio electronics to reach the home. The laser optics, servo system for automatic focusing and tracking, control microprocessors, and output digital-to-analog circuitry arc all high, high tech. On the other hand, they are amazingly robust, as digital electronics are wont to be. With a little consideration, your player will consistently and without complaint continue to deliver its 4.3218 million bits per second.

### Installation

When installing a CD player, avoid heat sources, including radiators and even power amplifiers. Heat is circuitry's worst enemy: it causes premature aging and failure. Ventilation is circuitry's best friend. Make sure air can flow over, under, and around the back of your player. Avoid placing the player on rugs, sofas, or in stacks of equipment. Racks, bookcases, cabinets, and built-in installations are certainly convenient, but unless they are well engineered, they can spell trouble. Heat build-up can happen all too easily. Avoid racks unless they contain fans to move the air. Otherwise, the thermal stress will shorten the components' lifespan.

Also avoid areas subject to direct sunlight, excessive dust, cold, moisture, mechanical shock, or vibration. Keep the player away from sources of 60 Hz electrical hum, such as transformers or motors. Of course, AC-powered CD players should never be used near water.

Hooking up a CD player is an easy task. First, check for transport screws. Many players have one or more screws (or buttons) on the bottom panel that are used to lock the optical pickup in place to prevent damage during transport. The pickup must be unlocked before you attempt to play a disc.

The electrical connections are located on the player's back panel. Most players have two cords to deal with: AC power and audio. If you're the cautious type, check to make sure its power requirements correspond with that supplied by the country you're in (e.g., 120 volts, 60 Hz in the U.S.A.). The player's power requirements are printed on back or clearly marked on players with switchable power supplies.

An accessory that is highly recommended is an AC line noise filter and surge suppressor, sometimes called a spike filter. Invest your money in a high-quality unit, perhaps shopping for it in a computer store. It should be inserted in-line prior to all of your audio components. No, it won't improve frequency response or clean up error concealments, but next time your power company delivers a wad of bad voltage, it might save you from a big repair bill.

The player's audio outputs contain the left and right audio signals; in most players these are analog signals, using two phono connectors. In some cases, the level of the audio outputs can be varied from the front panel. Some players have a digital output that accepts a single phono plug which carries both audio channels to an external D/A converter. Some players also feature an optical connector. A fiber optic cable is used to convey data from the player. Often there is also a digital data output on/off switch. Digital data should be switched on only when you use this output; otherwise, it could interfere with the analog output.

The analog outputs should be connected to your preamplifier's CD inputs. A digital output should be connected to the input of an external D/A converter. The converter's analog outputs are then connected to a preamplifier. Of course, switch off system power before making or breaking any connections. Finally, take time to study the owner's manual accompanying your player; you'll probably uncover some subtlety you would otherwise have overlooked.

## Other Considerations

The pickup's laser diode produces a strong electromagnetic field. This is harmless for human lifeforms, but may affect magnetic media such as audio or video cassettes, floppy disks, or even some wristwatches. In other words, don't store cassettes on top of a CD player. The field is probably significant only when the player's shielding covers have been removed, but you never know until it's too late.

The digital processing circuits inside a CD player, with their clocks clocking in the megahertz range, make ideal radio stations, jamming channels used for legitimate radio and television broadcast. CD players must be tested and must comply with Federal Communications Commission guidelines for a Class B computing device; that is, they must reasonably limit the amount of radio frequency interference they generate. In general, a player will not broadcast signals strong enough to bother your neighbors, but might very well interfere with your own reception. Several measures can be taken to minimize the trouble: reorient the receiving radio or television antenna, relocate the player with respect to the receiver, move the player away from the receiver, or plug the player into a different AC outlet so that the player and receiver are on different branch circuits. Finally, of course, interference can be terminated by turning the CD player off.

Moisture condensation can cause temporary problems. If the player is brought in from a cold to a warm location, or is placed in a very damp room, moisture may condense on the lenses inside the pickup. Should this occur, the player may not operate. Fortunately, the cure is quite inexpensive: remove the disc and leave the player turned on for about an hour. The heat generated will evaporate the moisture. Discs with condensation can be wiped dry (always wipe a disc with radial motions) and played immediately.

Although some components, such as preamplifiers and power amplifiers, may be left on—indeed, professional audio gear is specifically designed to be powered indefinitely—a consumer CD player is best turned off when not in use. This will extend the life of the player. On the other hand, some audiophiles believe that CD players require a thorough warm-up (an hour or so) before their sound quality becomes optimal. To avoid the wait, they keep their player's power on. This may have merit. For example, D/A converter manufacturers recommend a one-half hour warm-up before service technicans calibrate their devices.

The outer cabinet, front panel, and controls may be cleaned with a soft cloth lightly moistened with a mild detergent solution. Do not use any type of abrasive pad, scouring powder, or solvent such as alcohol or benzine; the latter can melt or discolor cabinet paint. If any liquid should spill into the player, unplug the unit and have it cleaned and checked by qualified personnel. Incidentally, soft drinks such as colas are particularly renowned for their ability to quickly corrode contacts and connectors.

The pickup's objective lens should be kept clean for best performance. However, never touch the lens; it is far too delicate. A little compressed air, like that used to clean a camera lens, is recommended. If absolutely necessary, an objective lens may be cleaned with lens-cleaning paper, wetted with a 50/50 mixed solvent of IPA (isopropyl alcohol) and Freon (Freon 113 CC1 F-CC1F). In the preventative maintenance department, except when inserting or removing a CD, keep the disc drawer closed to keep out dust.

If a player won't be used for an extended length of time, unplug the player from the wall outlet. This will protect the player from lightning strikes which could easily jump the player's on/off switch and cause havoc. As noted, an AC line filter is always recommended for any audio gear. When installing an audio system, route the power supply cords so that they are not likely to be stepped on or pinched by doors.

If your player has one or more transport screws, be sure to secure them prior to any transporting. Their job is to secure the sled or swing arm housing the laser pickup. Without the screws, in some models, the sled or arm is free to move about when the player is moved. Carelessness in this matter could result in a misaligned or broken laser pickup. You may well find the cost of replacing a pickup is more than the price of the player itself.

### Repairs

Depending on your own handyman abilities, a trip to the service shop might be required in the following situations: the power supply cord or plug has been damaged; objects have fallen into the player; liquid has been spilled into the player; the player has been exposed to rain; the player has been dropped or the cabinet damaged; the player does not appear to operate normally or exhibits a marked change in performance. Conversely, an unnecessary trip to the repair shop, wasted money, and incredible embarrassment can be saved by a little common sense troubleshooting.

Unless you are qualified, home repairs on broken CD players are not recommended. Be warned: there is very little inside that is user-friendly, nothing that is user-useful, but numerous things that are user-dangerous. In general, the pickup and electrical circuitry are quite sophisticated and will defy most casual attempts at calibration or repair. For the qualified, or the foolish, the player's service manual is prerequisite to attempting any major repair.

Care must be taken when working near a pickup's laser beam. The laser beam diverges as it leaves the pickup, so after the light passes through the focus point (a few millimeters from the objective lens), the light's intensity rapidly decreases with the inverse square law to an inconsequential intensity. However, the intensity at the focused spot may reach a value of $1.3 \times 10^4$ W/cm$^2$. This could damage the human eye. It would be hard to get your eye close enough to the objective lens to run any risk. Even so, to be safe, do not look at the laser light through the objective lens directly, nor through a lens or mirror. Most players have a safety interlock to defeat the laser. A disc must be loaded, and the play button must be pressed before the laser turns on. Note that, unlike videodisc players, the laser beam in a CD player is invisible to the eye.

The laser diode could be damaged by a surge current or an electrostatic discharge. For safe handling, grounding of the human body and service equipment is strongly recommended.

In general, a CD player should last a long time. The electronics are long-lived, particularly because they operate at fairly low temperatures. The laser diode will eventually burn out, but life expectancy is between 10 and 25 thousand hours of operation. When a laser burns out, the entire pickup assembly is typically replaced. Perhaps the most troublesome aspect of player longevity is the alignment of the laser pickup. Misalignment would result in mistracking or increased error concealment. Rough handling or simple drift of the servo circuits (from age and temperature) can also cause tracking and focusing problems. That would mean a trip to the repair shop.

Aside from the normal considerations of reasonable handling and the use of transport screws when shipping, there is no preventive maintenance required. Even a yearly checkup is probably not worthwhile. CD players truly exemplify the rule that if it isn't broken, don't fix it.

## DISC NOTES

Despite manufacturers' assertions that compact discs sound perfect and are indestructible, it's worth looking at imperfections in discs as well as disc mortality. Specifically, the highly complex process of disc manufacturing inevitably introduces errors into discs. For a consumer, it is important to be able to identify such errors and, if they are excessive, demand an exchange or money back from the record store. In addition, in spite of the remarkable robustness of discs, certain precautions should be observed in handling them. It's important to minimize the chances for damage after it's too late to get your money back.

### Compact Disc Defects

The manufacture of CDs, as we shall see in Chapter Seven, is a highly complex operation, and there are numerous opportunities for defects to creep into the product. Theoretically, the quality control personnel at the factory reject all substandard work, but in practice some clunkers slip through.

Problems can occur anywhere in the manufacturing chain. The master tape or the master disc itself could be defective. If it is, every CD made from that master would contain the same defect. For example, there might be a drop-out on the tape, or a dust particle on the master disc, which could cause an error in all the production discs. For that reason, quality control is very rigorous at this stage, and errors here are unusual. It's a little more likely that defects could appear in the molds used to make the CDs. These metal replicas of the original glass master disc might have a flaw, and every disc made from that mold (perhaps 10,000 CDs per mold) would duplicate the error.

An injection molding machine forms both the disc substrate itself as well as the billions of pits on the substrate's surface. If the resulting disc is warped, optically distorted, or has impurities such as contamination or air bubbles trapped inside, the laser might not be able to see the pits properly.

Any badly formed pits, perhaps caused by temperature inconsistencies in the mold, would translate into bad data. It is particularly important that the pit walls be clearly defined, because the transitions from pit to substrate surface (and vice versa) signal binary 1s. Dust is particularly troublesome to the naked discs that are still warm; when they leave the mold they hold a high static charge which attracts dust particles. A dust particle would disrupt large amounts of data.

Dust particles are problematic to the metalizing process. Any dust particles on the disc prevent the metal molecules from adhering to the disc substrate properly, creating a pinhole in the metal layer. The reflection of the laser beam will be disrupted by the pinhole, and the data in the pits will be lost. Pinholes occur all too often. Check your discs for yourself. Hold them up to a bright light, and you'll sometimes see several (or many) holes in the aluminum layer, letting the light shine through. On some discs, the printed label conceals the pinholes. Other metalizing problems, such as a pebbly "orange peel" surface, can reflect the laser beam unevenly.

The final production steps are not especially prone to errors. The top protection layer is applied as a fast-drying plastic liquid; as long as it spreads evenly and covers the disc's entire surface, there should be no problem. The printed label is even easier; problems typically yield only cosmetic defects.

In some manufacturing methods, the center hole is molded during the injection molding process (the hole is smoothly shaped), while in other methods, the center hole is punched out after the top layer is applied (the hole is often rough). Either way (more likely in punching), the center hole could be off center or misshapen, resulting in an unplayable disc.

At the end of the manufacturing process, discs are checked by both automated and human checkers. While many bad discs (perhaps 10 percent) are rejected, random errors on individual discs can pass by unnoticed. If defects are detected before metalizing, the rugged polycarbonate is sometimes sold to companies which make football helmets.

## Evaluation Criteria

The complexity of CD manufacturing makes it an imperfect art, and the reproduction system has been designed with this in mind. As we have seen, all discs contain error correction encoding, and all players use error correction decoding to correct many errors. Error concealment methods, by which players use cunning strategies to hide flaws, can minimize larger problems. In short, although a disc may contain thousands of small errors, few or none of them are typically audible. An especially bad disc, however, played on a player with less than adequate error concealment ability, can result in audible errors.

It is wise to check a few quality criteria (if possible, before you buy). Although they are audibly insignificant, look for cosmetic defects such as a poorly printed label or rough edges. Any defect in the data area that is visible might cause an audible error. Check the disc for pinholes in the metal layer by holding it up to the light. A few are permissible; many are not. Use a magnifying glass to look for particles, scratches, bumps, or roughness on the reflective surface or on the substrate.

Load the disc in your player and check to see that it initializes and plays all tracks properly without skipping. If the player gets stuck, skips, or emits bursts of clicks, the disc is obviously defective. If a disc plays improperly, and no scratches are visible, the problem may be a warped disc. This can upset the laser readout considerably. To check for warpage, lay the disc on a flat surface, such as glass, and press down in the center. Turn the disc over and press again. If you detect movement of over one millimeter (about 1/32 inch), the disc is defective.

Finally, listen to the disc carefully. Errors will most likely be subtle. Preferably through headphones, listen for errors such as soft, quick clicks and pops and poorly concealed errors that occur as short bursts of distortion. How often do such audible disc errors occur? Very rarely. Depending on your perception, perhaps one out of 100 discs might require exchange.

An almost random variable in diagnosing bad discs is the player you're using. There are sometimes surprising irregularities between players' error correction performance and the type of error. A player might be a champion at handling a badly metalized disc, yet mistrack on a simple scratch. The point is that pickup and error correction circuit designs vary among manufacturers and have different performance results. Until types of errors are classified and standardized, it will be difficult for consumers to consistently evaluate a player's abilities.

It is ironic that, because of the CD's fidelity, it is often very difficult to differentiate between extraneous noises present in the original recording and disc problems. For example, in orchestral recordings you'll often hear squeaking chairs, respiratory and intestinal problems, singing conductors, air conditioning rumble, randomly slamming doors, and even outside traffic noise—things obviously beyond your control.

To help advise consumers of the technical origins of a disc, many record labels have adopted a code similar to one proposed by SPARS (Society of Professional Audio Recording Services). Its three letters describe the type of tape recorder technology used at the three primary stages of a recording: session recording, mix down and editing, and mastering. For example, a CD labeled ADD would indicate that it had been originally recorded on an analog tape recorder, mixed down to a digital recorder, and mastered to a digital recorder. Since all CDs are derived from a digital master, the code's third letter is always a D. Thus a CD labelled with an AAD code is purely an analog recording released on CD. Of course, there is no guarantee that a DDD recording will sound any better, nor does the code provide information on any analog signal processing devices or mixing consoles used, or transfers that may have taken place during an "all-digital" DDD recording.

### Disc Care

Of course, aggressively abusive treatment will ruin even the most perfectly made disc. Although impervious to conditions that annihilate other audio media, a CD is best treated with the kind of respect that its high technology deserves. The following guidelines for disc handling should guarantee that your CDs will still sound just as good for your grandchildren. Of course, by that time they will be terribly obsolete, interesting only as curiosities.

1. Handle the disc by its edge or center hole. To keep the disc clean, avoid touching the data surface.
2. Do not stick paper or tape on the label surface; this probably won't hurt the disc, but might jam the disc drive.
3. Because the CD's data surface is embedded directly beneath the label, protected by only a thin layer, this top surface is more vulnerable to catastrophic damage. A scratch that penetrates the label will directly destroy a considerable amount of data, whereas a scratch on the bottom data layer can often be overlooked by the optical pickup.
4. Do not write anything on the label surface with a ballpoint pen. This certainly will hurt the disc. Furthermore, do not use a marking pen; the solvent could penetrate the top layer and deteriorate the metalization layer. However, the polycarbonate (substrate) side of the disc is chemically impervious to most everything.

5. Do not expose the disc to high temperature or humidity for an extended time—for example, in a car parked in direct sunlight. The considerable rise in temperature could warp the disc. Polycarbonate begins to soften around 220 degrees Fahrenheit.

6. After subjecting the disc to extreme cold (which is not recommended), give it half an hour to return to room temperature before you play it.

7. If you must, clean a disc with a soft, moistened cloth. If possible, pat it dry. Otherwise, wipe the disc from the center out (like spokes in a wheel), and never wipe across the disc as you would an LP. This will prevent scratches from paralleling a pit track and impeding error correction. A scratch across the pit tracks is easier to correct. Modest fingerprints or smudges will not overly affect the quality of reproduction; their scrupulous removal might cause more permanent harm (in the form of scratches, for example) than good. To reiterate, preventive cleaning is unnecessary and potentially harmful. Clean only when it is required.

8. Do not use solvents such as benzine, thinner, volatile solvents, commercially available cleaners, or antistatic sprays intended for analog discs. These could irreparably damage the CD's surface.

9. After cleaning a disc, return it to its case. To prevent warpage, make sure the disc is not subjected to stress.

Although largely unnecessary in this author's opinion, a commercial cleaning solution might be useful in cases of particularly dirty discs (the surfaces, not the lyrics). A liquid cleaning fluid, a soft cleaning pad, and a soft brush should do the job. Avoid aerosol sprays; the resulting evaporation off the disc rapidly cools it, possibly leading to minute surface cracks.

There are also numerous disc cleaning machines on the market. Although most are suitable (at least for the incurably lazy), some are potentially dangerous to your discs. They wipe the disc with either a circular motion or straight across, potentially creating microscopic scratches along the pit track. Make sure any disc cleaning machine wipes the disc only radially.

If the data side of a disc is badly scratched and all else fails, you might try removing the scratch: apply a little polishing compound, such as the presoftened white variety, with a soft, dampened cloth. Never use a rubbing compound. Rub the damaged area with a light motion until you restore the plastic's shine. A little water on the cloth prevents the compound from drying. Remove any residue when you have finished. If that doesn't help, nothing will. If the scratch is on the upper label side, abandon all hope immediately and panic.

## FOR FURTHER READING

Audio Precision. "Application Note 1: Compact Disc Player Testing with the Audio Precision System One, Revision 1." Beaverton, Oreg.: Audio Precision, December, 1987.

EIAJ (Electronic Industries Association of Japan). "Methods of Measurement for CD Players." *EIAJ Document CP-307.*

EIAJ (Electronic Industries Association of Japan). "Test Disk for CD Players." *EIAJ Document CP-308.*

FCC (Federal Communications Commission). "How to Identify and Resolve Radio-TV Interference Problems." Washington, D.C.: US Government Printing Office, Stock Number 004-000-00345-4.

Feldman, L. "A New CD Test Standard." *Audio Magazine* 69(12):54–58, December, 1985.

Finger, Robert. "On the Use of Computer-Generated Dithered Test Signals." *Journal of the Audio Engineering Society* 35(6):434–45, June, 1987.

Ford, H. "CD Test Discs." *Studio Sound* 29(1):62–63, January, 1987.

Halbert, Joel M., and R. Allen Belcher. "Selection of Test Signals for DSP-Based Testing of Digital Audio Systems." *Journal of the Audio Engineering Society* 34(7/8):546–55, July/August, 1986.

Halbert, Joel M., and M. A. Shill. "An 18-Bit Digital-to-Analog Converter for High-Performance Digital Audio Applications." *Journal of the Audio Engineering Society* 36(6):469–80, June, 1988.

Lenk, J. D. *Complete Guide to Compact Disc (CD) Player Troubleshooting and Repair.* Englewood Cliffs, N. J.: Prentice Hall, 1986.

Sony. *Compact Disc Technology Update.* Sony White Paper, March, 1988.

Sweeney, D. *Demystifying Compact Discs: A Guide to Digital Audio.* Blue Ridge Summit, Penn.: Tab, 1986.

Takai, M., and S. Matsuoka. "Real Time Measurement of Jitter in CD Players." *AES Preprint No. 2414,* 81st Convention, 1986.

Yamaha. *Yamaha Hi-Bit Technology.* Yamaha White Paper, June, 1987.

*Chapter Six*

# Diverse Disc Formats

## INTRODUCTION

The versatility of the compact disc has quickly become apparent to manufacturers and users alike. Since music is an extremely storage-hungry phenomenon, the CD must have a tremendous storage capacity. To take further advantage of that capacity, other CD formats have been devised. CD-ROM was devised, incorporating non-audio data, such as data base and software data. CD-I and DVI are specific applications of CD-ROM. Their data storage opportunities include audio-visual information stored in a user-interactive manner. CD-V merges the compact disc audio format with the Laservision video format. CD-WO is a write-once format allowing users to store their own data. In addition, recordable/erasable CD formats have been developed. CD + G features storage for graphics and other non-musical data. A smaller diameter compact disc, the CD-3 is used for applications requiring shorter playing time.

## CD-ROM

The information storage and retrieval industry is characterized by some mind-boggling statistics: the Library of Congress has 83 million items on its 535 miles of shelves and 6 million microfilms. The library houses 21 million books, 400,000 newspapers, and 10 million movies, photographs, and other artifacts. The National Archives has about 6 billion pages of images, 16 million photographs, and 5 million maps and charts in its collection. The Internal Revenue Service has about 2 billion completed tax forms on file. In 1985, 18 million American office workers each generated enough paperwork to fill 4 file cabinets.

Clearly, the need for large-capacity, fast-retrieval storage is critical. The compact disc offers several advantages over paper or magnetic storage. Foremost is its high data density. An audio CD contains a large amount of data, deceptively consolidated into a few tracks of music. The CD-ROM standard is derived from the audio CD standard, but defines a format for general data storage. For example, a CD-ROM telephone book for the United States would be feasible. Assuming 100 million listed telephones, and 40 bytes of information associated with each one, the total of 4 Gbytes could be stored on about seven discs—a stack about 1/2 inch high. Moreover, any telephone number could be accessed in a few seconds. This kind of storage is the intent of the Compact Disc-Read Only Memory (CD-ROM) format.

### Applications

CD-ROM is the logical extension of the compact disc format toward the much broader application of information storage in general. Rather than being used to store music, the CD format can be treated as a read-only memory system used for any kind of program material. It is intended mainly as a medium for professional databases and mass storage for computer-related applications. In short, CD-ROM is a cost-effective way of distributing large amounts of information, especially information not requiring frequent updating.

The amount of data stored on a CD-ROM is, of course, equal to the amount of information stored on an audio CD, but a ROM underscores just how information-hungry a music recording is. For example, if you were to download all the information from one fully loaded CD-ROM at 300 baud (for example, transmitting it to a friend by means of a modem) for 24 hours a day, it would take 184 days to transmit the contents.

Think of CD-ROM as electronic paper (and a lot of it); anything publishable is a candidate for CD-ROM. However, a CD-ROM is much more efficient than paper. For example, the Grolier Academic Encyclopedia is available on a CD-ROM, but the text occupies only about 60 megabytes, or 1/10 of the disc storage space. A comprehensive index, occupying another 60 megabytes, greatly facilitates data access. You enter a subject and a listing of entries comes up on the screen. These entries are far more detailed than those in a conventional encyclopedia because the system's catalog can access many entries, comparing your request with the contents of the entire encyclopedia. A phrase like "freedom of speech" might have only a few citations in the index of a conventional encyclopedia, but in a CD-ROM-based system every mention of that phrase in the entire encyclopedia would be displayed. You can scroll to any entry and read the full text. The words you searched for are highlighted in the text.

In short, CD-ROM forms the basis for a new electronic publishing medium applicable to book publishing, dictionaries, technical manuals, business catalogs, computer storage, expert systems, artificial intelligence, and so on. It represents an entirely new technology of information dissemination.

### Data Format

Although a CD-ROM disc is visually identical to a music CD, it employs a modified data format; a CD-ROM disc automatically identifies itself as differing from an audio CD (through the Q subcode channel). Data in a music CD is derived from the 44.1 kHz sampled signal, with 16-bit quantization. The 16 bits are divided into higher and lower 8-bit bytes. These data bytes (before EFM modulation) are grouped into frames of 24 bytes, and parity and a synchronization word are added. While satisfactory for music applications, a frame is too short for numerical applications, and there is no provision for addressing. A solution was derived from the subcode field in which subcode from 98 frames is summed. In CD-ROM, 98 24-byte frames are summed; thus the effective size for the data area becomes 2352 (24 bytes × 98 frames), a workable area. This data format is shown in figure 6.1.

This 98-frame area is called a sector and it forms the basic CD-ROM data unit. This block is sufficiently long to handle numerical data as one sector without altering the audio CD format. Audio data is replaced by user data and system data that occupy 2048 bytes. The remaining 304 bytes are used for synchronization, headers, mode selection, and extended error detection and correction. Because there are 74 blocks output per second, a disc could theoretically hold a maximum of 333,000 blocks, each with 2048 bytes of user data, for a total of 681,984,000 bytes. A 60-minute equivalent disc would hold 270,000 blocks, or 552,960,000 bytes.

In practice, a storage capacity of approximately 550 megabytes is often utilized. In this way the outer 5 millimeters of the disc data area (equivalent to 14 minutes of music) are not used. This area is the hardest to manufacture and the hardest for users to keep clean. In any case, this is a large storage area, approximately equivalent to 1500 half-megabyte floppy disks, 275,000 pages of alphanumerics, 18,000 pieces of computer graphics, or 3,600 still video pictures.

With CD-ROM, PCM data is recorded with EFM, as in audio CDs. The first 12 bytes from the 2352 byte block are used as a synchronization word. The next 4 bytes form a header field used for time and address flags. Specifically, the header contains three address bytes and a mode byte. The address bytes store location as time: one address byte holds minutes (74 minutes maximum), the second byte holds seconds (0 to 59), and the third

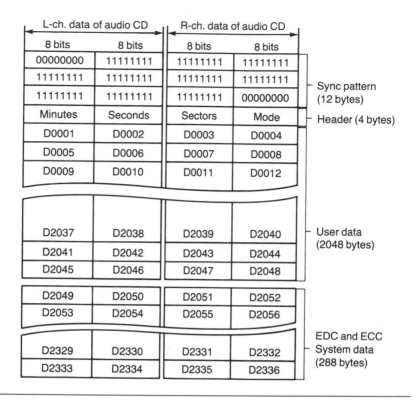

Figure 6.1 *CD-ROM data sectors are formed from 98 consecutive CD frames. (Courtesy Nippon Columbia)*

holds the block number within the second (75 blocks per second). For example, an address of 59-20-45 denotes the 45th block in the 20th second of the 59th minute on the disc. Although this repeats information already found in the Q subcode channel, it speeds and provides greater accuracy for searching.

The mode byte indicates the nature of the user data; for example, computer data is distinguished from audio-visual data. Figure 6.2 shows the three modes that are used. The Mode 0 format is used for null data. The Mode 1 format specifies that 2048 bytes of each block are devoted to user data. The Mode 2 format allows for 2336 bytes of user data. The difference between Mode 1 and 2 is that Mode 1 uses 288 bytes to provide an additional layer of error detection and correction (EDC/ECC). This is in addition to the basic error correction used on all compact discs, ensuring a level of data integrity essential for information that does not degrade gracefully, such as text and database binary code. Mode 2 trades this benefit of data security for maximum data rate by making the additional 288 bytes per sec-

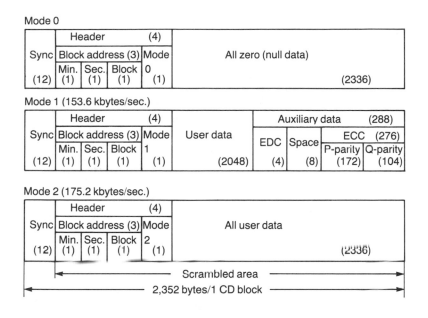

Figure 6.2 *Three modes are defined in the CD-ROM format. Mode 1 provides for extended error detection and correction. Mode 2 permits more user data. Mode 0 is a null mode. (Courtesy Nippon Columbia)*

tor available for user data. The basic error correction encoding is suitable for gracefully degrading data such as video and audio. Because of extended error correction, Mode 1 will have the most numerous applications; each block contains exactly 2K (2 × 1024) bytes of user data. The 2048-byte area is where the actual CD-ROM data resides.

### Error Correction

As noted, the remaining 288 bytes, called system data, provide for a higher degree of error detection and correction (EDC/ECC). This is a prerequisite to successful numerical data storage, which is more demanding than audio data. This system data forms an extended error correction code (EDC and layered ECC) existing independently and in addition to the cross interleave Reed-Solomon error correction code already encoded for each CD frame. The error rate is improved over that of an audio CD. Theoretically, CD-ROM bit error rates will be between $10^{-16}$ and $10^{-17}$, or one uncorrectable bit in every $10^{16}$ or $10^{17}$ bits. The extended code may be processed either by hardware circuitry contained in the CD-ROM player or by a host computer.

The CD-ROM standard recommends that burst errors in the RF signal due to local defects should include almost no C2 uncorrectable errors. Two methods may be used to define the required disc quality: (1) With a simple C1 and C2 error correction decoder, no more than one symbol error may occur in a data block measured at the input of the C2 decoder. (2) The number of successive C1-uncorrectable blocks should be less than seven. A block is called C1-uncorrectable if more than one symbol is erroneous. A symbol is called erroneous if one or more bits are erroneous.

CD-ROM production begins with a master data tape or tapes, recorded in computer magnetic tape format. The data is entered into a pre-mastering minicomputer where the data is placed into the CD-ROM format (header, error correction, subcode, and so forth are generated). Following pre-mastering, actual disc production is identical to that of audio CDs, albeit with greater quality control to ensure accuracy of data.

### CD-ROM Players

While CD-ROM uses a data format similar to that of music CDs, the players are not compatible. A CD-ROM player contains laser optics, modulation, and error correction, but D/A conversion and audio output sections are replaced with a computer interface to output the ROM data to a host computer, such as the one shown in figure 6.3. Data is transferred to the host computer in blocks of 2K bytes. Using the header field, the host computer verifies the sector address in minutes, seconds, and blocks. The disc table of contents (TOC) can be transferred to the CD-ROM player and used to locate a requested track.

The average data transfer rate is 75 sectors per second, or 153.6 Kbytes per second for a constant linear velocity (CLV) of 1.2 meters per second. Access time for any point on a disc is less than a second.

Because it is not tied to one specific operating system or data processor, CD-ROM devices can be interfaced with all existing and future computer systems. CD-ROM is limited only by the capabilities of the operating system and microprocessor in the host computer.

### The CD-ROM Standard

It is important to note that the CD-ROM standard as specified in the *Yellow Book* available to licensees, unlike the audio CD standard, does *not* link CD-ROM to any specific application. The format is thus transparent. It does *not* define the type of information that is stored in the user areas of Mode 1 and Mode 2. Hence the user data may be text, video, software, graphics, audio, and so forth. Nor is the encoding principle for various types of information defined. The means for encoding or compressing text,

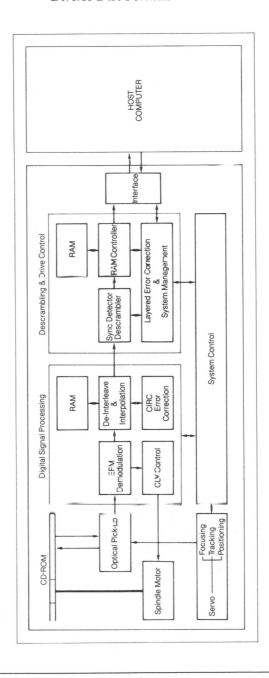

Figure 6.3    *Block diagram of a CD-ROM drive and interface to host computer.*
*(Courtesy Sony)*

graphics, audio, or video are not specified. Furthermore, the layout of information on the disc is not defined. The standard does not indicate where and how to store the directory, how to identify the beginning or end of a file, or how to open a file. The CD-ROM standard has been enhanced to include the CD-ROM XA (extended architecture) format. It incorporates some of the audio and video technology of the CD-I format to form a bridge between CD-ROM and CD-I. CD-ROM XA Audio contains CD-I's B- and C-level audio standards, and CD-ROM XA Screen Presentation contains CD-I's 640 × 480 pixel resolution CLUT, single-plane graphics, and ISO 8859/1 character set. As with any CD-ROM disc, CD-ROM XA is not dependent on a specific operating system.

Because the CD-ROM standard does not provide a logical file structure for CD-ROM media, software developers have implemented their own file formats, as well as extensions to common operating systems environments such as MS-DOS, VMS, etc. One group of vendors, the High Sierra Group, developed a proposal for a standard CD-ROM logical file structure. This has been codified by the International Standards Organization (ISO) as standard ISO/DIS 9660, "Volume and File Structure of CD-ROM for Information Interchange." All information on CD-ROMs that follow this standard can be made readable as standard files in all operating system environments. In addition, the logical file structure proposed by the High Sierra Group is forward compatible with CD-I equipment, so that CD-ROM discs will operate on CD-I systems. On the other hand, a CD-ROM system will not be capable of processing information on a CD-I disc, unless the CD-ROM system uses the processor, operating system, and audio and video encoding as specified in the CD-I format.

## CD-I

Compact Disc-Interactive (CD-I) is a special application of the CD-ROM format. Rather than store specific data on a CD-ROM, or music on an audio CD, CD-I permits storage of a simultaneous combination of audio, video, graphics, text, and data, all functioning in a defined, interactive format. CD-I is thus a multimedia extension of digital audio found on CD-Audio discs. Because CD-I players will reproduce conventional CD-Audio discs, CD-I is also an upscale CD-Audio system.

The CD-I format defines both hardware and software standards, much like the audio CD format. Although CD-ROM can also store text, graphics, and so forth, CD-I defines a special integration of such functions. Because CD-I is an interactive medium, its information may be accessed through a dialogue procedure. The system can present the user with alternatives that can be used to steer the user to the desired information.

The specification for the CD-I standard is detailed in the *Green Book* available to all CD-I licensees. CD-I is a specific application of CD-ROM, with rigidly defined implementations as in the audio CD format. The CD-I standard defines the following:

(1) How various types of information, such as video, audio, text, executable code, and graphics, will be distinguished and identified on the media.

(2) How each type of information will be encoded, including specification for several formats of high-, medium-, or low-resolution video, audio, graphics, data compaction, and so forth.

(3) How the logical layout of files will be handled on the disc.

(4) How hardware will read discs and decode the contained information.

CD-I is specified in detail because it is targeted for the mass consumer market as a user-friendly, standardized system. It is thus important for all present and future CD-I discs to be interchangeable and to play in all present and future CD-I players.

### Applications

CD-I systems are single-medium systems, containing both the operational program and the information itself, so that no secondary media such as floppy disks are required for boot-up. In addition, CD-I is intended to ride piggyback on other electronics products, such as CD-Audio players and television, for multimedia presentation. CD-I uses include automotive applications such as maps, navigation, real-time animation, and diagnostics. Education and training applications include do-it-yourself formats, home learning, interactive training, reference books, albums, and talking books. Entertainment applications include music plus text, notes and pictures, action games, strategy games, adventure games, and activity simulation. Creative leisure applications include drawing and painting, filming, and composing. Work applications include document processing, and information retrieval and analysis.

A single CD-I disc might contain over 17 hours of audio, 7,000 color pictures, 150,000 typed pages, or any combination of the three. Thus CD-I applications are diverse. For example, a CD-I dictionary might contain a word and its definition, as well as spoken pronunciation, pictures, and cross referencing to synonyms, antonyms, word relationships, origins, and translations into foreign languages.

A single CD-I disc could contain a biography of a composer, providing textual information, pictures, recorded examples of his music played while the score is displayed, and a complete catalog of his musical works, as well as available recordings. Another application is the "teach-yourself" or "how-to-do-it" field; the CD-I's ability to convey text, pictures and diagrams combined with sound make it ideally suited. For example, the sound of a motorcycle engine in various stages of tuning could be reproduced on the disc. A hobbyist's book on ornithology could reproduce bird calls. Tourists could obtain a multimedia preview of popular vacation spots. Music lovers could define the parameters of reproduced music using elastic music programs. Fictional works could be provided with a labyrinth of plot deviations, differing each time the book is read, steered at the discretion of the reader.

### Data Format

These applications require flexibility in audio and video quality levels. Thus audio fidelity, or video resolution and color coding, can be selected. Longer playing times are achieved by dividing a disc into channels, the number of which would depend on the quality of the audio and video programs. In addition, real-time requirements for interactivity necessitated the adoption of executable object code as the coding method for application software. Multimedia applications also call for physical interleaving of the three basic types of data (audio, video, and text/binary) to ensure synchronized presentation of different data types. Finally, the disc must provide efficient storage for both data that degrades gracefully (audio and video) and data that does not (text/binary). The former thus requires maximum bandwidth, while the latter requires extended error detection and correction.

The CD-I data format may be considered a subset of the CD-ROM data format. A CD-I system is designed to read CD-I discs, compatible CD-ROM discs, and audio CD discs. The CD-I format provides for this three-way compatibility. It uses a sub-header and two physical formats (referred to as Forms), as shown in figure 6.4. The sub-header (SH in the figure) is used for real-time physical interleaving of data, while the two forms define two levels of data integrity.

Form 1 is intended for text, computer data, and highly compressed visual data; EDC/ECC (extended error detection and correction) is used.

Form 1                                    Form 2

Figure 6.4    *The CD-I format uses two forms for extended error detection and correction, or for greater storage capacity. (Courtesy Philips)*

The extended error code (CIRC encoding) used is the same as for CD-ROM Mode 1. In Form 1, user data occupies 2048 bytes, and 280 bytes are reserved for extended error detection and correction codes. Form 2 is intended for real-time audio and video; EDC/ECC is omitted. In Form 2, user data occupies 2324 bytes. Data is recorded to disc with EFM modulation.

To differentiate one kind of CD-I data from the other, a sub-header is placed immediately after the regular 16-byte CD-ROM sync/address/mode header. Depending on the kind of data in that block, the data is directed to the appropriate circuitry for reproduction, display, or processing. In Form 1, the 8-byte space usually found between the header and the data area is omitted to compensate for the eight bytes used by the sub-header. This yields 2048 bytes. Otherwise, in Form 2, 2324 user bytes are available, which is eight less than in CD-ROM Mode 2.

The compatibility hierarchy of the CD family is summarized in figure 6.5. When only a physical format compatibility is required, then specific

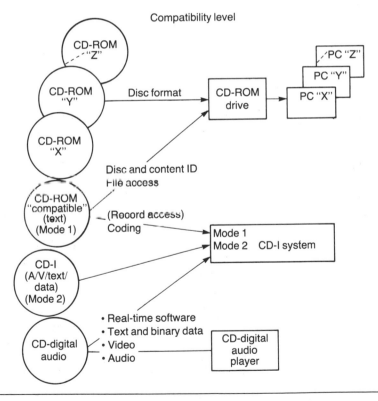

Figure 6.5 *A compatibility hierarchy exists between CD-Audio, CD-ROM, and CD-I. (Courtesy Philips)*

CD-ROM discs may be associated with specific systems, as shown at the top of the figure. At a second level, with professional text-oriented contents, a bridge exists between CD-ROM and CD-I, based on the Mode 1 format. For the consumer marketplace, a further level of compatibility is required so that all CD-I discs are playable on all CD-I systems. However, some discs may contain data not recognizable by a lower level (base case) player. In addition, audio CD discs may be played on CD-I systems. To summarize, CD-I discs are based on the CD-ROM Mode 2 format. CD-ROM/CD-I compatible discs are based on the CD-ROM Mode 1 format as specified by the High Sierra Group. The CD-I system is capable of reading audio CD discs.

The CD-I format calls for a total storage capacity of approximately 650 Mbytes. Because a CD-I disc is recorded with constant linear velocity, a constant readout rate of 75 sectors (or frames) per second is achieved. This results in a data transfer rate of 150 kbytes per second for Form 1 (and Mode 1) and 170.2 kbytes per second for Form 2. In both cases, this represents user data, excluding headers, and so forth.

### CD-I Audio

The CD-I format offers five levels of audio quality, to be selected according to the need for fidelity. These levels are shown in table 6.1. To allow for extended video information, data compression techniques may be used to reduce the storage space required to encode the audio program. A CD-DA mode uses linear 16-bit PCM with 44.1 kHz sampling rate, yielding an audio bandwidth of 20 kHz. The quality duplicates that of stereo audio CDs. Alternatively, 8- or 4-bit adaptive delta pulse code modulation (ADPCM) is used for three levels of varying fidelity. The "A" Hi-Fi audio level uses 8-bit ADPCM with a sampling rate of 37.8 kHz, yielding an audio bandwidth of 18 kHz. The quality is similar to that of vinyl LP records. The "B" Mid-Fi audio level uses 4-bit ADPCM with a 37.8 kHz sampling rate, yielding an audio bandwidth of 18 kHz. The quality is similar to that of an FM broadcast. The "C" Speech audio level uses 4-bit ADPCM with an 18.9 kHz sampling rate, yielding an audio bandwidth of 9 kHz. The quality is similar to that of an AM broadcast. The CD-I format also supports an "information audio level" in which phonetic information is encoded. Its quality is similar to that of a telephone. Because the data is not fully decoded by hardware, but uses both the microprocessor and the ADPCM audio decoder, there is a slight delay during which the phonetic information is synthesized for output.

An audio program may be divided into multiple channels (each with a maximum of 74 minutes of playing time) stored in parallel across the disc playing surface. The 16-bit PCM channel is stereo; the three ADPCM modes can be recorded in either stereo or monaural. The number of chan-

| Level | Encoding | Sampling Rate | Word Length | Signal-to-Noise Ratio |
|---|---|---|---|---|
| CD-Audio | PCM | 44.1 kHz | 16 | 98 dB |
| A | ADPCM | 37.8 kHz | 8 | 90 dB |
| B | ADPCM | 37.8 kHz | 4 | 60 dB |
| C | ADPCM | 18.9 kHz | 4 | 60 dB |
| Information | phonetic | – | – | – |

| Level | Bandwidth | Number of Channels | Data for 1 Second of Sound | Typical Playing Time |
|---|---|---|---|---|
| CD-Audio | 20 kHz | 1 stereo | 171.1 kbytes | 1 hour |
| A | 17 kHz | 2 stereo | 85.1 kbytes | 2 hours |
|  |  | 4 mono | 42.5 kbytes | 4 hours |
| B | 17 kHz | 4 mono | 42.5 kbytes | 4 hours |
|  |  | 8 stereo | 21.3 kbytes | 8 hours |
| C | 8.5 kHz | 8 stereo | 21.3 kbytes | 8 hours |
|  |  | 16 mono | 10.6 kbytes | 16 hours |
| Information | – | – | – | 10,000 hrs |

Table 6.1 *The CD-I audio format provides for five audio quality levels.*

nels increases as the fidelity level decreases. Of course, there are always twice as many monaural channels as stereo channels. Based on a CD-Audio stereo program length of 1 hour, the "A" Hi-Fi level would permit two stereo or four monaural channels of 4 hours; the "B" Mid-Fi level would permit four stereo or eight monaural channels of 8 hours, and the "C" Speech level permits eight stereo or sixteen monaural channels of 16 hours. The Information audio level permits storage of 10,000 hours of speech database. The parallel audio channels may store simultaneous data (e.g., a story in different languages) or sequentially-played data. With the latter, there is a 1- to 3-second pause when switching from the end of one channel to the beginning of the next channel.

The audio information on a disc might share its storage capacity with video or other information. Given the different quality levels, one hour of audio leaves greater or lesser storage space for video information. Figure 6.6 illustrates the ratios. Similarly, the amount of video information depends on its quality level.

### The CD-I ADPCM Audio Format

ADPCM combines elements of pulse code modulation (PCM) encoding and delta modulation (DM) encoding. Because of its ability to store digital data with fewer bits, ADPCM is extremely efficient. On the other hand, ADPCM requires additional processing beyond regular PCM for both encoding and decoding. With PCM, the audio signal is sampled, and the amplitude is quantized and coded into binary pulses; the code permits the determination of the quantized value. With delta modulation the audio signal is sampled, but the size of each quantized staircase step is kept constant. Furthermore, the staircase can move by only one quantization level at a time. Thus the quantized signal must either increase by one step size or decrease by one step size at each sample time. Delta modulation thus encodes the difference from one sample to the next, as shown in figure 6.7.

Unfortunately, delta modulation faces several problems. The accuracy of the encoding is directly dependent on the size of the positive- and negative-going steps—the smaller the steps, the better the approximation to the audio signal. However, when the signal is changing rapidly, small steps cannot keep up, as shown in figure 6.8. The problem can be solved by

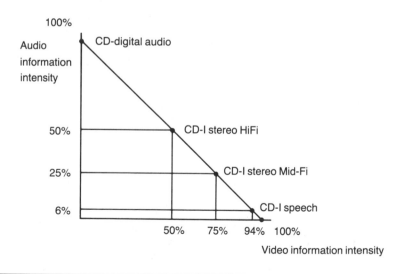

Figure 6.6 *Disc storage space dictates a trade-off between video and audio information capacity. (Courtesy Philips)*

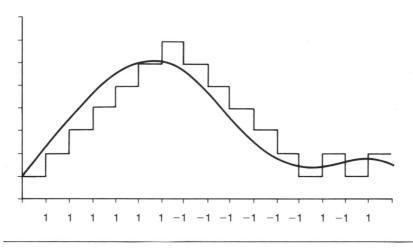

Figure 6.7    *Delta modulation encodes the difference from one sample to the next.*

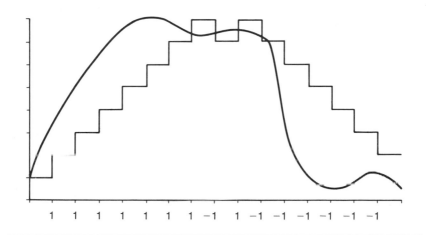

Figure 6.8    *A delta modulation system may not be able to respond to a rapidly changing audio amplitude. The result is slope overload distortion.*

increasing the sampling rate, but this detracts from the efficiency of the scheme.

One variation on delta modulation is adaptive delta modulation (ADM). With ADM the quantization step size is varied according to the behavior of the audio signal, illustrated in figure 6.9. Large steps are used for fast-changing waveforms so the system can keep on track. Similarly, small steps are used to maintain resolution for slowly changing waveforms.

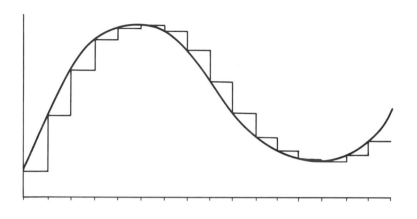

Figure 6.9    *With adaptive delta modulation, step size can be varied.*

Various algorithms may be used to select the proper step size. For example, alternating data polarity would indicate good tracking, and the increment size would be reduced for even greater accuracy. When continuous polarity is present, the waveform's amplitude is clearly changing quickly, so larger steps are selected. However, certain conditions, such as simultaneous high frequencies and high amplitudes, demand large steps which increase quantization noise. This can produce modulation noise in which the noise floor becomes a function of the signal itself.

Adaptive delta pulse code modulation (ADPCM) combines the difference signal of DM with the binary code of PCM; instead of a 1-bit correction signal, a greater number of bits are used. A PCM word is recorded or transmitted and used to reconstruct the audio staircase. The ADPCM used in the CD-I format uses 4- or 8-bit words, depending on the level of sound quality required. With a 4-bit system, correction information is available at one of sixteen levels, which provides better resolution. Since each of the quantization levels is assigned a step size scale factor, step sizes may be adapted with greater accuracy, because more step size information is available. The scale factors are based on the statistics of the signal itself; for example, scale factors for an ADPCM circuit designed to process speech would be selected differently from those for a system designed to process music.

The ADPCM system employed in the CD-I format may be considered a bit rate reduction technique. This technique is based on the fact that the amplitude and spectrum distribution of audio signals tends to be concentrated in a specific region. The scale factors and other coding elements in the CD-I ADPCM format take advantage of these statistical properties of audio. During encoding, the original audio data has a sampling rate of 44.1

kHz. So a sampling rate converter is used to reduce the sampling rate to 37.8 kHz or 18.9 kHz, depending on the CD-I audio quality level to be used. Word length is then compressed from the original 16 bits to either 8 or 4 bits per sample. A bit rate reduction (BRR) encoder accomplishes this. According to fluctuations in the frequency distribution of the audio signal, it selects different delta PCM modes. It also employs companding to increase signal dynamic range. Range and filter information, along with other residual data, are added at the block encoder. A subheader is added. Audio data is multiplexed with video or computer data, a sync word and header are added, and error detection/correction and EFM encoding are performed during disc mastering.

Decoding is accomplished in the CD-I player. EFM demodulation and error detection/correction decoding are effected, and headers are removed. Interpolation is performed if error flags are present, and ADPCM audio data is block-decoded and expanded to linear 16-bit form by the BRR decoder. D/A conversion, low-pass filtering, and de-emphasis completes the audio processing.

At a proper sampling rate ADPCM performs competitively with regular PCM. If the signal were always near its maximum frequency, ADPCM's performance would be similar to PCM's. With audio signals, however, this is almost never the case. Since the instantaneous audio frequency is relatively low, the signal is changing more slowly. Amplitude changes are therefore smaller, so ADPCM's quantization error is less than that for PCM. Thus in theory, ADPCM can achieve better signal resolution for the same number of quantization bits.

As implemented in the CD-I format, ADPCM's fidelity is lower than the PCM signal on an audio CD, but it is suitable for many CD-I applications, particularly when speech comprises the audio program. ADPCM is well suited for the CD-I format because relatively fewer bits are needed to achieve good performance.

### CD-I Video

A CD-I disc can store video material compatible with both the NTSC (America and Japan) and PAL/SECAM (Europe) television standards. CD-I discs may be manufactured to provide either 525 scanning lines (NTSC) or 625 scanning lines (PAL). Because CD-I visual information is coded digitally and because the digital coding is the same for all television standards, either type disc is playable on any standard television. When a standard disc is played on a corresponding standard television (525 through 525, or 625 through 625), negligible visual distortion is produced. When a disc is played through a television adhering to another standard (525 through 625, or 625 through 525), approximately 7% visual distortion results. Generally, the eye is able to perceive 5% distortion in a side-by-side comparison, or 10% distortion otherwise. Alternatively, a CD-I disc may be produced with a 525/625 "compatible" video format, playable on either a 525 or 625 television with 3.6% distortion.

The CD-I format calls for varying quality levels for resolution and pixel coding. Three standards of video resolution are supported: Normal Resolution of 360 × 240 pixels (NTSC) and 384 × 280 pixels (PAL); Double Resolution (twice the horizontal resolution) with 720 × 240 pixels (NTSC) and 768 × 280 pixels (PAL); and High Resolution (twice the horizontal and vertical resolution) with 720 × 480 pixels (NTSC) and 768 × 560 pixels (PAL). Normal Resolution corresponds to the best resolution achievable with present television receivers, while Double and High Resolution represents the quality of future enhanced or digital receivers. Pictures are generally non-interlaced, although interlacing can be used.

Image coding provides for three picture qualities: studio picture quality and two graphics qualities. Natural (photographic) pictures use DYUV (Delta YUV) coding in which Y represents luminance and U and V are chroma. Using statistical properties of pictures, a data compression of 3 over RGB (red-green-blue) coding is achieved. Pictures occupy about 325 kilobytes per picture without interlacing (650 kilobytes with interlacing). All natural pictures are compressed with DYUV coding to about 85 kilobytes (NTSC) and 105 kilobytes (PAL). At a data rate of 170.2 kilobytes per second in Form 2, one full frame natural picture is transferred in about 0.5 seconds.

The first graphics mode is designed for end-user manipulation applications; it is based on RGB 5:5:5 coding, and supports 16-bit/32,768 colors, with 5 bits for each of the R, G, and B components, and one bit for transparency. A 16-bit RGB graphic would occupy about 170 kilobytes per NTSC picture and 210 kilobytes for PAL.

The second graphics mode is based on CLUT (color lookup table) graphics which permit 4-bit/16, 7-bit/128, or 8-bit/256 color full screen animation. Up to 8 colors may be redefined per scan line. Because 256 levels may be defined for each R, G, and B element, the total number of colors available for a single image is 256 × 256 × 256, or about 16 million. The CLUT 8-bit mode requires 108 kilobytes per picture. Taking advantage of the statistical properties of pictures, a data compression of 2 over RGB is achieved. With compression, the interleaving of sound and CLUT picture results in the ability to provide full screen animation in Form 2. Both 7- and 8-bit CLUT pictures (like DYUV) occupy about 85 kilobytes in NTSC and 105 kilobytes in PAL.

Run-length CLUT coding may be used for cartoon-like animation or average resolution pictures. Taking advantage of the statistical properties of pictures, it achieves a data compression of between 8 to 12 over RGB. Either 3-bit/8 or 7-bit/128 color coding may be used. A drawing requires only 10 to 20 kilobytes of data.

CD-I developers have also proposed a high resolution extension to the CD-I video standard which yields high picture quality without the need for large data storage or long loading time. The system is called QHY (Quantized High-resolution Y). It is a new method of coding the digital data on the disc to produce more distinct images on the screen. The edge of an image defines its cleanliness. QHY uses pixel manipulation on image edges to remove redundant data from a high resolution picture with only a slight increase in storage data and loading time over normal resolution.

### CD-I Text

Text encoding can be visualized either as a bit-map process, or by character encoding via systems software. The bit-map process requires 5 bytes per character, resulting in about 120 million characters per disc (if only 16 colors are used in an $8 \times 10$ matrix). These characters cannot be manipulated under program control. Up to 4 overlaying planes are defined, with both transparency and translucency for all except the background plane. One plane is reserved for external video and another for the cursor.

Character-encoded text can either be system text or application text in standardized form, using 1 byte per character, yielding over 600 million characters on a disc. The ISO 8859/1 standard character set is available in the CD-I format. Application text can be encoded with 2 bytes per character, specifying factors such as color, font type, and character size, resulting in over 300 million characters per disc. In both cases, it is possible to manipulate text via software—for example, copying text from disc to external storage.

In the normal mode, text is limited to 40 characters on 20 lines. The high resolution mode allows 80 characters on 40 lines. Compatibility is maintained between the two text formats. A wide range of visual effects are defined, including cuts, scrolls, overlays, dissolves, fades, and so forth.

### Interactivity

The CD-I format permits a high degree of real-time interactivity. The extended data physical format allows for real-time switching between sectors. Thus it is possible to have sectors with different information content and with a different physical format. Sectors may be interleaved at the file level, channel level, or at the coding information type level. File level interleaving allows interspersing of nonrelated information of two or more files in a constant sector stream, thus better utilizing the disc area. Channel interleaving allows real-time selection when one is playing a disc. It is possible to switch between different types of information according to the desired application.

The compact disc real-time operating system (CD-RTOS) is based on the OS-9 operating system, a multi-tasking operating system suited for real-time capability and synchronizing diverse data. Synchronization is achieved with synchronization control data at the beginning of a real-time record. This indicates how the audio data is synchronized to the video data. The CD-RTOS is comprised of four major blocks: libraries to assure that specialized user functions, math, I/O, and synchronization are available; a CD-RTOS kernel derived from OS-9; managers to define virtual device levels and provide software support; and drivers to interface between virtual and hardware systems.

### Implementation

CD-I is not a peripheral, but a self-contained system. To ensure universal disc/drive compatibility, dedicated hardware and interfaces are specified. A CD-I player contains a CD-ROM disc drive as the system's input, decoder chips for text, graphics, video, and audio, and microprocessor controllers. The CD-I system uses the Motorola 68000 microprocessor family. A CD-I player could be interfaced to a television and stereo. Although it could also be interfaced to a personal computer, it would not be cost-effective, and such interfacing would miss the medium's intent. A CD-ROM drive alone would make a better computer peripheral.

Because the CD-I format recognizes 16-bit PCM data (the first audio quality level), a CD-I player can play regular CD-Audio discs. An audio CD player cannot play CD-I discs. As specified in the High Sierra Group proposal, CD-ROM Mode 1 discs can operate on CD-I systems. On the other hand, a microcomputer with a CD-ROM drive is not always capable of processing the information on a CD-I. Universal players capable of playing any kind of CD may appear.

The CD-I disc layout and file structure specifies a number of criteria. The first track (track 0) of a CD-I disc is a mandatory CD-I track, complying both physically and logically with the CD-Audio standard, according to which a maximum of 99 tracks may be encoded on a disc. If CD-Audio tracks are also present on a CD-I disc, then the first CD-I track must contain, at the very least, the disc label information. It is recommended that all CD-I information be placed in the first track, and that the second and subsequent tracks be used as CD-Audio tracks. In this way, if a CD-I disc is played on a CD-Audio player, the CD-I track can be skipped.

The beginning of a CD-I track always contains a disc label that contains the file structure volume descriptor, boot record, and terminator record which are required to initialize the CD-I player. The disc label also contains directory information that specifies the disc type and format and identifies the disc as being individual or part of a collection.

The scope of the CD-I specification is obviously considerable. The system's designers anticipated that a number of diverse players with different performance features and levels would be developed. Therefore, to ensure basic compatibility, the CD-I specification provides a minimum set of requirements for CD-I systems. The basic system must be able to read the following: CD-Audio tracks; CD-ROM Mode 1 tracks (as defined by the High Sierra Group Level 2 format); and CD-I tracks. The basic system must be capable of performing the following functions: decoding CD-Audio and CD-I audio information; interfacing with a single TV with normal resolution and any coding, or high resolution with a 4-bit pixel depth and CLUT coding; decoding DYUV; decoding RGB 5:5:5; decoding 8-bit CLUT; decoding one dimensional run length; handling special effects (e.g., cut, scroll); multiplane overlays; performing equivalent to or better than a 68000 processor operating at 8 MHz without MMU, 10 MHz with MMU, and OS-9-based CD-RTOS with a 16-bit data bus; carrying two DMA channels; storing at least two banks of 512 kilobytes each in system RAM and having a direct RAM expansion slot; and providing at least 8 kilobytes of non-volatile memory.

The CD-I format thus presents considerable opportunities for hardware, software, and publishing industries to provide consumers with new forms of interactive entertainment and education. However, there are not many existing, readily transferable programs that take advantage of the video, graphics, audio, and text capabilities supported by this new standard. There is thus a considerable amount of creative work ahead.

## DVI

Digital Video Interactive (DVI) is an all-digital optical disc format capable of reproducing full-motion, full-screen video, computer-generated video graphics, and digital audio via a CD-ROM drive. A DVI disc is, in fact, a CD-ROM disc containing DVI-specific data. This data specification permits motion video to be combined with foreground video objects, text, dynamic graphics, and multitrack audio—all under the user's control. Data compression techniques permit the system to utilize disc storage space more effectively, and output relatively large amounts of data more quickly. Although data on DVI discs is formatted to CD-ROM specifications and can be played on a CD-ROM drive (other digital media may be used as well), special DVI decoding technology is also required. The DVI format is thus incompatible with other interactive compact disc formats, such as CD-I and other CD-ROM implementations.

### Data Compression

Working in the David Sarnoff Research Center in Princeton, New Jersey, GE and RCA Laboratories attacked the essential problems of storing video information on CD: too much data in too little space and output at a rate that is too slow. A screen of analog video measuring 512 by 400 pixels (a pixel is the smallest measurable picture element) requires 600 kilobytes of data per frame for digital storage. With the NTSC standard, 30 frames are displayed each second; this works out to about 30 seconds of digital video per CD. Furthermore, because the data readout rate of the CD is only about 150 kilobytes per second (5,120 bytes each one-thirtieth of a second), it is not fast enough to show video at real-time speed; it would take over an hour to show that 30 seconds of digital video. In other words, the normal disc playing time limits the transfer rate.

Clearly, storage of raw video data is not the answer. Consequently, developers searched for a method of compressing data prior to storage and decompressing it during playback. They conceived the idea of performing non-real-time compression of video frames, with custom VLSI chips for real-time decompression. Compression is accomplished before mastering. Since it is done once and need not be done in real time, expensive computers may be used.

Each frame is digitized to 512 horizontal pixels by 480 lines vertical by 24 bits of color. Next, each frame is filtered and subsampled to reduce resolution to 256 by 200 by 24 bits. Filter choices to remove high-frequency data affect quality.

The basis for video compression is the fact that one video image is usually related to the previous image. Therefore, rather than storing each image in its entirety, only the difference between successive images is needed. Using a pyramid delta encoding compression scheme, a video frame is compressed to only 4500 bytes, or about 1100 four-byte words per frame (it is well known that a picture is worth a thousand words). However, the first frame of a new scene requires about 15 kilobytes. Required capacity of 4500 bytes per frame represents a reduction to 2.5% of the original size. Finally, data is formatted to CD-ROM specifications, and video and audio data are merged. The result is an hour of full-screen digital video with audio storage and a data rate supporting 30 frames per second.

### DVI Playback

Upon playback, the compressed data must be decompressed in real time each time the CD is played. Two VLSI chips form the VDP (video display processor). The first chip, VDP1, is the pixel processor that runs the decompression algorithm and is designed to operate at a rate of 12.5 MIPS (million instructions per second). Its instruction set contains several proprietary video/graphic instructions which permit simultaneous operations. This increases processing power and allows DVI to combine full-motion video with video overlays, text, and dynamic graphics all in the same video frame. A new program can be loaded in 120 microseconds (two scan lines) for rapid updates, a requirement of interactivity.

A second chip, VDP2, handles output display processing. It determines the resolution modes and pixel formats. Its resolution ranges from 256 to 768 pixels horizontally and up to 512 pixels vertically. The VDP2 pixel formats use 8, 16 or 24 bits per pixel; with 24 bits, any one of 16 million colors are available in each pixel.

Multitrack, multichannel digital audio is available on DVI. Up to four tracks are dynamically mixable down to two output channels. Audio encoding utilizes ADPCM, the same method used in CD-I technology, to compress audio data to about 500 bytes per frame, or less. As is the case with CD-I, DVI offers various audio bandwidth and dynamic ranges. The standard audio data rate is 128K bits/second (4 bits/sample × 32K samples/second) for an audio bandwidth of 16 kHz. Other rates provide audio bandwidths of 4 kHz and 8 kHz per track. Stereo audio is also available.

One DVI disc could hold a full-motion, full-screen video program (256 × 240) with a playing time of about 74 minutes. With an hour of video, the remaining disc space could be used for ADPCM audio, perhaps using its 4-bit mode. Of course, a higher audio quality level could be traded for less video playing time or reduced video quality. Storage capacity increases proportionally as the size of the video display decreases; up to two hours of half-screen video or four hours of quarter-screen video may be stored.

A DVI disc could also store still images. With compression techniques, a disc could contain 7,000 high resolution (768 × 480) stills, 10,000 medium resolution (512 × 480) stills, or 40,000 low resolution (256 × 240) stills.

### Implementation

DVI is designed with a computer bus interface compatible with several computer architectures, including the IBM PC AT. The first commercial incarnation of DVI consisted of two plug-in boards designed to fit into an IBM PC AT. As with CD-ROM and CD-I products, a microprocessor-based hardware player (with disc drive) is required. The result is a personal computer which integrates software programs, text, graphics, sound, and full-motion video. It is the latter which differentiates DVI from CD-ROM and CD-I systems; without DVI's data compression methods, video storage is limited in playing time and quality. Even CD-V, a format designed with video in mind, offers only a few minutes of full-motion video on a CD.

The video signal on DVI is full-screen and full-motion, but the data compression methods do have drawbacks. Not all scenes are encoded equally well. Particularly busy scenes suffer picture deterioration. On the other hand, simpler or more slowly moving scenes are very good. In other words, like all technologies, DVI will have its limitations and its applications.

DVI thus opens up several opportunities for product developers. For example, the educational market may use DVI as an affordable interactive video system (video tape is cumbersome, and video discs are expensive). Training systems must provide a high degree of realism in their simulations; often the poor quality of graphics-based pictures is inadequate for applications such as medical, aviation, and maintenance training. DVI could remedy this.

In another application, many retail stores are turning to in-store marketing with video systems which allow buyers to configure their purchases. DVI could be used by customers in clothing stores and automotive showrooms to check out their order before purchase. Of course, the biggest market is the consumer's living room. Its developers expect that DVI prices will reach consumer affordability. Interactive games and personal education packages are two potential markets.

Like CD-ROM, DVI is a format standard for placing any kind of digital data on a compact disc. However, the compressed data format used in DVI is incompatible with other CD specifications, such as the data formats and hardware used in CD-I. Because DVI specifies its own hardware requirements, it stands apart from the rest of the CD family. Recognizing that any format's success hinges on its universality and its acceptance by the manufacturing community, developers have invited participation in developing DVI technology. DVI is intended to be neither a competing format, nor a new standard. Rather, it is hoped that DVI chips can be incorporated into existing CD formats in which case this data algorithm technology could gain wide acceptance.

### CD-V

Compact Disc-Video (CD-V) is a combination of audio and video technology—specifically, a combination of the compact disc and Laservision (LV) systems. From this merger comes a new medium, the CDV-Single, and a new hardware product, the CD-V "combi-player," which is a combination CD and LV player. It plays 12-centimeter video "CDV-Singles," along with conventional full-length audio-only CDs, and all 20- and 30-centimeter LV video discs as well. The audio portion of a combi-player is identical to that of an audio CD player, and the audio quality of the CD-V duplicates that of an audio CD player. CD-V thus retains full compatibility with existing CD-Audio standards.

However, because of incompatible analog television standards, both NTSC and PAL/SECAM players and discs must be produced. Thus CD-V violates the universality of the compact disc—the unique advantage of playability and interchangeability between any discs and any players worldwide. When the CD was standardized, designers were free to design universality into the product. Thus any audio CD disc may be played on any CD-Audio player. In CD-I, because video is stored digitally, compatibility also exists. This is not so with CD-V. Because CD-V video information is stored and reproduced in analog form, a CD-V player, as well as CD-V discs, must be configured for one standard or another. In other words, the video portion of a PAL/SECAM CD-V disc is unplayable on a NTSC player and vice versa. In addition, the audio portion of the video program is incompatible because it is integrated into the video signal. The audio-only CD tracks on a CD-V disc will be playable on any PAL/SECAM or NTSC or CD-Audio player.

### *CDV-Single*

CD-V introduces an entirely new software format, the CDV-Single. The CDV-Single appears similar to an audio CD, although the substrate and top lacquer are gold-tinted to distinguish it visually. The disc is the size of an audio CD but contains approximately five minutes full motion NTSC video (encoded as an analog signal) with a CD digital audio soundtrack, as well as an extra twenty minutes of digital audio only. A PAL/SECAM standard disc encodes approximately six minutes of video material. CD-Audio standards are used for the digital audio, including a scanning velocity of 1.2 to 1.4 meters/second and a track pitch of 1.6 micrometers. Because the audio portion of the CDV-Single disc is placed on the innermost portion of the disc (from 50 to 74 millimeters), the audio portion may be played on a regular CD player. Similarly, the CD-V player may play any audio CD. The video signal on the outer portion (from 78 to 116 millimeters) is read only by the CD-V player. The placement of digital audio and video programs on a CDV-Single is shown in figure 6.10.

The video information on the outer portion is encoded as an analog signal according to the LV format. In the NTSC standard, disc speed ranges from 2700 to 1815 rpm, yielding a scanning velocity of 11 to 12 meters/second. In the PAL/SECAM standard, disc speed varies from 2250 to 1512 rpm, with a scanning velocity of 9.2 to 10.2 meters/second. The track pitch is 1.6 micrometers in either case. All CD-V specifications are defined in the *Blue Book* standards document.

The player must sense the presence of either digital audio-only or video signal and adjust its operating parameters accordingly. Typically, the player's pickup would read the audio lead-in area, skip to the video portion to begin playback, and then return to the audio-only portion.

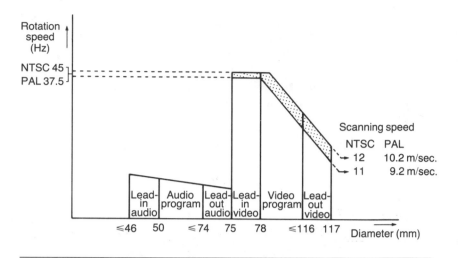

Figure 6.10 *Disc layout for a CDV-Single. Digital audio data is contained in the inner area, and analog video data is contained in the outer area.*

### CD-V/LV

The 20- and 30-centimeter diameter discs are denoted as CDV-EP (extended play) and CDV-LP (long play), respectively. As with the smaller CDV-Singles, they contain audio conforming to the CD-Audio standard and video conforming to the LV standard. Analog audio may be used in lieu of digital audio. The CDV-EP plays two twenty-minute sides, and the CDV-LP plays two sixty-minute sides. Obviously these discs cannot be played on an audio CD player. Scanning speed in the NTSC format is 10.1 to 11.4 meters/second. In the PAL/SECAM format it is 8.4 to 9.5 meters/second. Because of their long playing times, these discs will contain material such as concert videos, classical music videos, and feature films.

In the NTSC format, the audio portion of LV discs is encoded with two FM carriers placed at 2.3 and 2.8 MHz, which is below the FM picture signal. In the PAL/SECAM format, the FM carriers are placed at 648 and 1066 kHz. In either case, the digital audio signal in CD-V discs is placed in the 1.75 MHz band below the FM picture signal carriers. NTSC discs may therefore be encoded with both analog and digital sound. Digital audio NTSC CD-V discs are playable on existing LV players with analog audio circuitry. An NTSC CD-V player will play existing LV discs. However, in the PAL/SECAM format, the digital audio signal replaces the analog FM carriers. Thus a PAL/SECAM digital audio CD-V disc may not have analog audio as well. A PAL/SECAM CD-V player is able to reproduce both digital audio LVs and existing analog audio LVs. Existing LV players cannot reproduce the audio portion of new digital audio CD-V discs.

In addition to the CD-V combi-player that plays all four optical disc formats, there are CD-V dedicated players, able to play only CD-Audio and CDV-Single discs; they feature a small LCD screen and are available as portable players. CD-V players use audio circuitry identical to that of CD-Audio players including, for example, 16-bit D/A converters and four-times oversampling digital filtering. Their features encompass those of both CD and LV players, such as programmability, picture search, fast/slow motion, stills, and speed increase/decrease. Although primarily using constant linear velocity (CLV) scanning, CD-V also provides for constant angular velocity (CAV) scanning. Future enhancements call for CDV-HD (high definition) formats, CD-I controllers, and dual language software.

From a manufacturing standpoint, CD-V discs must be mastered on a dual-speed lathe using video from a 1-inch C-type machine and audio from a 3/4-inch U-matic machine synchronized with time code. The high bandwidth of 10 MHz (versus 1.5 MHz for CD-Audio) necessitates manufacturing procedures closer to those of video discs (as opposed to those for audio CDs); still, CDV discs are manufactured at audio CD plants.

## CD-WO

In its earliest incarnations, the CD was a playback-only medium. However, development in optical technology soon led to a writable CD format known as CD-WO (Compact Disc-Write Once). A write-once optical disc is exactly that. Data is written permanently, can be read many times, but cannot be erased, in much the same way that a photograph is a permanent record. Such systems are sometimes also referred to as WORMs, for *Write Once, Read Many*.

A write-once optical disc may be implemented in a variety of ways. In some systems a process called ablation uses a laser writer to burn holes in a thin film. Other mechanisms include lasers which cause bubbles or blisters to form in the medium. Tellurium and tellurium alloys have been chosen by many manufacturers for the thin film because of their low melting points and high sensitivity. In other systems, an irreversible phase change is used to provide a change in the index of reflectivity of the medium at the point where the laser strikes. Some systems using this method employ a thin metallic recording layer which changes its physical property from amorphous to crystalline when it is thermally heated (to approximately 170 degrees centigrade) by the writing laser. The phase transition alters the reflectivity of the recording layer at written spots, thus allowing laser reading of the data. In some systems a layer of antimony-selenium is employed, evaporated onto a hard plastic disc substrate. An alternative to metal film is the use of polymer dye binder bi-layer media. Colored dyes in a plastic medium over a reflective material are written with infrared light and read with red light. Unlike metal film discs, polymer dye technology can use a flexible substrate.

Philips and Sony, co-inventors of the CD, released a tentative CD-WO standard in February, 1988. The CD-WO format encompasses both CD-Audio and CD-ROM applications, and a disc may contain both user-recorded and prerecorded material. To ensure compatibility among users, the format uses a pre-grooved disc. As with other write-once systems, a variety of materials may be used. The recording layer may undergo a decrease or increase in reflectivity during recording. In CD-WO, to simplify the servo system design, the high-to-low reflectivity transition materials are used in a narrow pre-groove system, and low-to-high transition materials are used in an alternative wide pre-groove disc. The disc also contains CLV clocking information (as a radial groove wobble) and timecode (as a modulation of the groove wobble) over the entire disc surface.

This is how a CD-WO disc is laid out. First, there is a prerecorded lead-in area holding the TOC (table of contents). Next, there is the pre-grooved program area holding user-recorded (after recording) information; the area consists of an optional prerecorded area user table of contents (UTOC) and recordable user area. Finally, there is a prerecorded lead-out area. Any prerecorded data, including the optional prerecorded area, would be stored as CD pits. All user data is stored as a reflectivity change. Figure 6.11a shows the layout of a CD-WO disc without prerecorded tracks, and figure 6.11b shows the layout of a disc with prerecorded tracks.

The prerecorded TOC in the lead-in area contains the start position of the optional prerecorded CD tracks, the position of the UTOC area, the start position of the recordable user area, the position of the lead-out area, and information on the physical parameters of the recording layer, such as required laser recording power and the polarity of the recorded information (reflectivity increase or decrease). The start position of the user recordable area is also stored in the UTOC.

Both CD-Audio and CD-ROM data can be recorded in one track. Tracks in the user recording area can be created at will through pointers in the UTOC. A single track numbering system is used for all prerecorded and user recorded tracks. A disc can contain a maximum of 99 tracks of any duration. A disc may be recorded entirely at once, or discontinuously over a period of time, with new tracks starting at the end of previously recorded ones. In terms of disc dimensions, scanning velocity, encoding, error correction, subcode, and data structure, CD-WO is identical to audio CDs. Disc capacity is identical to that of CD-Audio or CD-ROM; a CD-WO may hold about 650 Mbytes of data, or about 74 minutes of audio.

a)

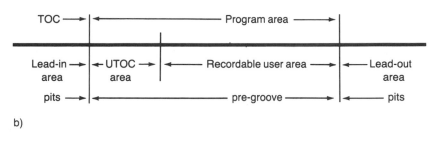

b)

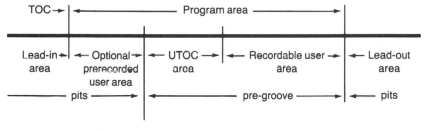

Figure 6.11   *The CD-WO format provides disc layouts for both discs without prerecorded tracks (a), and discs with prerecorded tracks (b).*

## ERASABLE CDS

Several recordable/erasable optical media technologies have been introduced. These formats provide complete liberty in the reading and writing of data to optical disc. Among them are magneto-optical, phase-change, and dye-polymer recording. Magneto-optics is a system using a combination of vertical magnetic recording and laser optics; it is sometimes called "optically-assisted magnetic recording." Magneto-optical recording is sometimes refered to as MOR, and the discs as MODs.

Magnetic storage is an effective way to record and erase data, but it suffers from basic problems such as medium and head wear. In addition, magnetic storage has hitherto used longitudinal recording, in which the magnetic particles are laid flat across the medium; this limits the density of particles and the amount of information stored in an area. Optical storage offers longevity of medium and pickup and high data density as powerful assets. However, optical properties of materials are not as easily changeable as their magnetic properties. Magneto-optical storage merges the record/erase properties of magnetic materials with the high density and contactless pickup of optical materials.

### Magneto-optical Recording

Fundamentally, magneto-optical recording is the same as any magnetic recording. However, vertical (sometimes called perpendicular or VR) recording is used. This differs from regular, longitudinal recording. In a vertical medium, magnetic particles are placed perpendicularly to the surface. This allows for much greater particle density, shorter recorded wavelengths, and, consequently, greater recording density. Vertical recording actually becomes more robust as recording density increases; as the cylindrically shaped particles are packed more tightly, they must be made thinner, which increases their magnetic strength. However, this great recording density is not fully utilized by conventional magnetic heads whose recording flux fields cannot be focused sufficently. In other words, the recorded area uses a far greater area than necessary.

With magneto-optics, a magnetic field is used to record data, but it is about one-tenth the strength of conventional recording fields. By itself, it is too weak to affect the orientation of the magnetic particles. However, a unique property of magnetic materials is utilized: as they are heated, their coercivity (the magnetic field strength required to bring a saturated medium to erasure) suddenly drops close to zero. The temperature at which a material's coercivity drops suddenly is called its Curie point. A magnet, for instance, heated to its Curie point, would lose its ability to attract metals. In the case of magneto-optics, at the Curie temperature (about 150 degrees centigrade), the magnetic particles on the disc are easily oriented by a weak field. A laser beam, precisely focused through an objective lens, is used to heat a minute spot of magnetic material to its Curie point. At that temperature only the few particles in that spot are affected by the magnetic field from the recording coil, and a very high-density recording results. After the laser pulse, the temperature decreases and the data is "frozen" into the magnetic layer. This is accomplished in one disc rotation. As in any digital magnetic storage, saturation recording is used. In this case, the aligned particles are reverse-oriented perpendicularly, as shown in figure 6.12.

### Magneto-optical Reading

Data readout utilizes the Kerr effect (or, alternatively, the Faraday effect), which describes the rotation of the plane of polarized light as it reflects from a magnetized material. Specifically, the reverse-oriented regions will reflect laser light differently than the unreversed regions. To

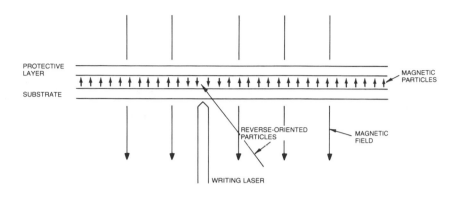

Figure 6.12    *Magneto-optical recording uses a laser beam to heat the recording layer, and a magnetic field to orient magnetic particles.*

read the disc, a laser is focused on it, and the angle of rotation of its reflection is monitored, as shown in figure 6.13. An analyzer distinguishes between rotated and unrotated light and converts that information into a beam of varying light intensity. Data is then recovered from this modulated signal. The intensity of the reading laser is much lower (perhaps by a factor of ten) than the recording laser, so the magnetic information is not affected.

To write data again, a magnetic field is applied to the disc, along with the laser heating spot, as illustrated in figure 6.14, and new data is written. However, in most designs an entire track must be erased on one rotation of the disc prior to writing new data; new data can only be written on the next rotation. Updating thus requires two disc rotations, which slows data writing. Future developments may allow the write operation to be accomplished in one pass, as with conventional magnetic media.

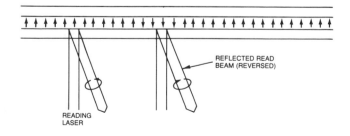

Figure 6.13    *Magneto-optical reading uses the angle of rotation of reflected light.*

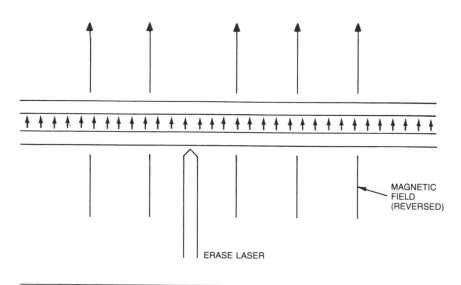

Figure 6.14    *Magneto-optical erasing is accomplished by writing new data.*

### A Magneto-optical System

Of course, any recording scheme is dependent on the modulation method used to write the data on the medium. There are several modulation methods suitable for magneto-optics. For example, the specific lengths of the input data code can be converted into a series of pulses which cause the recording laser to switch on and off, recording patterns of varying lengths corresponding to the input signal.

An important aspect of any recording medium is its compatibility with media from other recorders. To achieve this within the high tolerances of a magneto-optical medium, blank discs may be manufactured with prerecorded and nonerasable addressing. This method, called hardware addressing sectoring, uses a grooved disc in which address information is physically formed in the groove and detected by light beam reflection. Using this system, any magneto-optical player will automatically track both address and data information contained on any magneto-optical disc. By superimposing the hardware addressing information on the recorded data signal, playing time is not sacrificed.

A magneto-optical disc would retain the protective properties of other optical media. The recording layer would be sandwiched between a transparent substrate and a protective layer. The laser light would shine through the substrate, using its index of refraction to place surface dust and scratches out of focus with respect to the interior data. Although several magnetic materials could be used, the ultimate selection will be based on orientation properties, signal-to-noise ratio, and long-term stability. Magneto-optical discs use amorphous rare-earth transition metals, such as alloy coatings of gadolinium terbium iron, terbium iron cobalt, and terbium iron. Proprietary processing and chemical treatment have made these reactive elements stable. Tests indicate that a magneto-optical disc could be erased/recorded over ten million times and would retain its data for ten years or more.

The optical head and magnetic coils of a magneto-optical system require sophisticated engineering, both in terms of their design and the hardware and software which control them. In addition, a complete signal encoding chain is contained in every recorder. Some of the tasks a magneto-optical recorder must deal with include audio signal processing for both recording and playback; constant linear velocity (CLV) control of the disc; drive control of the optical head block for the focusing servo, tracking servo, and traverse motor; magnetic field control; laser drive control; disc loading and clamping mechanism; and system control of recording, reproduction, erasing, and access. Because of the similarity of their tasks, it would clearly make sense for a magneto-optical recorder to borrow some technology from the CD system and to emulate the CD format in terms of sampling rate and word length.

The CD system will be upwardly compatible with a magneto-optical system. Because much of the electronics are identical, all magneto-optical players could also play back CDs, in the same way that a cassette machine can record or play prerecorded tapes. They could share a common optical head, and even the difference between CD and magneto-optical discs would be automatically detected because of the differences in reflectivity. Of course, to record magneto-optical discs, or to play back magneto-optical discs that are already recorded, a magneto-optical recorder will be needed.

### Other Recording Technologies

Magneto-optics is not the only optical recording system being researched. Some systems use phase-change technology similar to that used in write-once systems. They use materials that exhibit a reversible crystalline/amorphous phase change when recorded at one temperature and erased at another. Typically, a high-reflectivity (crystalline) to low-reflectivity (amorphous) phase change is used to record data, and the reverse to erase. Information is recorded by heating an area of the crystalline layer to a temperature slightly above its melting point. When the area solidifies, it has become amorphous, and the change in reflectivity can be detected. Because the crystalline form is more stable, the material will tend to change back to this form; thus, when the area is heated to a point just below its melting temperature, it will return to a crystalline state, erasing the data. A recording layer comprised of gallium antimonide and indium antimonide has been developed. It has a long shelf life and is not affected by ambient temperatures and humidity. Over a thousand erasures can be achieved. Permanent recording may be achieved by simply increasing the power of the writing laser; this burns holes in the recording layer rather than changing its phase.

In another erasable technology, a dye-polymer recording layer is physically changed when recorded, and changed again when erased. The THOR-CD (THOR standing for Tandy High-intensity Optical Recording) uses this approach. A dye-polymer disc is made by sandwiching two layers of plastic materials coated with a dye that absorbs laser light. The medium is written by laser heating. Laser light of a specific wavelength heats the two-layered medium, causing the lower layer to expand and push up the top layer. The top layer cools faster than the lower, and retains the raised bump. This formation can be read by the read laser. Erasing and rerecording are easily accomplished: that is, when the surfaces are again heated—this time with a laser of a different wavelength—the bump flattens out again, leaving the surface in its original form, ready for rewriting of new data.

The recording surface forms a bump with one laser wavelength and flattens out with another. Moreover, the wavelength that flattens a bump does not affect the surface if it is already recorded. Thus data could be overwritten on a single disc revolution if the medium passes under the smoothing laser just before it encounters the laser writing new bumps.

Significantly, because THOR-CD medium is changed physically (that is, a pit is created) the disc can be read by a conventional CD player. Similarly, a conventional prerecorded CD can be played in the recorder. Thus the new technology is backward compatible.

However, a problem with this particular technology is that the layer can be erased only a few times, perhaps a hundred or less, before the recording layers become fatigued. While perhaps acceptable for some applications, this is certainly not acceptable for others. That problem, of course, has already been solved by magneto-optical recording.

Although the future is bright for recordable CDs, it is certain that playback-only CDs will remain popular as a medium for prerecorded optical reproduction. While many people will switch to CD recorders, one suspects that CD players will keep going strong, just as another great prerecorded software transport, the turntable, persisted for a number of years.

## CD + G

As noted in Chapter Four, every compact disc contains a subcode area. In addition to the P and Q channels used for conventional audio playback, there are other channels available for other applications. Compact Disc + Graphics (CD + G) takes advantage of this non-audio data area. Still color images, text, or other material may be stored on an audio compact disc and displayed on a television monitor while the music plays. Because this data area is already reserved in the CD standard, no music playing time is sacrificed when graphics data is inserted.

### Subcode Video

Every audio compact disc contains additional data capacity in the subcode bits. These six channels (R,S,T,U,V, and W) account for about 20 megabytes of 8-bit storage per disc, and are arranged in 98-bit words, as are the P and Q channels. The R-W subcode area was reserved as contingency storage by the original disc designers.

For video applications the data in these six subcode channels can be collected over thousands of subcode blocks to form an image. A CD holding a full program of audio data could hold hundreds of still video images, drawing a new image from the R-W bits contained in each frame every few seconds. All synchronization, error correction, and video data is self-contained in the subcode field. However, appropriate editors and master tape recorder formats are required to encode the information onto the PCM tape master.

CD graphics data is output from a player using a digital output port on the CD player. The hookup requires an external decoder/adaptor box which accepts the subcode signal from the player and converts it into a modulated video signal suitable for the television. Alternatively, a player could contain all necessary circuitry and output the video signal directly. The resolution of CD graphics is 288 × 192 pixels, and 4,096 colors are available when CLUT encoding is used. When a disc does not contain graphics information, the R-W bits are recorded with zeros, which does not affect playback.

The possibilities for R-W graphics are varied. Still pictures relating conceptually or directly to the audio material could be displayed, as could liner notes, lyrics, or other alphanumeric information. An opera recording could display the libretto in several languagues. A popular disc might have pictures of rock 'n' roll stars, or even a display of guitar or keyboard chords.

Another application is known as CD + MIDI, or CD + G + M. MIDI (Musical Information Digital Interface) information can be used to control external synthesizers. For example, using a listener's MIDI equipment, instruments and voices could be relocated in the playback mix, the sound of instruments could be changed by revoicing the parts in the arrangement, tempi and keys could be changed, a song could be restructured, or sheet music could be printed out—all using an external MIDI set-up. Up to 16

MIDI channels can be stored in the subcode area, along with a full audio program.

## CD-3

The ultimate in compact disc portability may be realized with the CD-3. It is identical to regular 12 centimeter diameter CDs; however, its diameter is only 8 centimeters, or about 3 inches. Its small size promotes greater portability as well as the use of smaller portable players. In addition, the CD-3 format has been approved for CD-ROM applications. Because the CD data spiral begins at the innermost diameter, and all CD formats use this standard dimension, CD-3s are compatible with regular discs and players. Most players feature a disc drawer with concentric wells able to accommodate both disc diameters. In some cases, an outer adaptor ring must be used to enlarge the CD-3's size so that players can properly load them.

Naturally, the CD-3 holds less music because of its smaller size; its maximum playing time is about twenty minutes. It is thus designed to replace the analog 7-inch, 45 rpm single, as well as to promote CD portability. A variety of CD-3 portable players has appeared, achieving truly shirt pocket dimensions. In some cases, these tiny players are also able to play 12-centimeter discs by sliding the disc spindle motor to one side.

Portable CD players also come packaged along with amplifiers, loudspeakers, cassette recorders, radios, graphic equalizers, and other assorted audio gear, as well as a handle. These "boom boxes" are useful for applications in which you are eager to share your musical tastes with as many other people as possible, such as at the beach or on the subway.

## FOR FURTHER READING

Bouwhuis, G., J. Braat, A. Huijser, J. Pasman, G. van Rosmalen, and K. Schouhamer-Immink. *Principles of Optical Disc Systems*. Bristol and Boston: Hilger, 1985.

Bouwhuis, G., and P. Burgstede. "The Optical Scanning System of the Philips 'VLP' Record Player." *Philips Technical Review* 33(7):186–89, 1973.

Compaan, K., and P. Kramer. "The Philips 'VLP' System." *Philips Technical Review* 33(7):178–80, 1973.

"CD-I—The Future" (Conference Proceedings). OnLine Conference and Exhibitions, San Francisco, May 11–13, 1987.

Cornyn, Stan. "CD-I and the Media." In J. Strawn, ed. *Proceedings of the AES 5th International Conference—Music and Digital Technology.* New York: Audio Engineering Society, 1987.

Denon Nippon Columbia. *CD-ROM Disc.* Technical Information. March, 1986.

Denon Nippon Columbia. *CD-ROM Drive.* Technical Information. March, 1986.

Denon Nippon Columbia. *Controller for CD-ROM Drive (SCSI/SASI Protocol).* Technical manual, March, 1986.

Dixon, D. F., S. J. Golin, and I. H. Hashfield. "DVI Video/Graphics." *Computer Graphics World,* July, 1987.

Freese, R. P. "Optical Disks Become Recordable." *IEEE Spectrum* 36(2)·41–45, February, 1988.

Hartmann, M., B. A. J. Jacobs, and J. J. M. Brant. "Erasable Magneto-Optical Recording." *Philips Technical Review* 42(2):37–47, August, 1985.

Isailovic, J. *Videodisc and Optical Memory Systems.* Englewood Cliffs, N.J.: Prentice-Hall, 1985.

ISO (International Standards Organization). "Volume and File Structure of CD-ROM for Information Interchange." *Standard ISO/DIS 9660.*

Janssen, P. J. M., and P. E. Day. "Control Mechanisms in the Philips 'VLP' Record Player." *Philips Technical Review* 33(7):190–93, 1973.

Lambert, S., and S. Ropiequet. *CD-ROM, the New Papyrus.* Redmond, Wash.: Microsoft, 1986

Lambert, S., and J. Sallis, eds. *CD I and Interactive Videodisc Technology.* Indianapolis: Sams, 1987.

Nishiguchi, M., K. Akagiri, and T. Suzuki. "A New Audio Bit Rate Reduction System for the CD-I Format." *AES Preprint no. 2375,* 81st Convention, 1986.

Philips International. *A General Introduction to CD-Interactive.* October, 1986.

Philips International, ed. *Compact Disc-Interactive: A Designer's Overview.* New York: McGraw-Hill, 1988.

Philips International. *Optical Media in Perspective.* March, 1987.

Philips International. "The CD Video System." Press release, Eindhoven, March, 1987.

Ropiequet, S. *CD-ROM Optical Publishing,* Volume 2. Redmond, Wash.: Microsoft, 1987.

Rosen, D. "GE/RCA Announces DVI." *CD-I News* 1(6):1, 4–5, 8–9, 1987.

Roth, J. P. *Essential Guide to CD-ROM.* Westport, Conn.: Meckler, 1986.

Rothchild, E. S. "Optical Memory: Data Storage by Laser." *Byte* 9(11):215–24, October, 1984.

Schouhamer-Immink, Kees A., A. H. Hoogendijk, and J. A. Kahlman. "Digital Audio Modulation in the PAL and NTSC Optical Video Disk Coding Formats." *Journal of the Audio Engineering Society* 32(11):883–88, November, 1984.

Schouhamer-Immink, Kees A., and J. J. M. Braat. "Experiments toward an Erasable Compact Disc Digital Audio System." *Journal of the Audio Engineering Society* 32(7/8):531–38, July/August, 1984.

Schwerin, J. B. *CD-ROM Standards: The Book.* Oxford (England): Learned Information, and Pittsfield, Vt.: InfoTech, 1986.

Thomas, G. E. "Future Trends in Optical Recordings." *Philips Technical Review* 44(2):51–57, April, 1988.

Van den Bussche, W., A. H. Hoogendijk, and J. H. Wessels. "Signal Processing in the Philips 'VLP' System." *Philips Technical Review* 33(7):181–85, 1973.

# Chapter Seven

# Disc Manufacturing

## INTRODUCTION

The compact disc has proved to be a technological wunderkind in the highly sophisticated and competitive field of music and data storage. Forecasters have projected a worldwide demand of one billion CDs annually by the mid 1990s. Established injection molding factories are expanding, and new facilities are coming on-line while efforts are being made to perfect other manufacturing methods offering a quicker and cheaper alternative. In this chapter we explore the CD manufacturing chain.

## PRE-MASTERING

Every CD begins life as a master tape and any CD is only as good as its master tape. Because mastering to CD cannot eliminate the faults on the master, the master tape must be selected carefully. With analog tapes, the original master should be used, never a safety copy. If the master is of poor quality, one should consider remixing. If such is the case, one should locate the original equalization settings; if they were used to compensate for LP deficiencies, new equalization should be considered. Never use a submaster equalized for LP. If the master is digital, one must avoid any transfer to the analog domain; for example, one should equalize digitally if possible. In accordance with *Red Book* standards, facilities can produce only CD-Audio CDs which are playable on any stereo or mono playback system without requiring modification. The audio program must fall into one of these categories: (1) regular stereo; (2) one mono signal, simultaneously encoded on both audio channels; and (3) one mono signal on one channel and no signal on the other channel. Thus the use of two audio channels for two different mono programs is not allowed. Nevertheless, some dual-mono CDs have been released.

In pre-mastering, the original master tape is copied to a specially prepared tape master, which is used to produce the master disc prior to replication. It is the first step in CD replication. The original tape (of any format) is referred to as the master tape. By means of a digital audio processor, the audio program is copied to a 3/4-inch U-matic tape referenced with SMPTE time code. This tape is called the CD master tape. When subcode data is added, it is called a CD tape master. This is the tape used to cut the CD master disc. The digital audio program is recorded on the helical scan video track, subcode is recorded on longitudinal channel 1, and time code is recorded on longitudinal channel 2. Figure 7.1 illustrates the three main steps in tape mastering. Although mastering facilities will accept master tapes (of various formats) along with required documentation, pre-mastering may be accomplished in a properly equipped recording studio. To achieve a properly prepared tape, one must observe the cardinal rules of CD pre-mastering listed in figure 7.2.

While the pertinent facts are contained in the cardinal rules, some points in the pre-mastering process merit further discussion. No matter what the original medium, the *de facto* standard equipment for CD mastering is the Sony PCM-1630 digital audio processor format, using a 44.1 kHz sampling rate and a 3/4-inch U-matic video recorder. Other (incompatible) digital audio processors are sometimes used. High-quality tape is crucial;

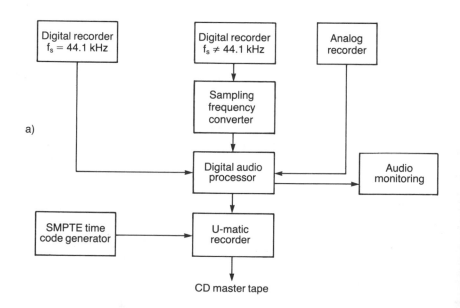

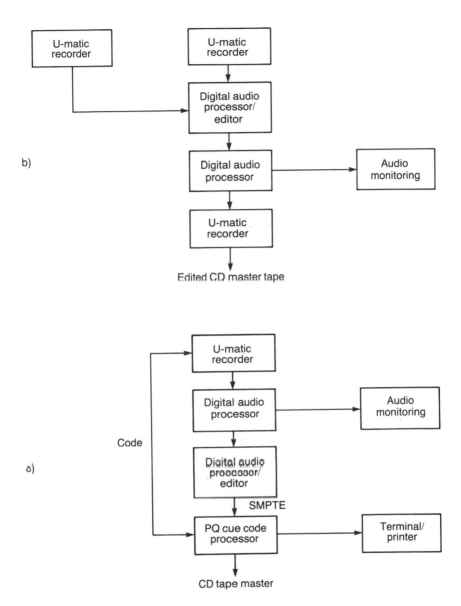

Figure 7.1   *The tape mastering process consists of tape transcription (a), track assemble editing (b), and PQ code generation and editing (c).*

1. Sampling rate must be 44.1 kHz.

2. Tape format must be 3/4-inch U-matic NTSC standard.

3. Time code must be SMPTE 60 Hz Non-Drop Frame time code.

4. Time code must be synchronized to the NTSC video signal.

5. Time code should run continuously and uninterrupted. Code should not cross over 00 hours, 00 minutes, 00 seconds, 00 frames.

6. Time code should be recorded on analog track #2 of the U-matic tape.

7. Record digital mute with time code for a minimum of 1 minute before the first track and 1 1/2 minutes after the last track.

8. A minimum of 2 seconds must be allowed for emphasis changes between tracks.

9. Prepare a list that is frame accurate to locate beginning and ending points.

10. Prepare a guideline of spurious noise information which indicates any unusual noises or general notes regarding the quality of the recording.

---

Figure 7.2    *Rules for CD master tape preparation.*

although 80-minute tapes are available, programs longer than 60 minutes are sometimes supplied on two 60-minute tapes and reassembled during tape mastering. Any recording must be auditioned carefully, with special attention to phantom dropouts caused by loose particles moving around the tape. The U-matic recorder must be checked for dirty heads or tape path, worn heads, and mechanical alignment. The U-matic should be NTSC format with the dropout compensator (DOC) switched out of circuit. In the case of V0 type U-matics, a modification should shift the crossover position of the head-switching servo (this is indicated by a "DA" on the model number). The dropout mute sensor on the 1630 must be set correctly; this is variable by the use of DIP switches inside the processor — many engineers consider a setting of 20 lines to be optimal. Before beginning recording, many engineers exercise the video tape by fast-forwarding it to the end and then rewinding it; this removes any packing irregularities.

### Tape Preparation

Whatever the master tape's format, the master CD will be cut from a U-matic tape through a PCM processor. To prepare a tape master, the time-code should first be recorded on channel 2 of the analog track at 0 VU, ±3 dB on the U-matic meter, nondrop frame (i.e. full frame). It should run across the entire tape length, or at least from the beginning, to one minute after the end of the audio program. This provides a SMPTE code and video sync pulse; the digital audio program will be recorded as an insert-type edit, leaving the video control track and timecode track intact. Timecoding can be done using a 1630 set in dubbing mode, which produces a digital mute picture for the video transport. The processor automatically sets itself for 60 Hz, nondrop frame code. Major axis crossings such as 23 hours, 59 minutes, 59 seconds, 29 frames, should be avoided; they might disrupt the encoder. When using a digital audio editor, track assembly may be accomplished without first striping the tape with timecode.

The original master tape is copied to the timecoded CD tape master. The CD master tape is assembled by performing the correct edits and inserting pauses between tracks. When dubbing from noisy analog tapes, fast fade-ins and fade-outs are preferable to tight leadering in order to avoid abrupt transitions in noise level. Of course, the analog tape machine must be aligned to the tape itself.

At least thirty seconds of digital zero (PCM data with no modulation) must be recorded at the beginning and end of the tape. This is a lead-in and lead-out period. The lead-in avoids potentially defective tape at the beginning of the cassette (cautious clients use two minutes or more of digital zero here). This is easily achieved with the 1630 input set for dubbing and the playback processor set for pause. When the audio signal is transfer/edited through the 1630, watch the levels carefully, adjusting for a decibel or two of headroom. (A peak level of $+18$ to $+20$ on the 1630's bargraphs will result in a fully modulated tape.) When digitally fading any program material, care must be taken to avoid granulation noise during fade-outs. Fader positions of more than 60 dB below system headroom can produce granulation noise and should be faded through as quickly as possible. Beware of any lapses in audio signal or clicks between tracks. Leave up to two minutes of lead-out at the end of the program. No alignment tones are required on the CD master tape. And of course, LP side breaks are no longer needed.

The audio program can be recorded either with or without pre-emphasis, or it may change between tracks, provided the begin-access point of the track is placed at least two seconds after the end-access point of the previous track (see below). Pre-emphasis boosts high frequencies during encoding and attenuates them upon decoding (at the player); this results in a slightly better S/N ratio. However, the boost also necessitates slightly lower levels on the master tape and the resulting CDs.

### Subcode Editing

After the master tape has been assembled, the music program is fully recorded on the U-matic tape. The next step in the pre-mastering process turns the CD master tape into a CD tape master, ready for mastering. Every CD contains a subcode (which was discussed in Chapter Four). Cue editors use user-input information and timecode numbers to generate the subcode. Using the CD subcode processor/editor, the engineer enters the preliminary required data that is requested by the system's menu: album title, artist, record label, catalogue number, UPC number, analog or digital source, and mastering engineer's name. All track titles are entered, along with other individual track information, including the ISRC number, copy inhibit, pre-emphasis, and index points.

### Access Times

The timecode points at the beginning and end of individual tracks must be entered. The concept of using timecode to select the proper begin-access and end-access points is critical in preparing a CD tape master, as well as its cue sheet. The start of the first track is located using the proper timecode numbers. Then the editor is used to rewind the tape fifteen video frames, and this new location is entered into the subcode editor. The added time is required to allow a player sufficient time to unmute and begin playing after it has located a track's beginning. It also provides a comfortable margin for the listener from the time the play button is pressed to the beginning of playback, and it protects against offset between the audio and video heads on the U-matic. Of course, any ambient noise before or after a track must be included in the track's time markings.

Next, the end of the track is located. The end-access point is the point where the access signal to the player is encoded. It signals the player when to go to the next track when the player is in random mode playback. It is not equivalent to the actual end point. The end-access point must be placed after the end of the program (including its decay ambience) or else the player might prematurely skip ahead to the next track when it is in random access mode. Some facilities suggest a full second between actual end point and end-access point.

This procedure is graphically represented in figure 7.3. In the first example (figure 7.3a), the tracks (TNO) are separated by intervals of two seconds or more. If access-begin points are placed a full second before actual-begin points, and access-end points placed a full second after actual-end points, then a comfortable margin is assured. In the second example (figure 7.3b), the tracks are merged with crossfades. In this case, the first begin-access point and the last end-access point get their one-second cushion. However, the begin-access points are placed fifteen video frames (thirty frames per second) before the crossfade begins, and access-end points may be omitted after tracks 1 and 2. In the third example (figure 7.3c), the intervals separating the tracks are less than two seconds. The inter-track begin-access points must be placed fifteen frames prior to the actual-begin points. Note that the begin-access point for TNO 2 is placed while TNO 1 is still playing.

A few specific caveats are worth pointing out. A track time length must be at least four seconds, and individual duration should be the time be-

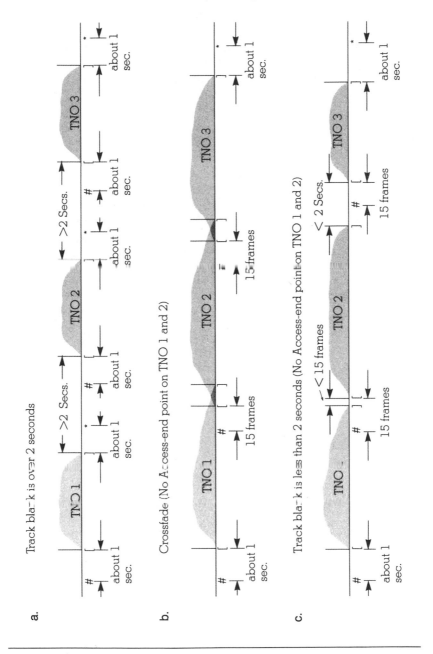

Figure 7.3   *Three examples showing placement of access points relative to actual program times. (a) two tracks separated by 2 or more sec. (b) tracks merged with a crossfade (no end-access points on tracks 1 and 2). (c) tracks separated by an interval less than 2 sec. (no access-end points on tracks 1 and 2). Key: # = access-begin point; \* = access-end point; [ = actual begin point; ] = actual end point. (Courtesy Sony)*

tween the begin-access and the end-access points. When a track is recorded with emphasis (but the prior track is not), the begin-access of the track should be placed at least two seconds after the end-access point of the prior track. When the interval between two tracks is less than two seconds, omit the end-access point for the former track and place the begin-access of the latter track fifteen frames before the actual begin point. As in a crossfade, when the track blank is less than two seconds and the end-access point is omitted, the individual time should be between the begin-access points of the two tracks.

Disagreement appears to exist between one pressing facility and another regarding the number of frames between the begin-access point, the end-access point, the actual begin point, and the actual end point. The result is an offset in which some players access a track after the start of program when they are in random access mode.

Some pressing facilities suggest that the begin-access point be placed one second before the actual starting point to provide the listener with a comfortable margin. This also aids slow players. However, this risks the possibility of an accurate player starting a track at a point where the previous track is still playing. In the case of a crossfade between two tracks, use fifteen frames before the beginning of the next track (not fifteen frames after the previous track's end). Other facilities call for only five frames between the begin-access point and actual begin point. In either case, the first track calls for a longer start delay than other tracks; two seconds or more gives the listener a chance to get settled.

The CD standard calls for players to mute/unmute the audio signal within fourteen milliseconds during track search operations and gives them two seconds to unmute at the first audio track. The standard also permits an inaccuracy of 150 milliseconds in locating a random start location. In practice, in any case, cheaper players can exceed tolerances. A difference of five frames generously covers these player tolerances. However, not all players are built to tolerance. When preparing your own CD tape master, the choice is yours. A consultative phone call to the intended pressing plant could prevent confusion.

When supplying a master tape to a CD pressing facility, and when in doubt, specify all timecodes without offset and clearly state this in your documentation. In any event, all timecodes must of course refer to the actual time of the program on the production tape master. Any error would result in errors in the disc's table of contents.

### Final Steps

When all of the track access points have been entered, the subcode editor calculates the playing time for each track and the total disc playing time, including pauses in minutes, seconds, and frames. Finally, the master tape is rewound, and the subcode editor writes a thirty-second header tone which is followed by the subcode information recorded on audio track 1 of the U-matic. The subcode section may extend past the start of the program; this is permissible. Subcode information is recorded at the beginning of the tape in a table of contents (TOC) format. This code is different from the disc subcode channels which are generated with the SMPTE timecode when the disc is cut.

A cue sheet contains a printout of the subcode from the editor. Copies should accompany the CD tape master to the pressing facility, a copy should accompany a safety copy, and the graphic designer could use a copy to properly list the titles and timings on the artwork. Naturally, the cue sheet should be checked carefully against the master tape for accuracy.

A spurious noise information sheet should accompany any tape sent to a pressing facility. The client should document the TNO and describe any noises on the tape (e.g., "TNO 3, click at 25 mins, 34 secs, 12 frames"). This lets the mastering engineer know that the tape has a problem that is already identified and that it has been decided to let it slide. Otherwise, the mastering engineer might contact the client to ask about the click, which would cause delay and further expense.

A summary of information to be supplied with the tape master is shown in figure 7.4.

Title, catalogue number, name of customer, etc.

Lettering for center of disc (if different from catalogue number)

Format of tape (PCM-1610/30, PCM-F1, analog, noise reduction, etc.)

Sampling rate

Whether time code or cue format present (PCM-1610/30 tapes only)

Barcode (optional)

Total playing time, including pauses (optional)

Starting point for all timings (tapes without time code only)

For each track:

    Track number

    Start time

    Stop time

    Times of index points (optional)

    ISRC (optional)

    Whether emphasized

    Length of track (optional)

    Title of track (optional)

Spurious noise information

---

Figure 7.4    *Summary of information that should accompany a CD tape master.*

Finally, after the tape master has been auditioned for dropouts, phantom or otherwise, and the cue sheet has been checked for accuracy, they may be forwarded to the CD pressing facility, along with the documentation. The only task left is the preparation of artwork; the pressing plant should be consulted regarding details of the disc label, the inlay card booklet, and restrictions on the use of the official CD logo.

## DISC MASTERING

The design of CD disc mastering systems presented a unique challenge to development engineers. Although much of the manufacturing chain could be assembled from existing equipment, such as injection molding, metallization, and label printing machines, the first link in the chain required a wholly new system. The precision required of the system is considerable; any defect introduced on the master disc will be replicated on all production discs.

CD mastering begins with a U-matic tape master and a glass disc. The PCM audio data contained on a tape master will be transferred to the glass master where it will be represented as pits. Three mastering methods, using photoresist, nonphotoresist, and direct metal mastering, have been developed. All CDs are ultimately derived from the resulting master disc. Figure 7.5 illustrates the manufacturing chain; in this case, photoresist mastering is shown.

### Glass Master Disc

Disc mastering begins with a glass plate, about 240 millimeters in diameter and 5.9 millimeters thick. It is washed, lapped, and polished. An adhesive (chrome film or a silane coupling agent) is applied, followed by a coat of photoresist that is applied by a spinning developer machine. The plate is tested for optical dropouts with a laser; any burst dropouts in reflected intensity are cause for rejection of the plate. The plate is cured in an oven and stored with a shelf life of several weeks; it is ready for master cutting.

### Photoresist Mastering System

In most cases, disc mastering is accomplished with a largely automated laser "cutting" machine which exposes the AZ photoresist on the master glass disc, followed by wet development. The encoded signal must meet the CD encoding standard, as discussed in Chapter Three. Figure 7.6 is a block diagram of a complete photoresist mastering system. The equipment is quite complex. The mastering machine is composed of two units: a control rack and a lathe. The control rack contains a minicomputer with video

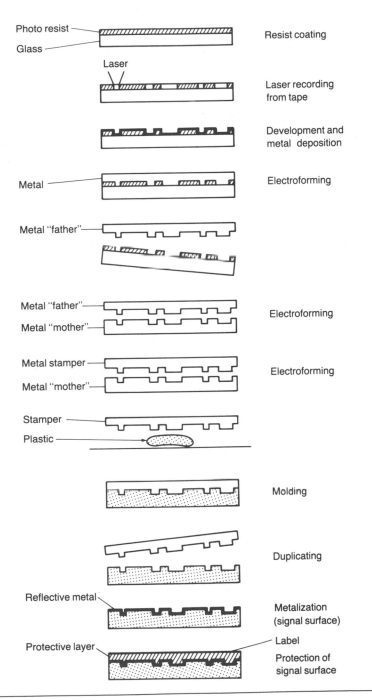

Resist coating

Laser recording
from tape

Development and
metal deposition

Electroforming

Electroforming

Electroforming

Molding

Duplicating

Metalization
(signal surface)

Protection of
signal surface

Figure 7.5 *Summary of CD manufacturing chain.*

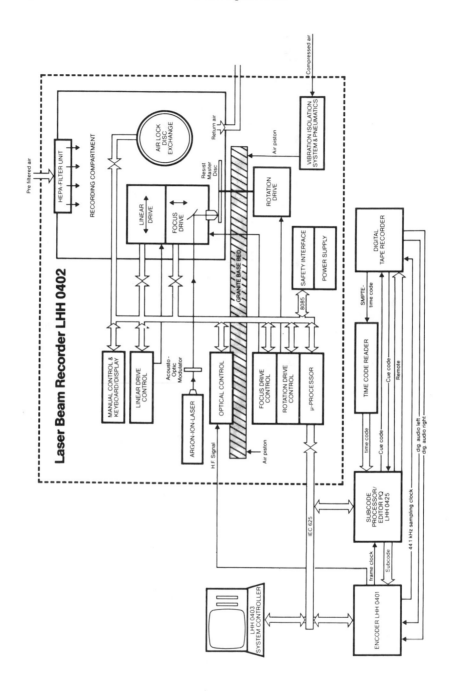

Figure 7.6    *Block diagram of a laser beam recorder. (Courtesy Philips)*

terminal and floppy disk drive, U-matic video transport, PCM audio processor, and diagnostic equipment. The master tape is loaded in the video transport, and the CD encoder uses subcode, timecode, and digital audio from the master tape to carry out multiplexing and CIRC encoding. The CD encoder generates the EFM channel bit stream signal. That signal modulates the cutting lathe's laser beam. In addition the CD encoder outputs signals used for automatic quality control.

The system controller in the control rack provides for automatic system operation. Recording operations are stored on floppy disk. Recording parameters, such as linear velocity, master identification number, and program length, are entered via controller keyboard. Track pitch, focus offset, and recording intensity can be altered from program defaults if necessary. A video display shows process status.

The master glass plate coated with photoresist is placed on the lathe and exposed with a "cutting" laser to form the spiral track, creating the disc contents in real time as the master tape is played through the PCM processor. The channel bit stream is input to an acousto-optical modulator that is used to intensity-modulate a laser which creates the cutting signal corresponding to the data on the original audio master tape. Audio data on the tape master is transferred, sample by sample, to the disc.

A second laser, which does not affect the photoresist, is used for focus and tracking. A focus monitor is used to confirm accuracy and recording spot quality. The spiral data track extending outward across the disc requires precise motion for both disc rotation and the linear speed of the sled carrying the cutting and focusing optics. To obtain frictionless motion, air bearings are used for both mechanisms.

Although the optics are similar to those found inside consumer CD players, the mechanisms are built on a grander scale, especially in terms of isolation from vibration. The entire cutting process is accomplished automatically under computer control. Not only are the contents of the CD exposed, but the test signals are recorded on the inner and outer diameters of the master disc data area.

*Developing*

After exposure in the master cutter, the glass master is developed by an automatic developing machine. The exposed areas are etched away by the developing fluid, creating pits in the resist surface. During development a laser monitors pit depth and stops development when proper engraving depth has been reached. The optimum data signal would result when a pit caused an absence of reflected light from the disc, thus distinguishing it from the surrounding reflective land. This is achieved when the pit depth is one-quarter of the apparent wavelength of the laser pickup, thus providing destructive interference, and the pit width is such that the intensity of the light reflected from the pit bottom equals the intensity of the light reflected from the surface. In practice, pit depth and width specifications must be modified slightly to provide a more robust tracking signal. This was discussed in detail in Chapter Three.

### Final Preparation

Following development, a metal coating, usually of silver, is evaporated onto the photoresist layer; the master disc is then ready for electroforming and replication. An important quality control check is performed at this point to ascertain the accuracy of the disc formation and pit geometry. The master disc is played on a master player, and test signals are derived to measure the high-frequency signal output. Track pitch and track stability are measured by monitoring the radial tracking signal during playback. In addition, errors are counted and subcode accuracy is verified. Finally, the master disc is auditioned for audio program quality.

### Facility Requirements

Even though mastering sounds fairly straightforward, most CD mastering facilities will attest to the difficulties involved. A laser beam mastering facility requires numerous subsystems, including a resist master preparation system, master recording system, developer system, master disc player system, and disc master electroplating equipment. Other items from a long list include microscopes, ovens, chemical preparation equipment, diagnostic and test equipment, glassware, cleaning and protective materials, desks and hoods, audio monitoring equipment, and dust-free paper.

Site requirements are carefully specified. Clean air is critical. CD pits are among the smallest of all manufactured formations — about the size of a smoke particle. Thus the entire mastering process must be carried out in a clean room environment, with the size and number of particles in the air strictly regulated. Clean room classifications specify the number of particles present in the air and their size. Class 100,000 for example, specifies no more than 100,000 particles 0.5 to 5.0 micrometers in diameter per cubic foot of air per minute. The air inside a CD mastering lathe is specified to be Class 100.

Temperature and humidity, along with ambient air pollution levels, must also be specified. With some systems the glass disc moves from one process stage to the next in a sealed cartridge. With each process step, the disc is automatically removed from the cartridge and then returned. This minimizes manual contact and air exposure, thus reducing the chances for contamination of the disc.

Vibration would be disastrous to the cutting process. The laser beam recorder is mounted on a massive baseplate, made from materials such as cast iron or granite, with a pneumatic vibration isolation system. Other requirements include a clean electrical system, demineralized and hot water, compressed air, filtered air, nitrogen, and a system ensuring the exhaust of contaminated air.

The facility could be housed in a clean room of 200 square meters. However, many disc manufacturers specify larger rooms, with an eye toward additional mastering equipment to accommodate the production of audio discs as well as CD-ROM, and future formats encompassing both constant linear velocity as well as constant angular velocity discs.

### DRAW Mastering System

A DRAW compact master disc recorder system uses a process quite different from conventional AZ photoresist mastering equipment. A non-photoresist (NPR) recording medium is used. It employs a direct-read-after-write (DRAW) technology which eliminates the developing processing required by photoresist methods after laser cutting. With a DRAW system, pits are formed on a plastic coated glass master disc; a 50 mW argon ion writing laser operating at a wavelength of 488 nm vaporizes points on the plastic layer to form the pits. A lower powered 5 mW helium neon reading laser follows the writing laser to control the focus of the writing laser and check the integrity of the cut immediately after it is made, reading back the cut signal. With modifications, cutting time can be decreased two or three times less than real time. The cutting lathe is enclosed in its own Class 100 air chamber with positive pressure, thus minimizing exterior room specifications. Because the lathe is designed to read the master disc while it is being written, even exposure power is servo-controlled, based on playback of the master disc in real time. This eliminates the need for a separate master disc player for the quality control operation following master disc recording.

The DRAW mastering process, originally developed for video disc mastering, offers several advantages over conventional AZ photoresist technology; there are fewer steps of critical nature. Preparation of the glass master is simpler; no adhesive layers are required and baking does not affect the sensitivity of NPR as it does AZ photoresist. Because NPR is self-developing, a separate developing step is not needed; moreover, disc exposure evaluation can take place in real time. The pit shape of an NPR master surface is uniform and not subject to variation due to exposure, baking, or development. All quality control can be carried out during data writing. One can expect improvement in yield, efficiency, and productivity.

### Direct Metal Mastering System

Alternatively, a direct metal mastering (DMM) process has been developed for producing compact disc masters. Instead of using a laser to expose a photoresist disc, DMM embosses the CD pits directly on a metal master disc. Because the embossing process is largely impervious to contaminants on the disc surface, a clean room is not required. Its developers claim lower investment and production costs compared to conventional photoresist CD mastering.

The process employs a piezoelectric electromechanical transducer, such as the type used in videodisc recording. Figure 7.7 shows a piezoelectric longitudinal transducer with an embossing diamond stylus attached. Deformation of the element occurs through the piezoelectric effect, according to the polarity of the bipolar applied potential. The assembly rests on the disc, pressing on the recording surface because of gravity. Because the center of gravity of the assembly cannot change instantaneously on account of inertia, the longer dimension causes the cutting stylus to press into the recording surface while the shorter dimension causes it to move away, lifting it from the disc.

The stylus thus presses into the disc during positive pulses and skips above it during negative pulses. The difference in length in the piezoelectric element and the maximum possible time between positive pulses can be calculated. This, in turn, is correlated to the lowest data frequency of the CD signal (196 kHz). The stylus is thus designed to successfully jump over (and onto) the disc surface within the constraints of the CD's EFM signal. The result is the impression of pits on the disc surface.

The shape of the diamond stylus is crucial, for it must create a pit geometry compatible with the CD system. An embossed pit has a geometry similar to that of an analog groove; a cross section view would reveal a "V" shape with walls at a 45 degree angle. By selecting a suitable stylus angle and optimizing the speed with which the cutting stylus is moving, engineers can create pits which modulate the pickup's laser beam with the same intensity and a similar phase characteristic as the pits from conventionally

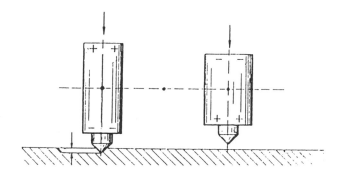

Figure 7.7   *A piezoelectric embossing element is used in the DMM CD mastering process. (Courtesy Teldec)*

mastered CDs. The manufacturer states that a CD player built with standard wavelength and aperture cannot distinguish between the two types of pits.

An embossed pit also differs from a photoresist pit because embossing results in a displacement of material; because of material flow, a ridge in created along the lateral pit edges. The pits on a conventionally mastered disc have a rounded contour because the polycarbonate cannot conform exactly to the mold geometry. Embossed pits produce a relatively sharp edge because of deformation after injection molding. Figure 7.8 shows a cross section of a mold and an injection-molded disc substrate. Ridges produced by embossing produce a hollow area in the negative area of the stamper. This encourages polycarbonate flow and, consequently, a sharper pit edge.

In direct metal mastering, a metal surface is used for mastering. A glass substrate disc is prepared with a separation layer a few nanometers thick A layer of copper approximately 300 nanometers thick is sputtered over the preparation layer and the data is embossed on this copper surface.

When the embossing is complete, a galvanic process is used to prepare the master for replication. The copper surface is covered with a layer of precious metal (gold or rhodium) a few micrometers thick. This layer is then covered with a layer of nickel approximately .25 millimeters thick; this may be used as a father or stamper after separation from the glass substrate. Finally, the electroplate must be released from the sandwich; both the copper layer and separation layer may be removed in a ferric chloride solution without damaging the gold or rhodium surface on the nickel backing. Using the resulting metal parts, engineers use conventional galvanic processes to generate mother and stamper tools. If rhodium is used, the

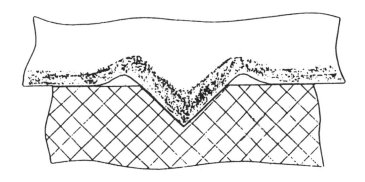

Figure 7.8 *A profile of a pit stamper shows the resulting "V" shaped pit, with a sharply-defined pit edge. (Courtesy Teldec)*

metal part may be used directly as a stamper, able to press 10,000 to 15,000 discs before deterioration.

The DMM CD master system is an ingenious and cost-effective product in the context of the increasingly vigorous introduction of new CD manufacturing equipment. Because it does not require clean room conditions, the DMM-CD system, along with many other products, will help lower the manufacturing costs of CDs.


## ELECTROFORMING

Electroforming, sometimes called matrixing, bears a close resemblance to the corresponding stages of vinyl LP production. The various aspects of electroforming, such as composition of the plating solution, temperature control, solution flow, and plating current distribution, are optimized to obtain a fine surface for CD replication. These adjustments are completely different from those needed for an analog disc. The electroforming plating process ultimately results in metal stampers used to replicate CDs.

Following mastering and developing, a silver (or nickel) layer is deposited with vacuum evaporation over the photoresist layer. The master is played on a master player system to assess aural and measured quality; it also serves as a reference to evaluate the quality of the final production discs. The silvered master is then transferred to the electroforming room. The silvered master disc, which is now electrically conductive, is placed in a galvanic nickel electrolyte bath. The master disc is the cathode ($-$) of an electric circuit. From a nickel anode ($+$) a nickel layer is electroformed onto the master disc.

In a typical application, a reservoir holding the electrolyte solution (nickel sulphamate) is located outside the clean room. It is held at a constant temperature, filtered for one or two micron maximum particle size, electrolytically purified, pH checked and held at a constant value by adding sulphamic acid, and circulated constantly. The master is placed in a sink and etched (activated) with a solution of sulphamic acid. It is rinsed and put in a holder to ensure uniform current flow over the master's face. The holder is placed on the shaft of the cathode drive in the plating tank, and the plating process is initiated.

The plating process starts with a low current which increases as the nickel plate grows thicker. The time required for plating depends on the thickness desired. Nominally, a maximum current of 100 amps produces a part in less than two hours.

After electroforming, the nickel part is separated from the glass master. It is rinsed in an electrolytic degreasing tank at high temperature, or with a solvent such as acetone, to remove any particles of photoresist. Since the master's photoresist layer is usually damaged when it is separated from the metal part, masters may be used only once.

Because the disc master has a positive impression of the CD pit track, the resulting nickel copy, called the "father," is a negative impression. In cases of limited production, the father can be used to replicate CDs. The father is inspected and used to galvanically generate a number of positive impression "mothers." Four or five mothers may be made from one father.

Each mother is inspected. If a mother is acceptable, it can then generate a number of negative impression nickel mold matrices, "sons" or "stampers," by the same process. Stampers are optically checked to ensure quality.

When it is separated from the mother, the stamper is rinsed, dried, and a protective layer (either a tape, form, or plastisol) is applied to its face. Next, a backsanding machine is used to polish its back, and it is put in a centering device. Using a reference mark on the stamper, the part is centered to within 1.0 micron, and the center hole is punched out. Next, the outside circumference is punched. The stamper is ready for mounting in an injection molding machine. Four or five stampers may be made from one mother. When mounted to a die, stampers are used in the replicating machines to produce CD discs.

The electroplating room requires a Class 1,000 environment. However, the electroplating process is carried out in enclosed electroforming consoles. They are placed in Class 100 laminar flow enclosures to maintain cleanliness. Often a HEPA (High Efficiency Particulate Air) filter and fan are used to circulate filtered air. Submicronic filtration systems are used to ensure that the chemical baths do not become contaminated. Moreover, the electroplating system must be able to produce disc molds that are flat to within ±3 microns over the entire disc surface.

In new generations of electroforming equipment, the emphasis is on speed. In some cases the father, mother, and stamper processing can be completed in less than an hour. This is crucial when small disc runs require a large volume of stampers. In particular, CD-ROM production would necessitate speedy electroforming.


## INJECTION MOLDING

Following the mastering and electroforming processes, the disc is ready for replication. Injection molding techniques are commonly used. Molten plastic is injected into a mold cavity, with the stamper on one face, producing a clear plastic disc with the pits impressed on one side. A polycarbonate plastic is used chiefly because of its high transparency, dimensional stability, accurate reproduction of the mold surface, minimum water absorption, good impact resistance, easy processing characteristics, and freedom from impurities. These characteristics can be achieved from a high-grade polycarbonate resin. However, polycarbonate material has certain inferior specifications, especially when handled by injection molding; we shall discuss these later in this section.

### Molding Considerations

The molding of compact discs presents great challenges; the disc must be flat and optically pure, and it must retain an accurate impression of the data pits. Furthermore, typical molding practices result in discs with deficient optical properties. To achieve satisfactory results, disc molding requires minimized plastic resin viscosity for good fluidity. To obtain low viscosity, good fluidity — and hence acceptable optical properties — the resin temperature must be raised considerably. However, the resin is easily decomposed, resulting in color change or bubbles. Because the disc volume is small and the amount of resin needed is small, heated resin is retained longer in typical molding machines, easily leading to degraded or burned resin. Furthermore, high-speed passing of resin causes mechanical shearing heat, which is another factor to be controlled.

Although problematic, high-speed filling is desirable in injection molding. High-speed filling prevents a drop in temperature of the polycarbonate and enables uniform melting temperature in the cavity. This ensures uniform force and density of the molded disc and makes possible uniform cooling speed across the entire disc surface, which in turn allows uniform shrinkage. High-speed filling also prevents pressure drop and assures that adequate pressure is applied even at the far edges of the cavity. Distribution of the pressure in the cavity is uniform, and molding shrinkage is small. Molding can be performed with lower pressure, resulting in discs with minimun warpage or deformation. Finally, high-speed filling permits molding at lower temperature and faster cycle times.

As cavity filling speed is increased, however, two problems arise. First, it is difficult to accurately control the amount of polycarbonate to be injected. Second, it is difficult to discharge air from inside the cavity. Sophisticated control systems and, in some cases, a vacuum in the cavity can be used to achieve very brief filling periods of 0.01 to 0.1 seconds at low pressure.

Because of these and other problems, use of typical injection molding machines results in discs with burned plastic and, consequently, contaminations or bubbles. If the resin temperature is lowered, strain or deformation of the disc after molding can result, along with a high birefringence. After experimentation with various polycarbonate resins, different kinds of injection molding machine designs, and mold shapes, techniques for producing a single piece polycarbonate disc were achieved. As a result, there is a considerable difference between standard polycarbonate and that used for making CDs in specifications such as melt flow rate.

### The Molding Machine

The heart of an injection molding machine is its plasticizing unit, shown in figure 7.9. Because polycarbonate is a hygroscopic material, it must be dried, stored at a high temperature, and then used without being exposed to ambient air. Thus pellets of polycarbonate (cleaned and dried) are drawn directly through the hopper and into a heating barrel; a screw moves the pellets through a series of heating coils to heat the plastic quickly and uniformly to a high temperature (approximately 660 degrees Fahrenheit) in order to achieve smooth flow properties into the mold cavity during injection. When the molten plastic is injected into the mold cavity at high pressure, it conforms to the stamper's contours, producing a substrate disc with pits. The mold is kept at a temperature of approximately 230 degrees Fahrenheit.

Some systems use an injection-compression molding process. The molten plastic is first injected into the mold, which is not yet completely closed. The final shape of the disc is accomplished during the subsequent compression step. With injection-compression molding, molded-in stress is minimized, but cycle times are somewhat longer than conventional injection molding, perhaps fifteen seconds as compared to seven seconds.

In some systems, the center hole is formed before the disc is removed from the mold. In other systems, the center hole is punched out of the disc

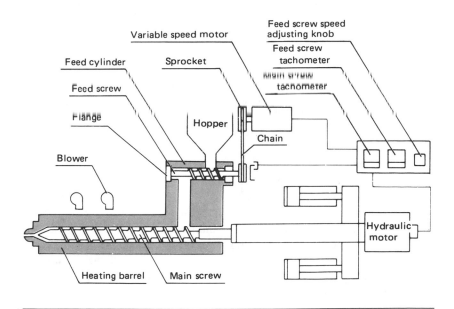

Figure 7.9    *Elements of an injection molding machine. (Courtesy Meiki)*

separately, after the top layer is applied but before the label is printed. Following molding, the warm disc is subject to static charge; any dust particles in the air are attracted to the disc. The molding room must be kept at Class 1,000, and special hoods are placed over the molding machines for an even cleaner environment at the molding head.

In summary, the injection molding process requires consideration of environmental cleanliness and temperature control, nozzle and hopper temperature regulation, mold temperature regulation, adjustment and stability of injection volume and time, removal of flashes from mold surface, and the quality of stampers.

## Birefringence

A form of optical distortion measured as birefringence can be introduced during injection molding of the polycarbonate substrate. Birefringence is an optical measure of material stress, measuring by the differences in the index of refraction in materials through which light passes. These affect the phase relationship of laser light and can result in reading errors. The amount of birefringence in a plastic material is related to its inherent optical properties, but more importantly to the internal stress in the plastic caused, in this case, by shrinkage, flow lines, and inclusions. Injection molding therefore greatly increases the amount of birefringence in polycarbonate.

Due to refraction, light rays bend as they pass from one medium to another with a different density. With birefringence (a kind of double refraction) light is refracted into two images. In refraction, light slows down as it enters a new medium. With birefringence, light is slowed down at two different rates, depending on the angle that it passes through the material. More specifically, the light is split into two perpendicular polarized components with different refraction and different wavelengths, as shown in figure 7.10. Birefringence causes a reduction in the intensity of laser light that is read from the disc by the pickup. This reduction in intensity is caused by the turning of the polarization direction away from that of the polarizer. Because the polarization direction is not aligned with the polarizer, less light is allowed back into the pickup. The effect is similar to the way polarized sunglasses reduce glare.

Birefringence also changes the critical phasing of the light as it reflects off the disc. The area of the laser spot simultaneously striking a pit relative to the surrounding land (refer to figure 3.3) and the carefully calculated pit depth causes destructive interference. This yields intensity modulation of the reflected light. Since birefringence causes deteriorated interference, the quality of the modulated light is degraded. In either case, birefrigence causes reduced signal response from the optical pickup. This can cause

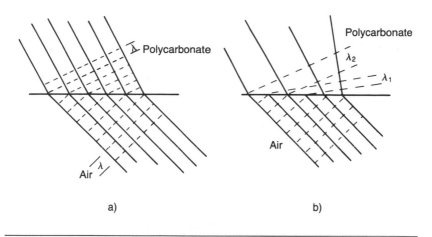

Figure 7.10   *Light rays bend in a result of refraction (a). Birefringence causes double refraction (b).*

data reading errors, as well as tracking problems, in all CD players with laser pickups which use a polarized, beam-splitting head to read polarized light as it passes through the disc. Pickups using holographic optical elements (HEM) technology are not affected by birefringence.

The wavelength of a pickup's laser light is 780 nanometers in air and approximately 500 nanometers in polycarbonate (the index of refraction is 1.55). Birefringence is measured in terms of the phase shift between the $x$ and $y$ components of light and is expressed in nanometers. It is measured by finding the amount of reduction of polarized light intensity through the disc. The birefringence specification calls for a maximum deviation of 20 percent (100 nanometers) from the 500 nanometer wavelength. In any event, when birefringence of a disc exceeds a normal amount, there is increased risk that not all players will play the disc.

### Future Considerations

The conventional method of injection molding of polycarbonate is inefficient in several respects. Polycarbonate is difficult to mold without introducing optical distortions, and basic materials and equipment are expensive. In addition, large floor space and manpower are required, to say nothing of expensive clean rooms. Given the difficulties in this replication method, improvements and innovations in the process are proceeding; for example, the increased use of robot workers, the consolidation of equipment into in-line configurations, and the placement of equipment inside small, self-contained clean areas are dramatically increasing efficiency.

## METALLIZATION AND SPIN COATING

After leaving the molding machine, the disc is wholly formed, but transparent; a player's laser beam could not read the impressed data because there would be no reflected beam to convey the information. Hence a reflective layer must be placed over the data pits. The reflective layer, typically aluminum, is very thin — on the order of 50 to 100 nanometers thick. To protect this thin layer from physical damage and oxidation, an acrylic plastic layer is applied over it.

### Metallization Layer

The reflection coefficient of the metal layer, including the polycarbonate substrate (note that the CD player laser must shine through the substrate to the metal layer), is specified to be between 70 and 90%. In addition, the metal must be chosen to be inert with the polycarbonate substrate. Three cost-effective metals qualify with the required reflectivity and stability: aluminum, copper, and silver. Gold could also be used as an expensive alternative. The fact that it is an inert metal may be of use in some applications. Reflectance values of 80 to 90% apply at the readout wavelength even with thin layers. Because of the physical appearance of the layer, aluminum and silver are preferred over copper. Metallization requires a clean room of Class 1,000.

### Vacuum Evaporation

With vacuum evaporation (vapor deposition) as the application method, aluminum has good adherence and is most commonly used. A spacer covers the center of the disc, and a ring masks the outer edge. Consequently, only the area containing the information is coated. In some systems, the evaporation is accomplished in a vacuum chamber with aluminum-coated resistance elements. Large racks of discs are treated simultaneously, and a good mirror coating results. Metallization may take about fifteen minutes, depending on the size of the vacuum chamber. However, a major production snag is encountered as the discs must be individually loaded onto the racks and batch-metallized. Then the pumping-down of the evaporation chamber must occur, followed by the readmission of air after deposition. These steps are not easily integrated into the otherwise continuous disc manufacturing process. Furthermore, any dust in the chamber, stirred up during pumping, may cause pinholes in the metal layer. This can be avoided only through stringent cleanliness.

Alternatively, some vapor deposition systems employ multiple prechambers in which a spindle loaded with discs may be undergoing metallization while another load in a prechamber is being evacuated. Discs are metallized individually, a process which takes about three seconds. With a capacity of 1,200 discs per hour and a target life of 40,000 hours, such a metallizer could run forty hours without interruption. In still other systems, discs are moved one at a time through the metallizer on a conveyer. In this way, throughput is further increased.

### Sputtering

Magnetron sputtering is another metallization method used for CDs. A cold solid target is bombarded with ions, releasing metal molecules which coat the disc. Using high voltages, a discharge is formed between a cathode target and an anode. Powerful permanent magnets behind the cathode form a concentrated plasma discharge immediately above the target area. Argon ions are extracted from the plasma. They bombard the target surface, thus sputtering it. The CD is placed opposite the target and outside the plasma region.

Discs can be metallized one at a time by loading them into a fast pump-down vacuum chamber; metallization takes only a few seconds. Because each disc sees exactly the same conditions each time (versus differing disc-to-disc conditions in a batch process), consistency is enhanced. Alternatively, a continuous sputtering machine with a permanent vacuum can be used for mass production. Discs are loaded at one end of a conveyer and passed through a series of bulkheads which create pressure gradients from ambient pressure down to a vacuum and back again to ambient pressure conditions. Sputtering is faster than evaporation and allows a choice of different metals or alloys.

### Wet Silvering

A metallic mirror can also be obtained by electroless silver deposition, often called wet silvering, a process long used to produce glass mirrors. In this process wet chemicals are combined to cause the formation of a thin layer of silver over the disc surface. Since the process is accomplished by spraying liquids, a continuous production machine can be used; the discs are placed on a conveyer belt and ride through the sequential processing stages. Wet silvering takes less time per disc than vacuum evaporation, and continuous rinsing of the disc minimizes the formation of pinholes.

### Spin Coating

The metal layer is covered by a plastic layer with a spin coating machine. This layer protects the aluminum layer from scratches and oxidation. The plastic layer can be nitrocellulose-based with air-drying, or an acrylic plastic cured in ultraviolet light. The latter is advantageous because of very short curing time, good bonding ability to aluminum, and the fact that it is a harder, more scratch resistant surface. However, it is more costly and difficult to print on.

At the spin coating machine, a small, metered amount of acrylic is sprayed on the disc just inside the inner diameter of the metal coat. The disc is then spun at high speed so that a very thin coat of lacquer, typically about six or seven microns thick, remains over the disc surface. The layer is then cured.

### Label Printing

The label is printed over the top acrylic layer. Two types of printing are in common use: silk screening and pad printing. Silk screening is very good when large surfaces have to be covered with an opaque layer of ink. A silk screening machine is somewhat slower and more expensive. Pad printing may be superior for reproducing intricate details. Both systems can print up to four colors and can be easily changed to new labels.

In the silk screening process, a screen with light-sensitive emulsion is exposed to light in order to transfer the image to the screen. The screen is then used as a stencil to mask printing ink to the disc surface. The ink must dry quickly. In some systems, ultraviolet-curing ink is used.

With pad printing, a coat of printing ink is spread on a cliche with recessed characters. The ink on this cliche is then scraped away with a knife, leaving only the ink in the characters. A cushion or pad is pressed onto the cliche and then transferred to the disc where it is pressed down again. In this way the ink is forced to adhere to the surface of the disc and remains there when the pad is lifted off. The disc is conveyed from one print position to the next for multiple colors.

In general, silk screening is the preferred method of labelling. It proves to be faster, with better yield. For example, a silk screen printer may process 2,500 discs per hour, as opposed to the pad printer's rate of 700 an hour. Printing may be carried out in a dirty room of Class 100,000. After printing, discs are ready for final quality control checks.

## QUALITY CONTROL

To ensure that all CDs successfully play on all CD players, a large range of optical, mechanical, and electrical criteria have been established for the CD system. The co-inventors and license holders of the compact disc, Philips and Sony, have published these specifications in the *Red Book*, the reference on standards available to all CD licensees. Some disc tolerances, such as disc eccentricity, have been established empirically; they represent a compromise between practicalities of manufacturing discs on one hand, and those of players on the other. Other specifications, such as error flags, are strictly theoretically determined. However, the implementation of this aspect, the number of errors permitted on any particular disc, again represents a compromise between media and players.

In any case, disc manufacturers and player manufacturers must agree on the facts to ensure that all disc tolerances are within the design limitations of all players. Moreover, quality control procedures are invaluable as an in-house means of diagnosing problems in the manufacturing process. Figure 7.11 shows the primary disc specifications and their relation to disc playback. Some of the primary specifications are examined below.

### Mechanical and Optical Specifications

Molded discs are checked for correct dimensions, lack of flash and burrs, birefringence, reflectivity, flatness (skew angle), and general appearance. The pit surface is checked for correct pit depth, correct pit volume or pit form and dimensions. The metallized coating is checked for pinholes and uneven thickness. As many manufacturers have discovered, one of the easiest ways to detect dust in the clean room is the appearance of pinholes. Birefringence can be checked with a circularly polarized light used to convert the phase change to an intensity variation measured with a photodiode. The disc can be scanned, creating a map of birefringence versus radius.

Angle deviation measures the angle formed by the normal to the disc in the radial direction as shown in figure 7.12. This angle is critical because any deviation causes the reflected laser beam to deviate from its return path through the objective lens. This angle deviation could result from an improper manufacturing method, specifications call for a maximum angle of 0.5 degrees. Because warpage could be introduced later in the field (for example, the extreme temperatures found in a car interior might cause bending), the specification allows a safety factor of 0.3 degrees.

Disc eccentricity measures the deviation from circularity of the pit track and the positioning of the center hole. The electroforming and molding processes introduce some eccentricity in the shape of the pit track. In addition, the player's positioning of the disc in the drive might introduce eccentricity. If it is excessive, it could exceed the ability of the radial tracking servo of the player. Tolerances for deviation from circularity call for maximum eccentricity of 140 micrometers.

Disc eccentricity must also account for alignment of the center hole. Specifications call for a center hole tolerance of 0.4 millimeters. A hole that is off center would lead to disc imbalance, and noise and resonance errors. In practice, an eccentricity of one millimeter would result in significant imbalance.

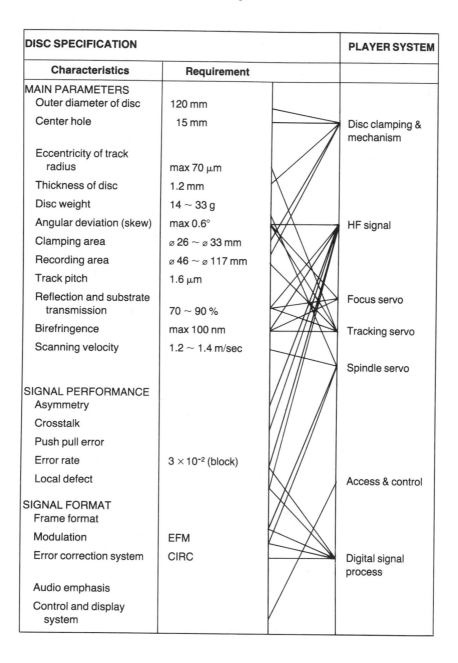

| DISC SPECIFICATION | | PLAYER SYSTEM |
|---|---|---|
| **Characteristics** | **Requirement** | |
| MAIN PARAMETERS | | |
| Outer diameter of disc | 120 mm | |
| Center hole | 15 mm | Disc clamping & mechanism |
| Eccentricity of track radius | max 70 μm | |
| Thickness of disc | 1.2 mm | |
| Disc weight | 14 ~ 33 g | |
| Angular deviation (skew) | max 0.6° | HF signal |
| Clamping area | ø 26 ~ ø 33 mm | |
| Recording area | ø 46 ~ ø 117 mm | |
| Track pitch | 1.6 μm | |
| Reflection and substrate transmission | 70 ~ 90 % | Focus servo |
| Birefringence | max 100 nm | Tracking servo |
| Scanning velocity | 1.2 ~ 1.4 m/sec | |
| | | Spindle servo |
| SIGNAL PERFORMANCE | | |
| Asymmetry | | |
| Crosstalk | | |
| Push pull error | | |
| Error rate | $3 \times 10^{-2}$ (block) | |
| Local defect | | Access & control |
| SIGNAL FORMAT | | |
| Frame format | | |
| Modulation | EFM | |
| Error correction system | CIRC | Digital signal process |
| Audio emphasis | | |
| Control and display system | | |

Figure 7.11 *Summary of primary disc tolerances and their relation to disc playback.*

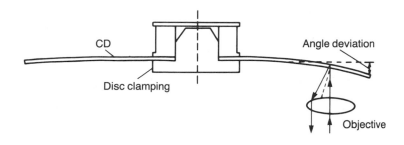

Figure 7.12 *Angle deviation causes reflected light to deviate from the objective lens.*

A distorted disc surface, such as one characterized by concentric waviness, results in reflection of the light beam at a deflected angle, as illustrated in figure 7.13. This, in turn, taxes the player's radial tracking servo circuit; a measurement of the radial error signal can be used to specify the tolerances for disc flatness. To measure the radial error signal for this specification (errors on the order of 0.1 to 1 millimeter) the error signal is filtered and processed to produce an RMS value. Standards call for a maximum radial tracking voltage of 250 millivolts. This represents the specification for radial errors, describing the maximum value the laser spot may deviate from the track. This maximum value is 0.03 micrometers. This

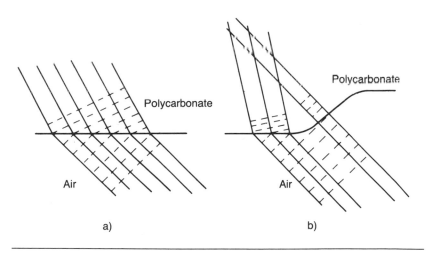

Figure 7.13 *A flat disc surface (a) permits normal refraction. A distorted disc surface (b) refracts light at a deflected angle.*

specification also accounts for other factors which affect radial tracking, including eccentricity and impurities such as bubbles, occlusions, or scratches.

### Error Correction Flags

Error correction flags generated during CD playback from the CIRC circuitry can represent the error rate (from sources such as pit structure, birefringence, pinholes, etc.) present on a disc. Thus the glass master, metal parts, and the finished disc may be checked for integrity via error correction flags. As discussed in Chapter Three, data is arranged in frames and corrected through two CIRC decoders, C1 and C2. The C1 decoder corrects minor errors and flags uncorrectable errors. The C2 decoder corrects larger errors, aided by the error flags. Uncorrected errors leaving C2 are flagged as well. Four flags are output from a measuring CD player: C1F1, C1F2, C2F1, and C2F2. They define the error conditions on the disc for every block of data as it is clocked through the decoders, as shown in table 7.1.

These flags can be counted over a time interval to obtain a measure of disc quality, as shown in figure 7.14. Three signals are derived from the C1 decoder. The first signal, E11, signals one defect symbol in a frame. The second signal, E21, signals two defect symbols in a frame. The third signal, E31, signals more than three defect symbols in a block. To evaluate the magnitude and quality of correction at C1, these signals are added, thus providing the block error rate (BLER). This measures the number of blocks per second containing any C1 errors (one block equals 588 bits/33 symbols). It is thus a measure of both correctable and uncorrectable errors at that decoding stage. A maximum BLER value of 220 pulses per second

| C1F1 | C1F2 | Status |
|------|------|--------|
| L | L | No errors detected in C1 decoder |
| H | L | 1 error corrected in C1 |
| L | H | 2 errors corrected in C1 |
| H | H | More than 2 errors in C1, data passed to C2 |

| C2F1 | C2F2 | Status |
|------|------|--------|
| L | L | No errors detected in C2 decoder |
| H | L | 1 error corrected in C2 |
| L | H | 2 errors corrected in C2 |
| H | H | More than 2 errors in C2 (uncorrectable) |

Table 7.1    *Four error flags derived from the error correction strategy are used to diagnose error conditions.*

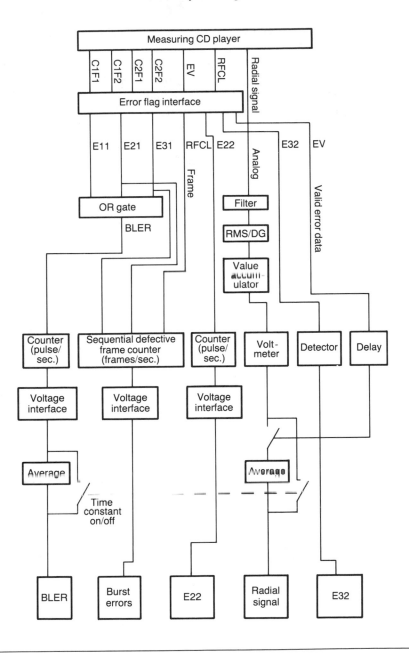

Figure 7.14 *Block error rate, burst errors, and other diagnostic signals may be derived from the measuring player.*

is permitted at the C1 decoder. High quality disc manufacturing facilities can achieve BLER values as low as 10 to 20.

The maximum value of 220 pulses per second shows that 0.03 percent of frames contain a defect. This defines the acceptable error limit, since greater frequency might lead to audible faults. The BLER does not provide information on individual defects between 100 to 300 micrometers, since the BLER responds to defects the size of one pit. BLER is often quoted as a one-second actual value or as a sliding ten-second average across the disc, as well as the maximum BLER encountered during a single ten-second interval during the test.

There are two error signals at the C2 decoder. The first signal, E22, signals two defect symbols in a frame. Empirical studies of inaudible faults have shown that a count of 100 pulses per second is permitted for E22. A quality control specification may allow eighty pulses per second. The second signal, E32, signals more than two defect symbols in a frame. These errors, which leave C2 uncorrected, are sometimes classified as noise interpolation errors (NI). The player must then interpolate; if there are multiple interpolations, the player may mute, or audible clicking may be heard. Thus, because E32 signals may indicate an audible fault, they are not permitted.

The E21 and E22 signals may be combined to form a burst error count (BST). It measures the number of consecutive block errors exceeding a specified threshold number. For example, if there are fourteen consecutive block errors, and the threshold is set at seven blocks, there will be two BST errors indicated. This count is often tabulated as a total number over an entire disc. A good quality control specification would not allow any burst errors (seven frames) to occur.

### Production Checking

In a production facility, finished discs are inspected for continuous and random defects using both automated and human checking. Birefringence, high-frequency signal, frame error rate, crosstalk, jitter, noise, presence of foreign particles, reflectivity, frame tracking, number of interpolations, and skew are checked on selected discs. As part of the quality control of master discs and finished discs, CD analyzers are used. These special players display the data recorded on the disc and provide a simultaneous printout. Often multiple players are used to check a percentage of several discs simultaneously, and then the results are combined for a composite report.

The analyzer indicates total playing time of the disc, the start time of each music selection as recorded in the table of contents, and the contents of the reference subcode. It checks for any subcode dropout or irregularities, noise generated by the error rate, and mistracking of the laser pickup.

All pertinent information, such the exact location of signal dropouts, can be printed out. The human eye is also effective for spotting defects; under polarized light, an area of defective pits is visible as a blemish.

## 100% Automated Inspection

In an automated quality control system, a rapid, automated device checks every disc for defects in less than one second. A laser beam scans each disc radially while the disc is rotated to produce 100% coverage of its surface. Defect detection is based on the normal reflection or transmission properties of the disc. Detection of all defects can only be achieved by using the optical properties of the disc itself, such as the diffraction grating formed by the pit and track structure. To perform this analysis, some systems use two or more optical receivers in combination. Sensors are placed to detect light reflected in the zero- and first-order diffraction angles. This may be extended to higher order diffraction angles as well.

Plane-polarized laser light is fitted to a polarization filter in the zero-order channel; it is sensitive to local birefringence and is thus able to detect small bubbles, inclusions, and other polycarbonate defects caused by localized stress. The first-order channel does not use a polarization filter; it is sensitive to metallization defects as well as faults in pit structure and track separation. Pinholes are detected with an optical transmission receiver shining on the disc.

Collecting the information from the light scattered by the different types of defects permits their classification and analysis. For example, damage on the upper surface of the disc produces a scattering in the incident light; this is recognized by a reduction in the amplitude of the first-order channel. Because the zero-order channel has a polarization filter, its amplitude will remain at zero unless birefringence causes a rotation in the plane of polarization. Thus an inclusion will cause an increase in the amplitude of the zero-order channel, while decreasing the amplitude of the first-order channel.

Scanning optics are used to provide a normal angle of incidence in the radial and tangential planes across the disc surface. This is required to reduce the refraction by the laser beam at the transitions between air, substrate, and metallized layer. Otherwise an error would occur in the measurement and location of defects due to distorting and de-focusing effects. A normal angle of incidence also prevents exaggeration of the local birefringence. The configuration of the laser scanning spot is crucial; experiments have shown that a rectangular spot is more sensitive to longitudinal defects, such as tangential scratches, than a circular spot of the same intensity. In one design, the rectangular scanning spot is thus made 10 micrometers radial by 150 micrometers tangential for audio CD checking. All optical scanning is controlled by extensive electronic evaluation equipment which permits quick analysis and adjustment of scanning parameters, as well as connection to a host computer for statistical compilation. In addition, options exist for reading a disc's alphanumeric code and automatically sorting discs from mixed production lines, while inspecting each according to different levels of quality.

Many facilities utilize this automated inspection method. One hundred percent automated disc inspection is recommended in addition to human visual inspection for causes of rejection such as cosmetic defects. After all the quality control checks have been completed, the disc is ready for packaging.

## *Disc Packaging*

Most CDs are packaged in a plastic jewel box which is made of transparent polystyrene, with a tray typically of opaque polystyrene. Printed inlay cards are inserted into the box, the tray is put on, and the box closed. This can be done manually, incorporating a final visual inspection, or by an automatic machine which can package up to sixty discs per minute. The finished jewel box may be blister- or shrink-wrapped, or inserted into a cardboard container. Following insertion into jewel box or other packaging and cellophane wrapping, the compact discs are ready for distribution to wholesalers.

## *Manufacturing Summary*

CD plants built from 1982 to 1984, so-called first generation plants, utilized large clean rooms, batch-type metallization systems, and little automation. Reject percentages were relatively high, and large amounts of downtime occurred. Plants constructed from 1984 to 1987 used second generation technology with large clean rooms, but with some isolation of heavy equipment outside of the clean areas to facilitate maintenance. Such plants generally employ in-line sputtering systems and some automation. However, similar to the first generation plants, high energy consumption, clean room costs, spoilage costs, labor costs, amortization of larger capital investment, and downtime dictate higher operating costs.

The design of third generation plants, first initiated in 1988, differs in a number of respects from earlier versions. First, they require about 25% less overall space, with very small clean rooms (about ten percent of the space required by a second generation facility). The replication processes are designed to be fully automated, including full integration of molding and metallizing, as well as automatic quality control sampling. As a result, because standby capacity is provided, plant downtime is minimized. In addition, the high level of automation reduces the number of production workers and eliminates rejects caused by contamination of the discs by workers.

Third generation plants employ a mono-line configuration which combines all the phases of CD replication into a single module. The time from raw polycarbonate to finished disc, including injection molding, metallization, spin coating, and labelling, is less than two minutes. Annual disc capacity of two million discs may be expected from a single line. The module is housed within its own clean room, protected by Class 100 HEPA filters, thereby reducing clean room requirements. The station may occupy a four by eight foot footprint. A module may be changed from one form of CD to another (e.g., 5-inch to 3-inch, or CD-Audio to CD-I) within one hour.

## ALTERNATIVE REPLICATION METHODS

Conventional CD manufacturing methods described previously incur both technical difficulties (e.g., bubbles in the substrate and static charge on discs attracting dust particles) and production limitations (e.g., batch evaporation to metallize discs), which yields a relatively inefficient manufacturing process. As an alternative, new manufacturing methods with increased productivity have been developed.

### 2P Process

The photopolymerization process (sometimes called the "2P" process) is not radically different from conventional injection molding of CDs. Instead of using polycarbonate thermoplastic resins, the 2P process uses a liquid photopolymer resin curable by ultraviolet light. Figure 7.15 shows the complete process. The liquid resin is injected into a mold with the pit stamper on one side and a prepared polycarbonate substrate on the other, and the mold is compressed. Ultraviolet light is radiated through the transparent substrate to cure the resin in the mold, and the hardened disc (pit formations on a 2P layer 30 micrometers thick, bonded to the substrate) is peeled from the mold. Subsequently, the disc is metallized, coated with a protective layer, and printed with a label, as with injection-molded CDs. Implementations of the 2P process have generally shown that it is cost-effective only for a relatively small production volume. Hence it is not an effective solution for the mass production of CDs.

### Continuous Methods

Rather than relying on batch processing, in which CDs are manufactured through a sequence of individual steps, alternative methods strive to produce CDs in one continuous process. One such method utilizes a proprietary photo-thermographic (PTT) process to produce stamped and laminated discs from extruded polycarbonate film and sheet. The process uses two layers of material, imprinted plastic film and polycarbonate, lami-

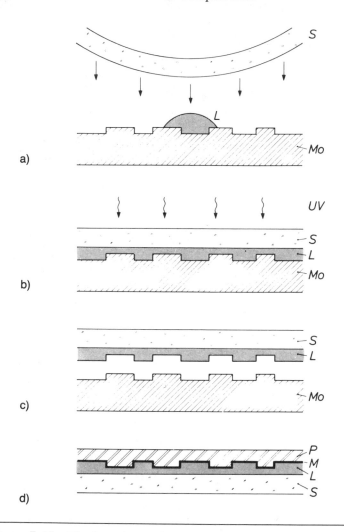

**Figure 7.15**  *The four phases of the 2P process: the liquid lacquer is spread over the mold by a slightly deformed substrate (a); exposure to ultraviolet light to cure the lacquer (b); substrate with lacquer separated from the mold (c); lacquer coated with reflective and protective layers (d). (Courtesy Philips Technical Review)*

nated together to form a disc, as shown in figure 7.16a. The pit data is imprinted on an optical-grade polycarbonate film with a nonmetallic stamper (made from a proprietary tool making technique), which is then coated with a reflective material through vacuum deposition or sputtering, illustrated in figure 7.16b. In a separate process, the imprinted reflective film is coated with an upper protective layer and then laminated to a sheet of

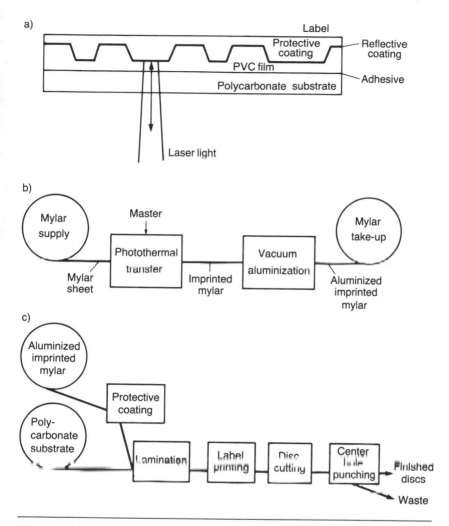

**Figure 7.16** *A continuous process in which an imprinted plastic film is laminated to a polycarbonate substrate (a). In the first manufacturing step, data is imprinted on the film and metallized (b). Finally, the film is coated with a protective layer and laminated to polycarbonate (c).*

polycarbonate. Conventional ultraviolet curing or electron-beam laminating resins are used. Finally, the discs are printed with a label and cut from the sheet as shown in figure 7.16c. The finished discs reflect laser light from the pickup identically to discs made from injection molding.

In another method, a machine turns out CDs from a continuous roll of polycarbonate substrate, operating much like a rotary printing press. Alu-

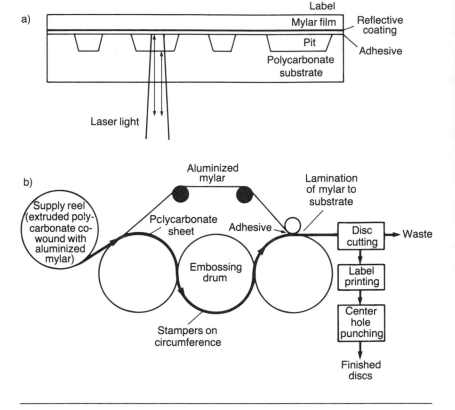

Figure 7.17    *A continuous process in which aluminized mylar is laminated to embossed polycarbonate (a). A rotary press is used to emboss the polycarbonate just prior to lamination (b).*

minized mylar is laminated to embossed polycarbonate substrate, such as the one shown in figure 7.17a. The data is embossed on the substrate and then laminated to a reflective and protective mylar layer. The finished disc is punched from the continuous ribbon as shown in figure 7.17b. Although the reflective film is flat, the light from the laser pickup undergoes phase cancellation as with a regular CD. The reflection from the flat bottom of the pit (aided by the change in refractive index between the polycarbonate substrate and the pit), is out-of-phase with the reflection from the reflective film, creating phase cancellation when a pit is read and hence an intensity difference between pit and land.

This system uses the same master disc as the injection molding process, but employs different stampers. Because the plastic substrate is first softened with a solvent and the stamping pressure is small, stampers have a long life expectancy. Because the pressing head is placed in a sealed environment, only a small, internal space requires clean room specifications. In theory, such a system could produce CDs at a rate of 1,000 per hour.

### Photolithographic Process

Another alternative manufacturing method uses photolithography to replicate discs. As with conventional CD mastering, a glass plate is coated with photoresist and exposed by a laser beam to produce a positive-impression disc. However, instead of using electroplating and injection molding, the pattern of pits is contact printed, by means of an ultraviolet light photoresist and exposing process, onto a plastic disc substrate previously coated with reflective material. The process is, in fact, quite similar to the the photographic process used to manufacture integrated circuits.

**FOR FURTHER READING**

Foster, Bill. "CD Mastering: How It Should Happen." *Studio Sound* 26(10):76 – 81, October, 1984.

Fox, B. "CD Video — The Technology." *One to One Magazine,* 28 – 30, May, 1987.

Herring, P. "Commitment to CD." *One to One Magazine,* 42 – 44, February, 1987.

LeBlanc, A. "Quality Control and Testing Procedures for Compact Discs." *AES Preprint No. 2511,* 83rd Convention, 1987.

Leonarz, P. "Toolex Alpha: Manufacturing CDs." *One to One Magazine,* 50 – 53, May, 1987.

Miyaoka, S. "Manufacturing Technology of the Compact Disc." In Blesser, B., B. Locanthi, and T. G. Stockham, Jr., eds. *Digital Audio.* New York: Audio Engineering Society, 1983.

Redlich, Horst, and Günter Joschko. "CD Direct Metal Mastering Technology: A Step toward a More Efficient Manufacturing Process for Compact Discs." *Journal of the Audio Engineering Society* 35(3):130 – 37, March, 1987.

Technoplas, Inc. "Cavity Pressure Control System for Injection Molding." November, 1986.

Technoplas, Inc. "Fast-Cycle Precision Injection Molding Machine." November, 1986.

Turner, Ben. "CD Mastering: How It Happened." *Studio Sound* 26(10):82 – 88, October, 1984.

Verkaik, W., "Compact Disc (CD) Mastering — An Industrial Process." In Blesser, B., B. Locanthi, and T. G. Stockham, Jr., eds. *Digital Audio.* New York: Audio Engineering Society, 1983.

# Glossary of Technical Terms

## A

**Access Time**  The time interval for the laser pickup to locate and begin reading data from any point on the disc.

**Acquisition Time**  The time duration required for a sample-and-hold circuit to capture an input analog value; specifically, the time for the output to equal the input.

**A/D**  See **Analog-to-Digital Converter.**

**Adaptive Delta Modulation (ADM)**  A variation of delta modulation in which the step size may vary from sample to sample.

**Adaptive Delta Pulse Code Modulation (ADPCM)**  A hybrid encoding technique that correlates successive data samples to adapt to changes in the signal.

**ADC**  See **Analog-to-Digital Converter.**

**Address**  A coded representation of the origin or destination of data.

**ADM**  See **Adaptive Delta Modulation.**

**ADPCM**  See **Adaptive Delta Pulse Code Modulation.**

**AES (Audio Engineering Society)**  A professional engineering society that, among other activities, helps establish standards, including a professional digital audio interface standard.

**AES/EBU Digital I/O**  See **Serial Transmission Format.**

**Aliasing**  Unwanted frequencies created when sampling a signal of a frequency higher than half the sampling rate (Nyquist Frequency).

**Algorithm**  A sequence of steps needed to perform a given task.

**Ambience**    The acoustical characteristics of an environment.

**Amplifier**    An electronic device for boosting signal strength.

**Analog**    A physical quantity or data characterized by being continuously variable (rather than discrete).

**Analog-to-Digital Converter (A/D)**    An electrial circuit which converts the instantaneous value of an analog signal to a digital word, represented as a binary. number.

**Anti-Aliasing Filter**    A low-pass filter used at the input of digital audio recorders to attenuate frequencies above the half-sampling frequency to prevent aliasing.

**Anti-Imaging Filter**    A low-pass filter used at the output of digital audio reproducers to attenuate frequencies above the half-sampling frequency to eliminate image spectra present at multiples of the sampling frequency.

**Antinode**    The point of maximum amplitude of vibration on a stationary wave.

**Aperture Circuit**    The sample-and-hold circuit used to buffer instability in the analog signal and correct for high-frequency roll-off following the D/A converter.

**Aperture Error**    The high frequency roll-off occurring during de-sampling.

**ASCII (American Standard Code for Information Interchange)**    A standard data transmission code consisting of seven information bits and one parity bit. (ASCII is pronounced ask-ee).

**Astigmatism**    The distorting property of certain lenses used in some optical pickups to generate a focus signal.

**Audio Frequencies**    Frequencies that can be heard by the human ear, approximately 20 to 20,000 Hertz.

**Authoring System**    Programs and equipment which enable nonprogrammers to write interactive and other programs, especially for CD-I.

**Auto-Focus**    The method used in CD player pickups to maintain the focus of the objective lens on the pit surface.

**Auto-Tracking**    The method used in CD player pickups to maintain tracking of the laser spot on the pit track.

**Auxiliary Data Field**    In CD-ROM Mode 1, a 288-byte field used for extended EDC/ECC. In Mode 2, a 280-byte field of user data.

# B

**Bandlimited**    A signal occupying a defined and finite frequency band.

**Bandwidth**  The range between lower and upper limiting frequencies; the width of a band of frequencies. Also, the maximum amount of information (e.g., bits) needed for transmission or storage.

**Base**  See **Radix**.

**Base Case**  The minimum equipment required to play a CD-I disc.

**Baud Rate**  The transmitted data rate in bits per second (Baud).

**Beam**  The laser light used in the optical pickup to recover data from the disc and to provide for focusing and tracking.

**Beam Splitter**  See **Polarization Beam Splitter**.

**Binary**  A condition in which there are two possible states; for example, the binary number system (base 2) using the digits 0 and 1.

**Bircfringence**  An optical distortion, such as the one in disc substrates.

**Bit**  The smallest amount of digital information. A bit can store only two states, a 0 and 1. Abbreviation for binary digit.

**Bit Error Rate (BER)**  The number of bits processed before an erroneous bit is found (e.g., $10^{13}$), or the frequency of erroneous bits (e.g., $10^{-13}$).

**Bit-Mapped Display**  A display in which each pixel's color and intensity data are stored in a separate memory location.

**Bit Rate**  The rate or frequency at which bits appear in a bit stream. The bit rate of raw data from a CD is 4.3218 MHz.

**Bits Per Second**  A measure of the speed of transmission.

**Bit Stream**  A binary signal without regard to grouping.

**Block**  Data that is addressed or moved as a single unit. A data block is composed of sets of words to generate a data format. A typical block consists of data words, parity words, subcode, and synchronization and error correction words.

**Block Error Rate (BLER)**  The number of blocks at the C1 decoder with one or more errors.

**Blue Book**  The Compact Disc-Video (CD-V) standards document.

**Brickwall**  Refers to the slope of a filter with steep attenuation. Some anti-aliasing and anti-imaging filters have brickwall characteristics.

**Buffer**  A memory used to provide consistent rate of data flow, such as from an inconsistent source. A crystal-clocked buffer virtually eliminates wow and flutter in digital audio systems.

**Burst Error**   A large number of data bits lost on the medium because of excessive damage to or obstruction on the medium.

**Byte**   A group of bits operating together, usually consisting of eight bits.

# C

**Capacitor**   An electrical component consisting of two metal plates separated by a nonconductor, used to store charge.

**Cassette**   A self-contained package of magnetic tape.

**CAV**   See **Constant Angular Velocity.**

**CD**   See **Compact Disc.**

**CD-DA (Compact Disc Digital Audio)**   System storing digital audio on a 12-centimeter diameter optical disc.

**CD + G (Compact Disc Graphics)**   System storing video and other non-audio data in a disc's subcode area.

**CD + MIDI**   System storing MIDI information in a disc's subcode area.

**CD-I (Compact Disc Interactive)**   System storing digital audio, video, text, and graphics information interactively, with user control over content and presentation, on a 12-centimeter diameter optical disc.

**CD-PROM (Compact Disc Programmable Read Only Memory)**   A write-once CD-ROM disc.

**CD-ROM (Compact Disc Read Only Memory)**   A method of storing digitally coded information, such as computer information or database, on a 12-centimeter diameter optical disc.

**CD-ROM XA**   An extended architecture format of CD-ROM containing audio and screen standards from the CD-I format.

**CD-RTOS (Compact Disc Real-Time Operating System)**   The software required to operate and manipulate CD-I or CD-ROM systems, based on OS-9.

**CD-3**   A system storing twenty minutes of digital audio on an 8-centimenter diameter optical disc.

**CD-V (Compact Disc Video)**   A system storing five minutes of analog video and digital audio plus twenty minutes of digital audio only on a 12-centimeter diameter optical disc, and longer times on 20- or 30-centimeter diameter optical discs.

**CD-WO (Compact Disc Write-Once)**   A system permitting audio or other data to be written once onto a 12-centimeter optical disc.

**Centi-**   Prefix for one hundredth, abbreviated c.

**Charge** A quantity of electricity in a body.

**Chebyshev** A type of filter used in digital design which can provide a steep filter characteristic.

**Checksum** The use of redundant data for error detection.

**Chip** See **Integrated Circuit.**

**Chrominance** The color information in a color electronic image.

**CIRC** See **Cross Interleave Reed-Solomon Code.**

**Circuit** A system of conductors and electrical components through which electricity flows.

**Clean Room** An area with strict cleanliness guidelines, used in CD manufacturing.

**Clock** A timing device that generates the basic periodic signal used as a source of synchronizing signals in digital equipment.

**Clock Rate** The time rate of pulses or events.

**CLUT** See **Color Lookup Table.**

**CLV** See **Constant Linear Velocity.**

**Code** A system of numerals or characters representing information.

**Collimator Lens** An optical component used in some pickups to make divergent light rays parallel.

**Color Lookup Table (CLUT)** A graphics encoding technique used in CD-I in which a table contains the colors for a particular image.

**Compact Disc (CD)** An optical disc storage system developed and licensed by Philips N.V. and Sony Corporation. The system stores 74 minutes, 33 seconds of digital audio and subcode information, or other non-audio data, on a 12-centimeter diameter optical disc. The disc is made of plastic, with a top metallized layer, and is read by reflected laser light.

**Composite Video** A video signal in which luminance, chrominance, and synchronization are combined.

**Compression** The reduction in the amount of data required to store information.

**Concealment** Strategy used to supply approximate data in lieu of missing or incorrect data. See **Interpolation.**

**Constant Angular Velocity (CAV)** A disc rotating at a constant number of revolutions per second. The LP is a CAV system at 33 1/3 rpm.

**Constant Linear Velocity (CLV)** A disc rotating at varying numbers of revolutions per second to maintain a constant relative velocity between pickup and track across the disc radius. The CD is a CLV system rotating from 200 to 500 rpm.

**CRCC**   See **Cyclic Redundancy Check Code.**

**Cross Interleave Reed-Solomon Code (CIRC)**   A method of error detection and correction using data delay, rearrangement, and the Reed-Solomon coding algorithm. Used in all CD formats.

**Crosstalk**   The undesirable interference of one signal into another signal path.

**Crystal Oscillator**   A circuit with an energized crystal producing fixed vibrations, as in a clock.

**Cutoff Frequency**   The frequency at which a filter effectively attenuates.

**Cycle**   A complete sequence of a waveform that repeats at regular intervals.

**Cyclic Redundancy Check Code (CRCC)**   An error detection code that is recorded with the original information at a specified interval. CRCC is used in CD subcode data.

**Cylindrical Lens**   An optical component used in some pickups to create an elliptical pattern through astigmatism in order to generate a focusing signal.


# D

**D/A**   See **Digital-to-Analog Converter.**

**DAC**   See **Digital-to-Analog Converter.**

**dB**   See **Decibel.**

**Decibel (dB)**   A measure of level equal to ten times the logarithm of a power ratio.

**Decimal**   The base ten number system, in which each numeral is multiplied by an appropriate power of ten.

**De-Emphasis**   See **Emphasis.**

**De-Interleave**   See **Interleaving.**

**Delta Modulation (DM)**   A single-bit coding technique in which a constant step size digitizes the input waveform. Past knowledge of the information permits encoding of the differences between consecutive values.

**Demodulation**   See **Modulation.**

**Demultiplexer**   See **Multiplexing.**

**Differential**   The encoding technique in which the difference from bit to bit forms the basis of encoding.

**Diffraction**   A modification in light or sound in which the incident rays are deflected.

**Diffraction Grating**   An optical component used in three-beam pickups to split the laser beam into secondary beams to be used for tracking.

**Digital**   The use of numbers (typically, binary numbers) to represent information.

**Digital Audio**   The use of sampling and quantization techniques to store or transmit audio information.

**Digital Filter**   Any filter accomplished in the digital domain.

**Digital Signal**   Any signal which is quantized at discrete points in time.

**Digital-to-Analog Converter (D/A)**   An electrical circuit that converts a binary coded word to an equivalent analog voltage.

**Digital Video Interactive (DVI)**   A system using data compression techniques to store seventy minutes of digital video and digital audio information on a 12-centimenter diameter optical disc.

**Digitization**   Any conversion of analog information into a digital form.

**DIN**   Acronym for *Deutsche Industrie Norm,* the West German standardization system.

**Direct Metal Master (DMM)**   An alternative CD mastering process.

**Directory**   Specification of the address of files on an electronic storage medium.

**Direct Read After Write (DRAW)**   An optical disc system

in which data may be written (recorded) and immediately read (played back).

**Disc**   A mechanical, optical, or magnetic storage medium.

**Disc Drive**   Mechanism for supporting and rotating a disc.

**Disc Mastering**   See **Mastering.**

**Disc Operating System (DOS)**   A software program controlling data in memory and disk storage.

**Discrete Time Sampling**   The technique of representing a waveform at discrete instants of time.

**Distortion**   Undesirable change in an output signal relative to the input.

**Dither**   The noise (typically analog) added to the input of a digital signal processing or recording chain to minimize the effect of quantizing error at low-level signals.

**DMM**   See **Direct Metal Master.**

**DRAW**   See **Direct Read After Write.**

**Droop**   An error condition in a sample-and-hold circuit in which the held analog value decreases.

**Dropout**   An error condition in which bits are incorrect or lost from a medium. A disc defect or obstruction could cause a dropout.

**Dual Slope Integrating Analog to Digital Converter**   A converter design which uses counters to time the output of integrators to yield a digital output word.

**DVI**   See **Digital Video Interactive.**

**Dye-Polymer**   An optical storage technology used in write-once and erasable systems.

**Dynamic Element Matching Digital-to-Analog Converter** A converter design which uses a series of current sources and switches to yield an analog output.

**Dynamic Range**   The amplitude operating range of an electrical circuit, from noise floor to overload condition.

**DYUV**   Delta YUV, a color encoding scheme for natural pictures with luminance encoded at full bandwidth and chrominance encoded at half bandwidth, storing only the differences between values.

# E

**EBU (European Broadcasting Union)**   A professional society that, among other things, helps establish standards.

**ECC (Error Correction Code)** See **Error Correction.**

**EDC (Error Detection Code)** See **Error Detection.**

**EFM**   See **Eight-to-Fourteen Modulation.**

**Eight-to-Fourteen Modulation** An encoding technique used in CD mastering to convert eight bits of digital data to fourteen bits. The player performs EFM demodulation.

**Electroforming**   The production of metal impressions from master or submaster CD discs, to be used for disc molding.

**Emphasis**   High frequencies in the audio signal can be boosted during recording, then de-emphasized or correspondingly attenuated during playback. This increases signal-to-noise ratio. A CD with emphasis is identified with a set emphasis bit, and the player automatically performs de-emphasis.

**Erasable Optical Storage**   Optical media upon which data can be written, read, and then erased and written again.

**Erase**   To destroy data stored on optical or magnetic media.

**Error**   A signal that is proportional to the difference between actual and desired conditions.

**Error Concealment**   A method used to "repair" an error in the audio signal. Through interpolation, new data is derived from adjacent error-free data blocks.

**Error Correction**   A method using a coding system to correct data errors by use of interleaved data or redundant data within a data block. Corrected data is identical to the original.

**Error Detection** A coding system which provides a method of determining errors that occur in a digital data stream. Accomplished prior to correction or concealment.

**Error Protection** The use of error detection, correction, and concealment to enhance the robustness of storage or transmission.

**Extension** Programs added to an operating system to augment its capabilities (e.g., an MS-DOS extension to permit access of CD-ROM files).

**Eye Pattern** The high-frequency or radio-frequency data signal output from the optical pickup.

# F

**FET** Acronym for Field Effect Transistor, a unipolar semiconductor.

**Fiber Optics** The technology of using glass fibers to convey light and modulated information.

**File Descriptor Record** A sector found in CD-I files containing information on data segments, needed to access the file.

**File Structure Volume Descriptor** A record of the CD-I disc label describing files.

**Filter** A circuit designed to modify certain frequencies.

**Flag** One or more bits used to store and indicate status of a circuit or system.

**Floating Point** An encoding technique in which a mantissa represents amplitude, and an exponent provides a scaling factor.

**Foldover** See **Aliasing.**

**Format** The order in which data is organized or recorded on a medium.

**Four Quadrant Photodiode** A component found in some optical pickups used to convert reflected laser light into data and focusing signals.

**Fourier Theorem** A mathematical theorem stating that any periodic function may be resolved into sine and cosine terms with known amplitudes and phases.

**Frame** The basic unit of data representation in the CD format, containing synchronization, subcode, audio data, and parity.

**Frequency** The number of recurrences of a periodic waveform in time.

# G

**Giga-** A prefix signifying one billion, abbreviated G.

**Glass Master** The glass disc used for CD mastering.

**Granulation Noise** An audible distortion resulting from quantization error.

**Green Book** The Compact Disc-Interactive (CD-I) standards document.

**Ground** The point in an electrical circuit at nominal zero voltage potential.

# H

**Hamming Codes** A class of error correction codes in which the error is self-locating.

**Hardware** The physical, mechanical, and electrical devices that form a system.

**Harmonics** A series of frequencies located at integer multiples of a fundamental frequency.

**Header Field** In CD-ROM, a 4-byte field of a data sector that contains the absolute sector address and the mode byte.

**Hertz (Hz)** A measure of frequency (cycles per second).

**High Sierra Group (HSG)** An ad hoc standards committee which established nominal data format and compatibility for CD-ROM.

**HF Signal** A high-frequency signal.

**HSG. See High Sierra Group.**

**Hygroscopic** Materials which readily take up and retain moisture.

**Hypermedia** Cross-linked databases possibly containing data in the form of text, pictures, and sound.

**Hz** See **Hertz**.

# I

**IC** See **Integrated Circuit**.

**IM** See **Intermodulation Distortion**.

**Index Numbers** Delineations found in the subcode of some CDs, marking points of reference in the audio program.

**Index of Refraction** The ratio of the velocity of light in one medium compared to a second medium.

**Information Exchange Protocol (IXP)** A protocol used in the mastering process for labelling data on a CD-I disc, describing media type and encoding techniques.

**Initialization** The process of reading the table of contents subcode when a CD is first loaded into the player, accomplished automatically.

**Injection Molding** Manufacturing process used to make CDs in which molten plastic is formed in a mold.

**Input** Any data entering a circuit or system.

**Input Filter** See **Anti-Aliasing Filter.**

**Input/Output (I/O)** Equipment or data used to communicate from a circuit or system to other circuits or systems, or the outside world.

**Integrated Circuit** A solid state device with miniaturized active components on a single semiconductor material.

**Interactive Media** Programs or courses of instruction with content and output controlled by the viewer.

**Interleaving** The process of rearranging data in time. Upon de-interleaving, errors in consecutive bits or words are distributed to a wider area to guard against consecutive errors in the storage media.

**Intermodulation Distortion (IMD)** Undesired sum and difference frequencies in an output signal relative to the input.

**International Standard Recording Code (ISRC)** A code used by record manufacturers stating country of origin, owner, year of issue, and serial number of tracks, used optionally in CD subcode.

**Interpolation** The method used to conceal errors by using adjacent data to determine the approximate value of missing data. An error concealment technique.

**I/O** See **Input/Output.**

# J

**Jack** A socket into which connectors are inserted to make electrical contact.

**Jitter** Timing error.

# K

**kHz** Kilohertz, or 1,000 cycles per second.

**Kilo-** A prefix signifying one thousand, abbreviated k.

# L

**Land** The reflective substrate between pits on the CD data surface.

**Laser** See **Light Amplification by Stimulated Emission of Radiation.**

**Laservision** The tradename for an optical video disk format.

**LCD** See **Liquid Crystal Display.**

**Lead-In/Lead-Out**   The non-audio program areas on a disc preceding and succeeding the audio program.

**Least Significant Bit (LSB)**   The bit within a digital word that is the least weighted.

**LED**   See **Light Emitting Diode.**

**Light Amplification by Stimulated Emission of Radiation (Laser)**   A device which generates coherent, monochromatic light waves. All CD players contain a semiconductor laser in their optical pickup.

**Light Emitting Diode (LED)**   A self-lighting semiconductor display of numerical or graphical information.

**Linear**   A device having an output that varies in direct proportion to the input.

**Linear PCM**   A pulse code modulation system in which the signal is converted directly to a PCM word without companding, or other processing.

**Liquid Crystal Display (LCD)**   A semiconductor display of numerical or graphical information, requiring ambient light or backlighting.

**Logic**   Systematized rules or interconnections of digital switching circuits.

**Low-Pass Filter**   A filter with a characteristic that allows all frequencies below a specified roll-off

frequency to pass and attenuates all frequencies above. Anti-aliasing and anti-imaging filters are low-pass filters.

**LSB**   See **Least Significant Bit.**

**Luminance**   The intensity or brightness component of an electronic image.

# M

**Magnetic Tape or Disc**   An analog or digital storage medium consisting of a magnetically coated substrate storing data as magnetic patterns.

**Magneto-Optical Recording (MOR)**   An erasable optical disc system using magnetic media and laser reading/writing.

**Master**   The original recording of a finished program.

**Mastering**   The process of encoding audio and control data on a glass master disc prior to CD replication.

**Matrixing**   See **Electroforming.**

**Medium, Media**   A material or basis on which information is stored or transmitted.

**Mega-**   A prefix signifying one million, abbreviated M.

**Memory**   Hardware used to store information.

**Menu**   A list of options displayed for a user.

**Menu-Driven** Software controlled through menus.

**Metallization** Step in the CD replication process in which the polycarbonate substrate is coated with metal to provide reflectivity.

**Micro-** Prefix for one thousandth, abbreviated μ.

**Microprocessor** An integrated circuit that performs a variety of operations in accordance with a list of instructions

**Milli-** Prefix for one thousandth, abbreviated m.

**Mode 1 and Mode 2** The two frame formats used in CD-ROM. CD-I is based on Mode 2.

**Modulation** The process of varying a carrier signal according to the instantaneous value of an input signal.

**Mono-Line** A CD manufacturing system in which replication processes are integrated, with automated control.

**MOR** See **Magneto-Optical Recording.**

**MOS** Acronym for Metal Oxide Semiconductor, a type of field effect transistor.

**Most Significant Bit (MSB)** The bit within a digital word that is the highest weighted.

**MSB** See **Most Significant Bit.**

**MS-DOS** An disk operating system used in many personal computers.

**Multiplexing** The process of combining independent signals and conveying them along a single conductor.

# N

**NA** See **Numerical Aperture.**

**Nano-** A prefix for one billionth, abbreviated n.

**Node** A point of zero amplitude of vibration on a stationary wave.

**Noise** Any spurious signal.

**Noise Floor** The lowest threshold of useful signal level.

**Noise-Shaping Circuit** A numerical feedback circuit used in some CD players to increase signal-to-noise ratio.

**Non-Photoresist (NPR)** An alternative CD mastering method.

**Non-Return-to-Zero (NRZ)** A digital code in which polarity changes positively with a 0/1 signal change, and negatively with a 1/0 signal change.

**Non-Return-to-Zero-Inverted (NRZI)** A digital code in which polarity is reversed each time a 1 occurs, and remains constant when a 0 occurs.

**NPR**   See **Non-Photoresist.**

**NRZ**   See **Non-Return-to-Zero.**

**NRZI**   See **Non-Return-to-Zero-Inverted.**

**NTSC Video Format**   The color television standard used in the U.S. and prepared by the National Television Systems Committee of the Electronics Industries Association (EIA).

**Numerical Aperture (NA)**   A measure of the relative capacity of an optical system to accept light from an outside medium.

**Nyquist Frequency**   The highest frequency that may be accurately sampled. The Nyquist Frequency is one-half the sampling frequency. The theoretical Nyquist Frequency of the CD system is 22.05 kHz.

# O

**Objective Lens**   The optical component used in pickups to focus laser light on the disc data surface.

**OEM**   See **Original Equipment Manufacturer.**

**Offset**   The difference in the number of frames between begin-access time and actual start time. A safety margin for player muting/de-muting.

**Omni-Player**   A CD-Video player that will play CD-I discs.

**Op Amp**   See **Operational Amplifier.**

**Operational Amplifier**   An analog device often used as a gain block.

**Optical Disc**   Any read-only, write-once, or erasable medium using laser light to convey data to or from the disc.

**Optical Pickup**   The optical device using laser light to convey data from a disc.

**Opto-Isolator**   Optical components which convert electrical signals to light and then back to electrical. Used in some CD players to isolate the noise of digital circuitry from analog circuitry.

**Original Equipment Manufacturer (OEM)**   A term used to describe how one manufacturer obtains finished parts of its equipment from another manufacturer, and then markets the assembled device under its own name.

**OS-9**   The real-time operating system on which the CD-I operating system is based.

**Output**   Any data leaving a circuit or system.

**Output Filter**   See **Anti-Imaging Filter.**

**Oversampling**   The technique in which the number of samples is multiplied to permit digital filtering of the signal prior to D/A conversion. A gentle analog low-pass filter is still required after oversampling to remove extreme supersonic frequencies.

# P

**PAL Video Format** The color television format used in Europe (except France), Africa, Australia, and South America. PAL is an acronym for phase alternation line.

**PAM** See **Pulse Amplitude Modulation.**

**Parallel** The simultaneous presence of bits in a data word on multiple conductors.

**Parity** A redundant error detection method in which the total number of binary 1's (or 0's) is always even or odd.

**PBS** See **Polarization Beam Splitter.**

**P Channel** Subcode channel carrying information on lead-in, lead-out, and play areas of a CD. See **Subcode.**

**PCM** See **Pulse Code Modulation.**

**Peripheral** Equipment physically independent of a controller.

**Phase Change Medium** An optical storage method used in both write-once and erasable media in which a change in reflectivity is used to encode data.

**Phase Shift** A displacement in the time relationship between two signals, or two components in one signal.

**Photodiode** A semiconductor device which generates an electrical current in proportion to received illumination.

**Photopolymerization (2P)** An alternative CD manufacturing method.

**Photoresist** A substance which becomes soluble (or insoluble) when exposed to light. Used in CD glass disc mastering.

**Pickup** See **Optical Pickup.**

**Pico-** Prefix for one trillionth, abbreviated p.

**Pitch** The distance between adjacent tracks of a data track. The pitch of the pit spiral on CDs is 1.6 microns.

**Pits** The physical impressions on a disc substrate. Viewed as bumps by the reading laser, they diffract the light, decreasing the intensity of light returned to the pickup.

**Pixel** A picture element, the smallest dot on a video screen.

**Player** The mechanical and electrical device used to recover data from a disc or other media.

**PNM** See **Pulse Number Modulation.**

**Polarization Beam Splitter (PBS)**   An optical component used in some pickups to conduct light in one plane of polarization, but reflect it in another.

**Polycarbonate**   The transparent plastic material used to form the substrate for CDs.

**Potentiometer**   A device with variable resistance.

**Power Supply**   A circuit that supplies proper voltages and currents as required by the system.

**PPM**   See **Pulse Position Modulation.**

**PQ Subcode**   See **Subcode.**

**Pre-Emphasis**   A high-frequency boost used during recording, followed by de-emphasis during playback, designed to reduce noise.

**Pre-Mastering**   The process of integration of digital data code, error correction and subcodes, and conversion to the CD data format prior to disc mastering.

**Psychoacoustics**   Study of the perception and response to sound.

**Pulse Amplitude Modulation (PAM)**   A conversion method in which the amplitudes of pulses in a pulse train represent the analog information.

**Pulse Code Modulation (PCM)**   A conversion method in which

digital words in a bit stream represent samples of analog information. The basis of most digital audio systems.

**Pulse Number Modulation (PNM)**   A conversion method in which the number of pulses in a pulse train represents the analog information.

**Pulse Parameter Modulation**   The general type of modulation in which information is encoded by pulse representation.

**Pulse Position Modulation (PPM)**   A conversion method in which the positions of pulses in a pulse train represent the analog information.

**Pulse Width Modulation (PWM)**   A conversion method in which the widths of pulses in a pulse train represent the analog information.

**PWM**   See **Pulse Width Modulation.**

# Q

**QC**   See **Quality Control.**

**Q Channel**   A subcode channel carrying information on track and index numbers, elapsed time, product codes, etc. See **Subcode.**

**Quality Control**   The series of tests and measurements used to maintain manufacturing tolerances — for example, those of discs.

**Quantization** The process of converting an infinitely variable amplitude of an analog waveform to one of a finite series of discrete levels. Performed by the A/D converter.

**Quantization Error** Error resulting from quantizing an analog waveform to a discrete level. The longer the word length, the less the error.

**Quarter Wave Plate (QWP)** An optical component used in some pickups to shift the plane of polarization of the laser light.

**QWP** See **Quarter Wave Plate.**

# R

**Radial Tracking Error** A measurement of a player's radial tracking servo signal, used to determine tolerance for disc flatness.

**Radix** The number of symbols used in a number system.

**RAM** See **Random Access Memory.**

**Random Access Memory (RAM)** A memory in which data may be read and written regardless of address or location.

**Random Bit Error** An error in a digital data stream in which only a few bits are lost. Corrected by error correction.

**R-DAT** See **Rotary Head Digital Audio Tape Recorder.**

**Read** The nondestructive reading of data from a medium.

**Read-Only-Memory (ROM)** A memory from which data, after initial storage, may only be read. The audio compact disc is a read-only system.

**Real-Time** Operation which is perceived to be instantaneous to a user.

**Red Book** The Compact Disc-Digital Audio (CD-Audio) standards document.

**Reed-Solomon Code** A cyclic, multiple-error correction code used in CDs. See **Cross Interleave Reed-Solomon Code.**

**Refractive Index** See **Index of Refraction.**

**Reverberation** Repeating echoes of sound, increasing in density, decreasing in amplitude.

**RF Signal** Radio frequency signal.

**RGB (Red-Green-Blue)** A type of color output to a display consisting of separate signals for red, green and blue — an alternative to composite video.

**RGB 5:5:5** An RGB encoding technique used in CD-I in which colors are each represented by 5 bits.

**ROM** See **Read-Only-Memory.**

**Root Directory**   The highest-level directory on a CD-I disc.

**Rotary Head Digital Audio Tape Recorder (R-DAT or DAT)**   A digital audio recorder utilizing a magnetic tape cassette system similar to that of a video recorder.

**RTOS (Real-Time Operating System)**   An operating system with real-time interaction.

# S

**Sample-and-Hold Circuit (S/H)** A circuit which captures and holds an analog signal for a finite period of time. The input S/H proceeds the A/D converter, allowing time for conversion. The output S/H (see **Aperture Circuit**) follows the D/A converter, smoothing glitches and compensating for aperture error.

**Sampling**   The process of representing the amplitude of a signal at a particular point in time.

**Sampling Frequency**   The frequency at which an analog signal is sampled. Expressed in Hertz. The sampling rate used on compact discs is 44,100 samples per second (44.1 kHz).

**Sampling (Nyquist) Theorem** Theorem stating that a bandlimited continuous waveform may be represented by a series of discrete samples if the sampling frequency is at least twice the highest frequency contained in the waveform.

**SAR**   See **Successive Approximation Register.**

**SCSI**   See **Small Computer Standard Interface.**

**SECAM Video Format**   The color television format used in France and Russia in which the three primary colors are sent sequentially, rather than nearly simultaneously. SECAM is an acronym for Séquentielle Couleur à la Mémoire.

**Sector**   In CD-ROM, a block or frame complete with synchronization and header field; a 2352-byte block.

**S/E Ratio**   See **Signal-to-Error Ratio.**

**Serial**   Sequential presence of data along one conductor.

**Serial Transmission Format**   A specification using bi-phase modulation for data, and balanced line drivers to transmit digital audio data.

**Servo Mechanism**   A control device or system which reads its own output to determine the degree of further output as compared to its input.

**Settling Time**   The time required for a circuit, such as a D/A converter, to reach a stable output value.

**S/H Circuit**   See **Sample-and-Hold Circuit.**

**Signal-to-Error Ratio (S/E)**   The ratio of signal voltage to quantization error voltage, typically expressed in decibels.

**Signal-to-Noise Ratio (S/N)**   The ratio of signal voltage to noise voltage, typically expressed in decibels.

**Sine Wave**   A fundamental waveform corresponding to a single frequency, without harmonics.

**Single-Beam Tracking**   An optical pickup design in which a single laser spot is used for data recovery, tracking, and focusing.

**Sled**   A mechanical chassis upon which the optical pickup is supported and moved along the disc surface.

**Small Computer Standard Interface (SCSI)**   A standard 8-bit parallel interface used to connect peripherals, such as connecting a CD-ROM player to a microcomputer. (SCSI is pronounced scuzzy.)

**Smoothing Filter**   See **Anti-Imaging Filter.**

**SMPTE (Society of Motion Picture and Television Engineers)** A professional engineering society that, among other activities, helps establish standards, including a timecode standard.

**S/N Ratio**   See **Signal-to-Noise Ratio.**

**Software**   A set of instructions or programs used to operate a data processing system. Also, precorded data or music programs.

**Sound**   A variation in air pressure within frequency limits from about 20 Hz to 20,000 Hz.

**Spectrum**   A distribution of frequencies in a bandwidth.

**Spin Coating**   A step in the CD replication process in which a protective layer is applied over the metallized disc surface.

**Spindle**   Part of the drive that spins the disc.

**Spiral Track**   The pit track spiral physically encoding data on a CD, running from the innermost region to the outermost.

**Sputtering**   A method used in the CD replication process to metallize a disc data surface.

**Stamper**   The metal mold used in polycarbonate plastic injection molding machines to replicate CDs.

**Subcode**   Data encoded on a CD that contains definable information such as track number, times, copy inhibit, copyright, etc.

**Subheader**   A field indicating the type of data in a sector.

**Substrate**   The material upon which a device is constructed and supported. A CD uses a polycarbonate substrate.

**Successive Approximation Register (SAR)**   A type of analog-to-digital converter using a digital-to-analog converter to determine the output word successively, bit by bit.

**Symbol**   An 8-bit byte.

**Synchronous**   A simultaneously timed operation in which a master clock is used to control events.

# T

**Table of Contents (TOC)**   Non-audio subcode data contained in the lead-in area of a CD, storing initialization data, including track and time information. Read during initialization.

**Test Disc**   A specially prepared CD containing signals and program material designed to measure and evaluate CD players and other equipment.

**THD**   See **Total Harmonic Distortion.**

**Three-Beam Tracking**   An optical pickup design in which a laser beam is split into three spots, the center spot used for data recovery and focusing, and the secondary spots for tracking.

**Time Sampling**   See **Discrete Time Sampling.**

**Total Harmonic Distortion (THD)**   Undesired harmonics on an output signal relative to the input. Often measured with corresponding noise (THD + N).

**Tracking Error**   An error condition in which the optical pickup deviates from the pit track, perhaps caused by an obstruction or disc defect.

**Track Numbers**   Numbering of songs or movements on a disc; this information is contained in the subcode.

**Track Pitch**   See **Pitch.**

**Transversal Filter**   A kind of numerical filter used in digital filtering CD players to perform low-pass filtering of the output signals; used in an oversampling-based architecture.

**Truncate**   To eliminate without round-off some low-order bits after performing an arithmetic computation.

**Two-Axis Actuator**   Mechanical device holding the objective lens of an optical pickup, able to move the lens horizontally and vertically for tracking and focusing.

# U

**Ultraviolet**   Electromagnetic radiation at frequencies higher than visible light yet lower than those of x-rays.

**U-Matic Tape Recorder** A rotary head tape recorder used for CD mastering.

# V

**Velocity of Sound** The speed of sound, 1087 feet per second at 32 degrees Fahrenheit.

**VMS** An operating system used in some minicomputers.

# W

**Waveform** A periodic propagated disturbance in a medium.

**Weighted Resistor Converter** A type of digital-to-analog converter using resistors with values varying as powers of two, used to generate a current proportional to the input word.

**Wet Silvering** A method of metallizing a disc data surface.

**White Noise** A noise with equal energy at any frequency.

**Word** A convenient collection of bits, commonly 16 bits.

**Word Length** The number of bits in a word.

**Wow and Flutter** Variation in transport speed from mechanical error. Negligible in the CD system.

**Write** To record data on a medium.

**Write-Once Media** Systems in which data may be written once, but not erased and rewritten.

# Y

**Yellow Book** The Compact Disc-Read Only Memory (CD-ROM) standards document.

**YUV** Video coding process used in CD-I in which the luminance signal (Y) is recorded at full bandwidth on each line and chroma values (U and V) are recorded at half bandwidth on alternate lines.

# Index